'An ambitious blueprint for post-Brexit Britain ... This is a book for its time.'

Patrick Mulholland, *National Review*

'[Nick Timothy is] one of our best current "One Nation" thinkers ... Politicians, advisors and commentators within the Conservative family would do well to read this book.'

Andrew O'Brien, *One Nation Economics*

Other Endorsements

'Refreshingly free from jargon, self-delusion or political partisanship, if you want to know why everything seems to be going wrong for the West, you must read this book.'

Tony Abbott, former Prime Minister of Australia

'A hopeful and compelling case for a modern state and revitalized communities, recognizing that markets alone will not create a fair and prosperous society. Essential reading across the spectrum.'

Claire Ainsley, Executive Director of the
Joseph Rowntree Foundation and author of
The New Working Class: How to Win Hearts, Minds and Votes

'This is an important attempt to chart a way forward for the Conservative Party by an author who has been at the heart of government. Nick Timothy seeks to do for the Conservative Party what Anthony Crosland tried to do many years ago for the Labour Party. I hope that he is more successful.'

Vernon Bogdanor, Professor of Government, King's College, London

'This is an essential book for anyone interested in understanding the forces driving this age of upheaval. It is a book about political power and the power of politics to effect lasting change. And it boldly explains why liberals keep getting it wrong.'

Jason Cowley, Editor of The New Statesman

'Nick Timothy has long been one of the most imaginative and important writers on the nature and future of conservatism. But this superb book should be read by anyone with an interest in our changing world, the political response to it, and the path forward from an era of turmoil.'

Matthew d'Ancona, Editor and Partner, Tortoise Media

'There is much in this book I don't agree with and much I do, but there wasn't a page I didn't find absorbing and challenging. I find Nick Timothy one of the most interesting modern Conservative thinkers and he has written a really interesting, important book which demands to be read.'

Daniel Finkelstein, Conservative peer and Times *columnist*

'Where does the anger come from? Should capitalism be tamed? Did liberal reform over-reach? Nick Timothy, reflecting in the calm after the storm of office, has produced an analysis that is essential reading, whether you're from the right or the left, or simply a "neutral" who is trying to understand our baffling times.'

Gary Gibbon, Political Editor, Channel Four News

'Nick Timothy is one of the few thinkers on the right who understands the dangers of untrammelled free-markets and the value of community. His ideas deserve a hearing from socialists as well as conservatives.'

Maurice Glasman, Labour peer and founder of Blue Labour

'Nick Timothy is Britain's leading conservative thinker if one's measure is a feel for real people rather than ease with arid theorizing. That this book sets out a trenchant yet sophisticated case for conservatism should come as no surprise. Nor should its stress on what is politically deliverable. But what is most striking is that it is also a serious attempt to find ways of making modern liberalism workable – and rescue it from itself.'

Paul Goodman, Editor of Conservative Home

'Nick Timothy is a brilliant analyst of our present discontents. His insights are sharp, his writing is compelling and his arguments are powerful. He knows the problems with our politics and takes no prisoners on his quest to put them right.'

Michael Gove MP

'Nick Timothy has given us a powerful critique of the simplistic liberal ideology that has ruled the right and the left for a generation or more. Analysing the destabilizing effects of unchecked free markets and an exclusive concern with individual freedom, he exposes the insecurities that have led to the dangerous rise of populism. Anyone who worries about the disordered state of politics today will profit from reading this hard-hitting book.'

Professor John Gray, author and philosopher

'Nick Timothy has written a clear, timely and thought-provoking book, providing a persuasive analysis of how the liberal consensus has lost popular support. Arguing that conservatism should always be focused on how we relate to each other, he points out that its adherents cannot be relaxed about the decline of community or the current extent of inequality. His recommendations will be important for political leaders and thinkers seeking a way forward that is neither veering towards populism nor doomed to be unpopular.'

William Hague, Conservative peer and former Conservative Party Leader

'Nick Timothy is that rare breed of politico, prophet and philosopher. After masterfully explaining what went wrong, he expertly lays out a new roadmap of how to stop the destruction of our culture and nation. To read this book is to feel convinced that Britain can, once again, lead the Western world back to sanity.'

Ed Husain, author of The House of Islam: A Global History

'The Conservative Party may now be master of all it surveys, but its obsession with Brexit has denuded it of a consistent and workable political economy – which certainly, as Nick Timothy argues, is not going to lie in reheating some combination of austerity and Thatcherism. In a *The State We're In* for the political right that looks unflinchingly at our ills, he sets out a reforming economic and social programme which may chime with Boris Johnson more than the consensus expects – a timely and must-read contribution to the national debate.'

Will Hutton, Principal of Hertford College, Oxford, author of
The State We're In *and* Observer *columnist*

'Nick Timothy's new book harnesses his unique combination of intellectual depth and practical policy experience to offer a bold and original diagnosis of the ills that bedevil today's polarized Western societies. He introduces the key idea of the "liberal ratchet", in which today's "meritocratic" elite seeks to untether itself from rooted majorities, working through institutions shielded from the electorate – courts, universities, agencies, parts of the media – to advance a universalist vision. Intellectuals are generally drawn to the individualisms of left and right, while their electorates yearn in vain for stability and community. Blending centre-left economics and small-'c' conservatism in culture, Timothy's new book speaks to today's forgotten majorities.'

Eric Kaufmann, Professor of Politics at Birkbeck College,
University of London, and author of
Whiteshift: Populism, Immigration and the Future of
White Majorities

'People on the left rarely read anything written by conservatives. They should make an exception for Nick Timothy's book. If they are smart it will make them think. If they are really smart they may be surprised at how much of it they agree with.'

Martin Kettle, Guardian *columnist*

'Readers on the right may savour Nick Timothy's savage take down of the political tribe he brands the "ultra-liberal" – the group he blames for many of the country's ills. What's more timely though is what he puts forward as an alternative. The label "One Nation Conservative" is all the rage in SW1, but even to many in Westminster, what it means in practice is still something of a mystery. In an extremely readable way, with the benefit of his experience and agony in government, Timothy defines what that mantra might mean for Conservative policy, and all of our real lives in the 21st century.'

Laura Kuenssberg, BBC Political Editor

'Nick Timothy has shed a bright light on the crisis facing liberal democracy. Without flinching from hard truths, he offers persuasive diagnoses and plausible prescriptions, where others offer only vitriol and venom. This is a must-read for those struggling to understand this era on both sides of the Atlantic.'

Yuval Levin, author of The Fractured Republic

'Caught between libertarian economics and social liberalism, contemporary conservatism is in need of a fundamental rethink to address economic and cultural insecurity. Nick Timothy's brilliant book combines a compelling critique of ultra-liberalism with a thoughtful restatement of One Nation Conservatism that can help to build a majority politics anchored in institutions enabling people to pursue the good life. This is a vital contribution to public political debate in Britain and beyond.'

Professor Adrian Pabst, co-author of The Politics of Virtue: Post-Liberalism and the Human Future

'Nick Timothy is one of Britain's most original conservative thinkers. His new book, informed by a near-decade of experience at the heart of government, draws on meticulously researched and well-presented data to examine the complex and chronic maladies of affluent liberal democracies. A must-read for anyone seeking to better understand the deep roots of Brexit and other contemporary political upheavals across the West.'

Bojan Pancevski, Germany Correspondent for The Wall Street Journal

'In recent years, British politics has blundered into a state of permanent crisis, whose roots run deep. And Nick Timothy didn't just have a front-row seat – he was on the stage. This book blends an insider account with years of thinking about how we got here and where we might go.'

Amol Rajan, BBC Media Editor

'Nick Timothy is the genuine Conservative modernizer, forensically challenging fashionable "ultra liberal" orthodoxies and putting the case for a more active state. This is both a gripping read and a route map towards an urgently needed One Nation Conservatism.'

Steve Richards, writer and broadcaster

'Much of the writing of political philosophy has been done by those who've never had to muddy their preconceptions with the grime of power and office. Timothy is unusual in that he combines a ferociously penetrating intellect with a period as a particularly influential chief of staff to the Prime Minister. The resulting book thus has particular authority. Like much of the best political philosophy over the centuries, it is written by someone with understanding.'

Anthony Seldon, Vice-Chancellor of the University of Buckingham, historian and author

'Combining philosophical insights with a wealth of policy experience, Nick Timothy offers a powerful critique of our current political malaise as rooted in the excesses of a distorted liberalism and offers a timely reminder of the intellectual and practical resources of a One Nation Conservatism. Those who want to understand where we are, how we got here, and what a future progressive conservative agenda should look like, will find this book a thought-provoking and rewarding read.'

Dr Matt Sleat, author of Liberal Realism: A Realist Theory of Liberal Politics

'The greatest threat to liberal democracies is when values and principles are neither articulated nor contested. This is a problem for the left and the right. Nick Timothy's book outlines a way forward for the conservatives, but also charts a path for restoring trust which transcends party politics.'

Gisela Stuart, former Labour MP

'True to form, Nick Timothy offers his readers an urgent critique of the limits of excessive liberalism that cuts to the heart of our broken political settlement. His ideas are incisive and radical – they should be listened to by anyone who wants to restore trust and sense to government.'

Will Tanner, Director of centre-right think tank Onward

'Across the Western world democratic states face mounting problems. Old identities dissolve. Disillusion increases. Here, Brexit is a body blow to old party loyalties and has created a new divide. Nick Timothy, both insider and analyst, has written a mordant dissection of the destructive ultra-liberalism that lies at the root of the problem with its "twin traps of impractical individualism and unrealistic universalism". He argues that a modern One Nation Conservatism is the practical way of repairing society. Brexiteers have put their faith in a rejuvenated nation state alive to the needs of all citizens. This tract for the times provides an ambitious agenda.'

Robert Tombs, Professor Emeritus of French History, Cambridge University

'A searingly honest and compelling account of an era-defining period of modern British political history. Nick Timothy's powerfully insightful re-evaluation of what it means to be conservative should be a must-read for anyone wanting to make sense of the failure of liberalism, and the future of centre-right thinking.'

Camilla Tominey, Associate Editor, Daily Telegraph

'This is a timely and thought-provoking book. Nick Timothy argues that the key question in politics today should not be whether the market or the state can do a better job but how we can reconcile both with community. For those of us who believe that strong communities are the key to our future happiness and prosperity, this book is a powerful call to action, by someone who has thought deeply about the challenges we face, during and since he worked in Number Ten.'

Tom Tugendhat, MP

'Conservatism is most real and interesting when it confronts the trade-offs between individual freedom and civic obligation, dynamism and rootedness, and seeks to reconcile them. This is why this is an important book on the future of conservatism and indeed the future of our country.'

David Willetts, Conservative peer and author

'This brilliant book makes a compelling and novel argument about the origins of the crises experienced in Britain and other liberal democracies. Its philosophical analysis is backed by robust empirical research, and its vision of a new conservatism is backed by creative new policy suggestions. Whether you agree with all of those suggestions or not, this is a must-read contribution to the debate that is raging all the way across the West.'

Gavin Williamson, MP

'The recent Conservative election victory is a complete vindication of the Nick Timothy approach. This book should be required reading for the new government on how to improve the lives of their new voters – and for the Labour Party to understand their seismic loss.'

Rachel Wolf, Partner at Public First and author of Boris Johnson's 2019 general election manifesto

'This book is an absolute must-read. It's both thorough and challenging. Inevitably there will be elements you'll disagree with but there are many others that are truly enlightening. The bottom line is that this is a vital contribution to a must-have debate.'

Sir Simon Woolley, crossbench peer and director of Operation Black Vote

REMAKING ONE NATION

REMAKING ONE NATION

The Future of Conservatism

NICK TIMOTHY

polity

First published in 2020 by Polity Press
This paperback edition first published in 2021 by Polity Press

Polity Press
65 Bridge Street
Cambridge CB2 1UR, UK

Polity Press
101 Station Landing
Suite 300
Medford, MA 02155, USA

ISBN-13: 978-1-5095-3917-8 Hardback
ISBN-13: 978-1-5095-3918-5 Paperback

A catalogue record for this book is available from the British Library.

Typeset in 10.75 on 14 Adobe Janson by
Servis Filmsetting Ltd, Stockport, Cheshire
Printed and bound in Great Britain by CPI Group (UK) Ltd, Croydon

For further information on Polity, visit our website: politybooks.com

CONTENTS

ACKNOWLEDGEMENTS

Many people have contributed in different ways to the production of this book. Any errors, needless to say, are my own. But I want to thank the friends and colleagues who have helped me along the way. I owe a debt of obligation to my publishers, Polity Press, and in particular to my editor, Dr George Owers, whose suggestions were indispensable. I owe an equal debt to Wadham College, Oxford, where between 2018 and 2019 I was a Keeley Visiting Fellow. In particular, I am grateful to the Warden, Lord Macdonald of River Glaven, for awarding me the Fellowship, and to Lord Wood of Anfield, who proposed me to the College. I am grateful, too, to Dr Paul Martin and Dr Tom Sinclair for their wise advice and support.

I want to thank Chris Evans, my editor at *The Daily Telegraph*, and Tom Welsh, the newspaper's insightful comment editor. I should also thank Tony Gallagher, the editor of *The Sun*, for whom I wrote between 2017 and 2019. It has been a privilege to write about many of the issues covered in this book in their magnificent newspapers. I am thankful to Matthew Taylor, who made me a Fellow of the RSA, which often provided me with a calm and quiet workspace in the middle of London. I should also thank the University of Sheffield, where I am a Visiting Professor, and in particular Professor Andrew Hindmoor and the brilliant Dr Matt Sleat.

Matt has been a wise counsellor throughout, as have Professor John Gray and Professor Vernon Bogdanor. Other friends and colleagues to whom I owe a particular debt for their thoughts and advice include Claire Ainsley, John Bowers, Matthew d'Ancona, Mike Flower, David Goodhart, Paul Goodman, Michael Gove, Tom Greeves, Ygal el Harrar, James Johnson, Professor Eric Kaufmann, Hans Kundnani, Baroness Meyer of Nine Elms, Sir Christopher Meyer, Rick Nye, Lord O'Shaughnessy of Maidenhead, Professor Adrian Pabst, Bojan Pancevski, Nick Pickles, Amol Rajan, Manveen Rana, Russell Rook, Gisela Stuart, Will Tanner, Niva Thiruchelvam, Nick Webb, Rachel Wolf, Sir Simon Woolley and my brother, John Timothy. It goes without saying that not everybody listed here agrees with everything I argue in the book.

In particular, I am grateful to Rick Nye for allowing me to reproduce the Populus 'Clockface' research in chapter 3. Nick Webb went far beyond the call of duty – especially given his own liberal beliefs – with his numerous comments and improvements. Adam Brown – my old friend 'Stumpy' – put me up for many Oxford nights and never hesitated to get the drinks in. And, of course, there is Martina, who advised and supported me through several draft texts and hundreds of conversations and email exchanges. It is to Martina, and to the whole of my family, that I dedicate this book.

INTRODUCTION TO THE
PAPERBACK EDITION

Events, dear boy

Publishing a book in 2020 was a risky business. Covid put paid to the launch party – thanks anyway to Rob Colvile of the Centre for Policy Studies for agreeing to host me, and to Michael Gove for agreeing to speak – but, more importantly, the proposition of the book was put to the test by fast-changing real-world events.

Fortunately, reviewers and readers agreed that *Remaking One Nation* passed its unexpected test. 'Nobody knows how the coronavirus pandemic will change politics', said the *Financial Times* upon publication, but the book was 'timely in ways that Timothy himself cannot have expected'. It is, of course, up to readers of this paperback edition to decide for yourselves as to whether this is true. But I want to dwell for a moment on those issues where the first edition was not contradicted by events, but where events moved so quickly that my arguments now require some reflection and expansion.

Since submitting my final draft, we have seen the British government agree a Brexit deal and new trading relationship with the European Union. We have had a historic general election, in which a new electoral coalition gave the Conservatives a thumping majority. We have lived through the emergence of Covid-19, lockdowns, worldwide recession, unprecedented fiscal interventions, the great scientific race to treat and halt the virus, and vaccine nationalism as leaders put their people before contracts and laws. We have watched the Black Lives Matter protests, the defeat of President Trump, and the deepening of a culture war in Britain as well as in America. We have grown more anxious about Scotland's place in the United Kingdom. And the whole world has seen the reality of the Chinese state: an alleged genocide in Xinjiang, the crushing of Hong Kong, aggression towards its neighbours, a Covid misinformation campaign, and a refusal to cooperate with other countries and international institutions over the virus that emerged in still mysterious circumstances in Wuhan.

The pandemic has prompted re-evaluation of many recent political assumptions. Politicians from across party divides now agree that there is a need for greater state capacity, for example, as the lack of such capacity was highlighted by some of the early failures in Britain's Covid response. There is recognition that global supply chains are too stretched, and Western economies too reliant on China. With vaccines the product of a successful partnership between the state and private business, there is increasing support for industrial intervention, even if some ministers prefer not to call it industrial strategy. There is even agreement among senior Conservatives that, while market-based health systems work elsewhere, it is neither practical nor desirable to marketize a national system like the NHS.

Not every Conservative is convinced, of course, but for those of us who do believe in the benefits of a strong state and active government, the task is to argue, not only that such changes need to be made, but also to suggest how we should go about making them. Industrial strategy, for example, requires government to make choices: investing in some sectors more than others, spending big on research and development, taking a call on the future skills needs of the country, identifying the infrastructure needs of different localities, and, where necessary, intervening to prevent certain mergers and acquisitions. Whether government, having grasped the need for an industrial strategy, is able to deliver such a strategy successfully is now what matters.

Of course, for some state interventions in the economy, there is still a question of degree. Conservative ministers remain nervous about being seen to 'pick winners' – normally a misunderstanding of industrial strategy rather than its repudiation – and many still worry about fiscal rectitude. But the possibility that Conservative politicians might support a more interventionist economic policy and tolerate higher public spending is greater now that the party's coalition of voters is more provincial, more working class and more in need of the security provided by the state rather than eager to win freedom from it.

This increasing appetite for state intervention may yet come a cropper. While some new and provincial Conservative MPs share the values of many of their voters, some are ideologically committed to shrinking the state and cutting spending and taxes. With some policy decisions, the values and interests of the party's new voters might clash with the values and interests of its more traditional supporters. And whether senior ministers – many of whom grew up on Hayek and Friedman – really have the appetite to change the Conservative Party, regardless of electoral or even empirical reality, remains to be seen.

Perhaps the biggest test will be the future of fiscal policy. The cost of locking down to avoid the worst of the pandemic was a record reduction in economic output and an unprecedented budget deficit. But it does not follow that austerity is what must come next. International institutions, like the IMF and OECD, recommend looser fiscal policies. The United States has launched a stimulus programme worth almost $2 trillion. And the markets are coming to terms with higher stocks of debt in the West. Unlike with the financial crash, which caused a credit crunch that undermined productivity, restricted economic growth and limited tax receipts, the fiscal effect of the pandemic is significant but not recurring. Governments can pay down their debts as future growth generates tax receipts.

And the broader needs of the country dictate that spending will need to increase, not decrease. If the Conservatives are to "level up" the country, as Boris Johnson has promised, they will need to spend big, not only on transport infrastructure, but digital connectivity, technical education, regeneration programmes and a range of different services. The important supply-side reforms the economy needs include some changes in tax and regulation, but more important are changes that require investment, such as in science and in research and development. Meanwhile, thanks to our growing old-age dependency ratio, demography determines that spending on pensions, health and social care will only go up. Many Conservatives may be reluctant to confront the question of how to raise the revenues, but Britain's fiscal future will require European levels of public spending.

Just as economic change has quickened, so too have cultural changes. The culture war has deepened dramatically and rapidly since the publication of the first edition. Traditional feminists are denounced as transphobes. Women's refuges are denied public money because they are not gender-neutral. August institutions from the Church of England to the National Trust are busily reviewing the histories of their buildings and apologizing for the conduct of generations long-gone. Academics argue about whether Winston Churchill was as big a villain as Adolf Hitler. Police forces warn members of the public – with no basis in legal fact – that 'being offensive is an offence'.

Issues of identity and culture are becoming more important, but our political classes have little idea of how to respond to them. The crisis of the white working class – in educational opportunity and attainment, in particular – continues. Yet frequently the crisis is ignored, denied or explained away. We are told, for example, that the reason white working-class children under-perform in national education statistics is that a disproportionate percentage of minority children live in London, where schools have improved most. This is part of the story, but official statistics show that, even in the capital, white children under-perform compared to others.

In Scotland, the increasing salience of identity takes the form of separatism, and the Union itself is now in grave danger. The argument I advance – that it is time for the United Kingdom to become fully federal – is still very much a minority opinion. But more and more there is recognition from thinkers and politicians across the ideological spectrum, and across the Kingdom, that the status quo cannot survive. Federation is a solution that corrects the constitutional imbalances created by the devolution settlement, brings government closer to the people, and recognizes better our identities as citizens of both the United Kingdom and its constituent nations of England, Scotland, Wales and Northern Ireland.

Perhaps the most rapid change since the publication of *Remaking One Nation* is the transformation of Britain's political classes from rampant Sinophiles to alarmed Sinosceptics. Since the emergence of

Covid-19, the conduct of the Chinese state has been shocking, but not surprising to those of us who have long warned about the true nature of Xi Jinping and his regime. And yet despite this conduct – tearing up international treaties, crushing Hong Kong, presiding over a genocide in Xinjiang, and much more besides – the West is divided. The European Union has negotiated a new treaty with Beijing, and British policy, like American policy, remains unclear.

A consistently Sinosceptic policy – which is now an urgent necessity – would require new alliances capable of sustaining a common approach to Beijing; the creation of new institutions to coordinate policies internationally; trade policies that minimize our dependence on China; the diversification of international supply chains; and industrial strategy to protect key industries and companies from Chinese ownership or espionage, and to maintain British and Western capabilities in strategic sectors, such as telecommunications and life sciences.

Throughout this century China will undoubtedly prove to be a powerful strategic rival to the West and democratic states around the world, but that does not mean there is nothing we can do. The Chinese regime needs high economic growth to survive, and for such growth it needs sensible relations with the rest of the world. Britain, as part of a wider alliance of countries concerned about Chinese power, has leverage against Beijing, and we should make sure it does not go unused.

On all these issues, and many others, the purpose of *Remaking One Nation* is to try to understand things in their proper philosophical context. That purpose is just as strong now as when the first edition was published. For so many of our contemporary problems and challenges stem from the flawed philosophical assumptions – adopted consciously or not – of the people who govern us. Those assumptions present themselves in different forms of ideological, ultra-liberalism that span left, right and centre. This book is an attempt to explore these bodies of ideas, identify their flaws, explain how they failed us in reality, and set out what conservatives – freed from the ideology that has captivated them for several decades – might do instead.

'Two nations [of rich and poor]; between whom there is no intercourse and no sympathy; who are as ignorant of each other's habits, thoughts, and feelings, as if they were dwellers in different zones, or inhabitants of different planets; who are formed by a different breeding, are fed by a different food, are ordered by different manners, and are not governed by the same laws.'

– Benjamin Disraeli, 1845

'We stand for the union of those two nations of which Disraeli spoke two generations ago: union … to make one nation of our own people which, if secured, nothing else matters in the world.'

– Stanley Baldwin, 1924

'We now speak as a one nation Conservative Party literally for everyone from Woking to Workington, from Kensington … to Clwyd South, from Surrey Heath to Sedgefield, from Wimbledon to Wolverhampton.'

– Boris Johnson, 2019

INTRODUCTION:
OUT OF THE ARENA

At two minutes to ten, my world fell to pieces. With a couple of hundred staffers watching us through the office glass walls, my friend and colleague Fiona read to me what the rest of the country would be told moments later. She had the exit poll result and it said the general election would produce a hung parliament. Our gamble had failed and we had lost our majority. It was a catastrophe.

The two of us strode through the throngs of volunteers and staffers, and made it through to the back room where the campaign directors were assembled. 'This is bullshit', spat Lynton Crosby, the Australian consultant, 'it's really wide of the mark.' Jim Messina, the American data expert, agreed. 'It's wrong', he kept muttering, over and over again. But Mark Textor, Crosby's business partner and polling expert, sat in stony silence. Stephen Gilbert, the veteran Tory campaigner and a personal friend for many years, took me to one side. 'Exit polls are never wrong', he warned, with the solemnity of a doctor declaring a death.

My phone rang. It was Theresa. 'They're saying it's a hung parliament', she said, barely audibly. I could hear the disappointment and hurt and anger in her voice. There was terror, too. I had seen or heard her cry on a few occasions before, but this was different. She was sobbing. I remember thinking she sounded like a child who wanted to be told everything was just fine. 'Lynton says the exit poll is wrong', I told her. 'We just have to see what happens.'

But by then I knew what was going to happen. We all did. The early results started to come in quickly. Newcastle, Sunderland. Labour holds, but significant swings to the Tories. The analysts fed the data into their models. 'You see!' repeated Messina. 'The poll's wrong!' But as more constituencies declared, the wishful thinking died, and the pattern became clear. We were increasing our vote, but so too were Labour.

Lynton showed me a text message he had received from Theresa. 'She's fucking blaming me!' he complained. Fiona got into a car and sped to Maidenhead, where Theresa was still awaiting her own constituency result. I was in a daze. Chris Wilkins, the Number Ten strategy director, knocked up a short speech for Theresa to make at her count. I went for a walk around the war room, the open-plan office where the campaign team had worked, and spoke to staffers. One senior party official – another long-time friend – had collapsed and looked as white as a ghost. An ambulance was called and he was whisked away to hospital.

Chris and I sat alone in the party boardroom as the hours went by. Ben Gummer, the MP for Ipswich and Minister for the Cabinet Office, texted to say he had lost. Other good friends were among the casualties. Chris White, in Warwick and Leamington. Simon Kirby, Brighton Kemptown. Nicola Blackwood, Oxford West and Abingdon. Edward Timpson, Crewe and Nantwich. There was a pathetic cheer from the war room as Amber Rudd clung on to Hastings and Rye. We won new, mainly working-class, constituencies in Mansfield, Middlesbrough and Walsall, but the gains were too few and the losses mounted. Constituencies that CCHQ thought we might win just a few hours earlier – including even Bolsover and Sedgefield – were declared. Labour hold. Labour hold.

Theresa spoke at her count. I watched on television. She was as she was on the phone earlier: teary and shell-shocked. Eventually she returned to CCHQ, and we sat, in awkward silence, around the boardroom table. 'We will have to resign to give you the space to carry on', I said. She didn't really reply. Her mind was fixed on the numbers. 'We need to talk to the DUP', she kept saying. 'We need to keep out

Corbyn.' Her phone kept buzzing with calls and text messages from MPs and others. Eventually, she read one out loud. 'The donors think you need to go', she said, staring at Fiona and me.

Riding high

One year earlier, things had been very different indeed. The referendum on Britain's membership of the European Union had been held in June 2016. David Cameron resigned and, after a short leadership campaign in which her rivals self-immolated, one after another, Theresa May became Prime Minister.

As she emerged from the car that had taken her from Buckingham Palace to Downing Street, it was difficult to hear anything from where I was standing, waiting, inside Number Ten. The shutters of cameras opened and closed, and helicopters circled above. At last, standing behind the official lectern for the first time, she addressed the country. 'If you're from an ordinary working-class family', she said, 'life is much harder than many people in Westminster realise ... I know you're working around the clock, I know you're doing your best, and I know that sometimes life can be a struggle.' Looking straight down the camera and into millions of living rooms, she promised, 'the government I lead will be driven not by the interests of the privileged few, but by yours.'

It was the shortest speech I had written for her, but it was by far the highest profile. As she spoke, Downing Street officials and her political team waited inside the Number Ten hallway. The Cabinet Secretary, the late Sir Jeremy Heywood, motioned to me to stand beside him. I was doubled over with anxiety, but as she spoke it became clear there was no need for nerves. The speech was a triumph. Theresa had been on the Conservative frontbench for nearly twenty years, and Home Secretary for the last six. But this was her introduction to the nation, and the public seemed to like what they heard and saw. The speech catapulted her to unprecedented approval ratings, which remained unusually positive all the way until the general election a year later.

The first job was to reshuffle her ministerial team. George Osborne, Cameron's Chancellor and author of 'Project Fear', the negative campaign against Brexit, was sacked. The media were led to believe he had resigned, and when a member of the Downing Street team corrected his version of events, he claimed to be the victim of vicious dirty tricks. Michael Gove, who had backed Boris Johnson's leadership bid before suddenly launching his own campaign, was also sent to the backbenches. Despite his intellect and talent, Tory MPs were angry about Michael's perceived treachery, which made it difficult to appoint him to a top job, but Theresa had never liked him and she played the role of executioner with enthusiasm.

The reshuffle was sweeping, and the media worked out that the Cabinet had more state-school educated ministers than any Conservative government before it. The front page of the *Daily Mail* hailed the 'march of the meritocrats'.[1] But it was bloodier than it was intended to be. Stephen Crabb, the Work and Pensions Secretary, resigned after failing to promise allegations about his sex life would not continue. Claire Perry and Anna Soubry refused frontbench roles as soon as it became clear they would not be given their own departments.

The summer passed quickly and quietly. Early Brexit talks with other European leaders began. Fairly minor policy announcements were made. Theresa's low-key and understated style seemed to mark a welcome change in the way the country was governed.

Then came the first controversy. In September, Theresa made a speech in which she said she wanted to make Britain 'the world's great meritocracy'. She outlined a new policy that would build on years of English school reform, and in particular free schools and academies, schools set up and sponsored by teachers, parents and community groups. Acknowledging that some communities lack the social capital to make free schools and academies a success, we wanted to get more groups into the system and running good state schools. Private schools and universities would be made to do more. Rules that effectively prevented Catholic – but not other faith groups – from setting up schools would be changed. And new selective schools would be permitted, on the strict condition that they also sponsored good primary schools and non-selective secondaries, and made sure their intakes included more children from poorer families.

The announcement blew up before it was even made. The Education Secretary, Justine Greening, turned out to oppose any new selective schools. She never said so to Theresa, but was less shy when briefing the newspapers. Shortly before the speech, Jonathan Slater, the Department for Education's permanent secretary, accompanied Greening on her way to a meeting with the PM in Downing Street. There, he was photographed with a folder exposing a sheet of paper revealing the Education Secretary's concern about new selective schools. Slater had not been invited to attend the meeting, and he did not try to come in. But the damage was done. The stunt was cynical, cheap and, coming from a senior official, completely inappropriate. But it worked: it sparked a row about grammar schools, and the policy never got off the ground.

Next came a warning sign about Theresa's own decision-making. In July, she had decided to 'pause' the process leading to the construction of a new nuclear reactor at Hinkley Point in Somerset. The project would be delivered by the French energy giant, EDF, and financed in part by the Chinese General Nuclear Power Group, a state-run business accused by the United States of stealing nuclear secrets.[2] It was eye-wateringly expensive, and relied on technology that had never been tried before. It also meant increasing Chinese involvement in Britain's critical national infrastructure. Under the terms of a 'progressive entry' agreement, Hinkley would be followed by new reactors at Sizewell in Suffolk and Bradwell in Essex. At each stage, the role of the Chinese in running the plants would deepen.

The decision to pause the deal was rancorous enough. The Chinese protested. A junior minister threatened to resign. And Theresa offended Jeremy Heywood when she questioned the contract: he thought she was accusing him of colluding with the French to push the deal through. But after all the hassle of the pause – the controversy, the bruised relations with China and France, and the clash with her most senior civil servant – in September, she backed down. Persuaded that cancellation would send a bad message to the markets so soon after the Brexit vote, and worrying about the need to keep the French onside through the Brexit talks, she let the deal pass. It would not be the last time she would be accused of talking tough before backing down. But at this stage, the criticism was fairly limited.

At the start of October, we headed to Birmingham for the party conference. 'A country that works for everyone', was emblazoned around the conference centre, and the mood was buoyant. Theresa spoke on the first day, the Sunday, and set out what would later be criticized as unnecessary red lines for the Brexit negotiations. 'Brexit means Brexit', she promised: Britain would take back control of its laws, its borders and its money. The audience was in ecstasy.

At the close of the conference, on Wednesday, she spoke again. This was the opportunity to set out her domestic priorities, and the way she intended to govern. Chris Wilkins and I had worked on the speech for weeks, and, in praising 'the good that government can do', it marked a clear break with recent Conservative thinking. The *Daily Mail* lauded its 'bold vision' and even the *Guardian* respected its ambitious attempt to recast conservatism.[3] As the draftsmen, I remember Chris and I were most pleased by praise from Peggy Noonan, the US columnist and former speechwriter to President Reagan, who from across the Atlantic declared it the 'beginning of a political future'.[4]

It was only later that the speech was attacked for its condemnation of 'citizens of nowhere'. It suited campaigners and political opponents to claim that Theresa had used this language to describe opponents of Brexit. But this was nonsense, as anybody listening at the time knew. Her targets were the more irresponsible and selfish members of big international business. The speech was absolutely clear. 'Today', she said, 'too many people in positions of power behave as though they have more in common with international elites than with the people down the road, the people they employ, the people they pass in the street. But if you believe you're a citizen of the world, you're a citizen of nowhere. You don't understand what the very word "citizenship" means.'[5]

The speech was an ambitious blueprint for what we wanted to do. But translating these promises into policy and reality would take more time. Consultation papers were launched on corporate governance, industrial strategy and schools. Fiona was developing a landmark domestic violence bill. In Downing Street and across Whitehall, work was underway on regional policy, market reform, workers' rights, housing, health, social care, racial justice and mental health. But to me it all felt like it was going too slowly. Behind the scenes, problems were mounting.

Behind the scenes

At the best of times, political parties find it difficult to renew themselves several years into government. If they are honest about problems that need fixing, the media and opposition ask why these things have not been fixed already. If they acknowledge past mistakes, their supporters criticize them for trashing their own record. If they change policies to suit the needs of the day, they are accused of U-turning. If they do any of these things quickly, without a longer conversation about the government's direction, they encounter resistance within their party. If they take time to build a consensus, they are accused of dithering. Former ministers and their allies guard their legacies jealously, and are quick to denounce perceived slights.

Prime ministers who arrive in Downing Street from opposition have usually had the time and space to develop their ideas and arguments. They can build up their policy programmes, and establish coalitions of supporters among experts, academics and journalists. New prime ministers who arrive straight from a government department have no time to do any of these things. They are thrust into Number Ten with no transition and little or no time to prepare their agenda.

The bold approach Theresa set out in the Downing Street and party conference speeches needed an equally bold policy programme. But here there was another problem. There was no mandate for a break with David Cameron's agenda. There had been little time to debate policy during the truncated Conservative leadership election. And several senior ministers opposed change. In particular, Theresa's Chancellor, Philip Hammond, refused to change fiscal policy and opposed reforms to corporate governance and competition policy. 'You don't need to actually *do* any of this stuff', he once said with a trademark smirk, 'you're miles ahead in the polls just talking about it.'

Theresa's relationship with Hammond was especially bad. At the point at which she made him her Chancellor, she believed she had a good personal relationship with him. But within weeks their relationship was bitter and rancorous. He showed little respect for Theresa or her intellect. He briefed the newspapers that she was 'economically illiterate', and he said the same about me. In his first Budget, he insisted on increasing National Insurance contributions for self-employed workers, against Theresa's advice and breaking a promise in the 2015 election manifesto. His response to the backbench rebellion he caused was not to show contrition but to become even more obstreperous and aggressive in his briefing against Number Ten.

Theresa's relationships with other ministers were little better. She got on badly with Justine Greening, Sajid Javid and Boris Johnson. Looking back, her relations with colleagues were often poor because she neither trusted them nor even knew them particularly well. She would often patronize Boris and put him down in front of his colleagues.

And what makes a minister successful running a government department – even a department as important as the Home Office – will not necessarily translate to Number Ten. In the Home Office, Fiona and I were able, on Theresa's behalf, to maintain a tight grip on departmental business. We were equals in everything we did, and worked fluidly across policy, political work, strategy and communications. In Number Ten, we tried and failed to work in the same way. Our status as joint chiefs of staff sometimes caused confusion in the command chain. With notable exceptions like JoJo Penn, James Slack, Will Tanner and Chris Wilkins, we did not build a strong enough senior team to delegate with confidence. We neglected our managerial duties because our other responsibilities overwhelmed us.

Compared to life in a department, the job in Downing Street is much more about setting a strategy and allowing ministers to deliver it, coordinating efforts across departments, solving problems and ensuring delivery, and constant, human communication. The complaint that Theresa – and we, her senior advisers – brought too much of the Home Office into Number Ten was justified. The role of the prime minister is not to play every instrument in the orchestra, but to write the score and conduct the musicians. Too often, Theresa was trying to play the strings, woodwind, brass and percussion all at the same time.

Yet she often backed down when confronted by opposition. She promised to 'repair the dysfunctional housing market', but was too nervy about agreeing the policies that would get more houses built.[6] She wanted 'an energy policy ... [with] lower costs for users', but ended up supporting unilateral climate change policies that will increase bills for households and industry.[7] When Hammond and others objected to her policies, she watered them down or gave up on them altogether. On each occasion I tried to convince her to change fiscal policy, she refused to do so. Only once the election had been lost did she accept the need to call time on the age of austerity.

Brexit

All the while, one issue more than any other loomed before us. Brexit was the reason Theresa had become Prime Minister. Yet she had been a Remainer. Back on 24 June, early on the morning after the referendum, I called her to talk about the leadership election that would soon begin. I was surprised to find she was crying. The tears, I judged, were caused by frustration, not grief. But her reaction to the result was to worry that the people who had voted for Brexit – especially manufacturing workers in the regions – were the people who stood to lose most from Britain leaving the European Union.

I thought about that moment many times as, after I left Downing Street, Theresa's negotiating strategy softened and softened. But at the time I had no cause to dwell on it. She came to terms with the result quickly. She stamped upon any suggestions that the referendum might be re-run. She rejected calls for different forms of associate EU membership. When ministers and officials proposed what she dismissed as 'clinging to bits of the EU we used to like', she relished reprimanding them. Taking off her reading glasses and waving them at her victims, she would explain that we needed to negotiate a close economic and security relationship, but we must be entirely outside the EU's laws and institutions.

When she became Prime Minister, Theresa created two new government departments to help deliver Brexit. The first was the Department for International Trade, whose responsibilities would include the negotiation of free trade deals with other countries. The second was the Department for Exiting the European Union. The logic for creating this department was to create a Whitehall institution with a clear interest in delivering Brexit, and to reassure Leave supporters about her good intentions. 'I will ... create a new government department', she promised during the leadership campaign, 'responsible for conducting Britain's negotiation with the EU and for supporting the rest of Whitehall in its European work. That department will be led by a senior Secretary of State – and I will make sure that the position is taken by a Member of Parliament who campaigned for Britain to leave the EU.'[8]

Strictly speaking, Theresa stuck to her promise. But the Secretary of State she appointed, David Davis, was never in charge of the negotiations. Brexit policy was discussed by the Cabinet and at regular meetings of a Cabinet sub-committee dedicated to leaving the EU. But the negotiating strategy was discussed in much smaller meetings between Theresa and her senior civil servants and political advisers. Olly Robbins, Theresa's Brussels 'Sherpa', was asked to lead the negotiations, not David Davis.

David Cameron had instructed the civil service not to draw up plans for leaving the EU, fearing that preparations would play into the hands of the Leave campaign by making Brexit seem realistic and safe. So it took a little time to get things moving along. During the summer, officials and ministers conducted talks with their opposite numbers across Europe and with officials in Brussels. Theresa had wanted to start informal negotiations before giving formal notice of Britain's intention to leave the EU. The mechanism for doing so, Article 50 of the Treaty on European Union, set a two-year deadline for concluding a withdrawal agreement. But by the end of the summer, the message from the Europeans was clear, and so was the official policy advice: there would be no negotiating until Article 50 was formally triggered.

In September, Theresa decided that she would have to invoke Article 50 to get anywhere with the talks. On the opening day of the Conservative conference, she announced she would trigger by no later than the end of March 2017. And she promised to repeal the European Communities Act, which gave direct effect to EU law in Britain. 'We will do what independent, sovereign countries do', she said. 'We will decide for ourselves how we control immigration. And we will be free to pass our own laws.'[9]

Later, it was claimed that this speech set unnecessary red lines that made the Brexit negotiations impossible. It was even claimed that the red lines were invented by Theresa and me alone, with no input from anybody else. Both claims are ridiculous. First, Brexit policy was discussed at Cabinet, in the Cabinet sub-committee, and in bilateral meetings between Theresa and her ministers. No Cabinet

Secretary, and certainly not one as experienced and as proper as Sir Jeremy Heywood, would have allowed new policy to be decided and announced in such a manner. And second, as any student of the European Union knows, the EU was established, in its original form, as a customs union. Its single market then developed over time. If Britain did not leave the customs union and single market – and the laws and institutions that underpin both – what would we be leaving? As David Davis said to me at the time, the speech was little more than 'a statement of the bleeding obvious'. And as Boris Johnson's Brexit deal proved, it is possible to leave the EU in full accordance with the so-called 'red lines'.

The speech was still a mistake, however. Theresa's first significant public intervention on Brexit policy should not have been made before a partisan audience. The Europeans perceived a prime minister playing to the gallery, and that caused some misunderstandings about the way she was planning to go about the negotiations.

The next big Brexit intervention was a different matter altogether. Theresa's Lancaster House speech was, if anything, tougher than what she said at the party conference. And yet it was received positively by Leavers and Remainers at home, and by Brussels and the remaining member states.

For the first time, Theresa explicitly ruled out membership of the customs union and the single market. She was robust with Brussels too. 'No deal for Britain is better than a bad deal', she warned. And if Britain was excluded from the single market, 'we would be free to change the basis of Britain's economic model.' But the tone was still constructive. 'We are leaving the European Union', she explained, 'but we are not leaving Europe.' She said she had listened to the EU, which was why she would not seek to divide its four freedoms of goods, capital, services and people. The days of British 'cherry picking' were over: we would seek fair access to the single market, but not re-join it.[10]

Theresa's next big speech – made in Philadelphia to an audience of Republican senators and congressmen – also went down well in Europe. Following the election of President Trump, many member states were worried that he was hostile to the EU and ambivalent about NATO. But in Philadelphia, Theresa came to Europe's defence. 'We are not turning our back on [Europe]', she declared, 'or on the interests and the values that we share. It remains overwhelmingly in our interests – and in those of the wider world – that the EU should succeed.'[11] In Washington, she pressed President Trump and won from him an unequivocal public commitment to NATO and the collective security of the West.

This was a real achievement, but behind the scenes, we were worrying. We had got off to a bad start with Sir Ivan Rogers, Britain's permanent representative in Brussels. His advice in meetings was pessimistic and bordered on the destructive. We could not negotiate before triggering Article 50, he said, but neither should we trigger Article 50, because it was a trap. Every policy option was impossible, he would argue: there was no way through the mess, because Brexit itself was impossible.

Ivan also had a strange relationship with the media. Former advisers to David Cameron warned us that he had briefed against them during the renegotiation prior to the referendum. 'He did it the whole time', one said. 'He is super smart, but prone to child-like tantrums and cannot pursue anything but his own personal agenda.'[12] During Theresa's premiership, newspaper reports by Brussels correspondents regularly contained quotations from 'diplomatic sources' that bore close resemblance to Ivan's private criticisms of Brexit.

Ivan's behaviour frustrated us all, including his fellow civil servants. Eventually, Jeremy Heywood suggested to Ivan that he should move on to another senior post. But very abruptly, Ivan instead resigned, writing an email to his team demanding that they continue to 'speak truth to power'.[13] Unsurprisingly, the email reached the media in no time at all. Ivan was quickly replaced by Sir Tim Barrow, a Foreign Office star, but he was to remain a prominent and trenchant critic not only of Brexit policy, but of Brexit itself.

Things were little better with some senior ministers. Meetings at Cabinet and with ministers were bad-tempered. Philip Hammond kept pushing for Brexit to be softer and softer. He wanted to make commitments about sticking with free movement rules, for example, and refused to consider alternatives to European regulations because he believed Britain would in the end have to accept EU rules anyway. Every attempt to take Brexit policy forward was an exhausting battle with one side of Cabinet pitched against the other.

In Parliament, it was clear that the House of Lords would do what it could to frustrate Brexit. In the Commons, Labour were gearing up to oppose whatever the Government did, and there were enough rebellious Tory Remainers to render the Government's slim majority meaningless. Fiona and I talked again and again about whether we needed an early election to help get Brexit through Parliament. But when we raised the question with Theresa, she was always quick to rebuff us.

The election campaign

I had first raised the question of an early election during the leadership campaign. Theresa was adamantly opposed: she wanted to use her launch speech to rule out any election before 2020. I thought that was a promise she might come to regret, because of the way Brexit divisions would inevitably cut across the parties in Parliament. Nonetheless, she made the promise, and I chose not to raise the subject again for several months.

But as time went by, the case for an election built. There was little sign of Parliament accepting the referendum result. Every vote in the Commons felt like a dangerous challenge, and we survived only through some deft tactics and the smart whipping operation led by Gavin Williamson. In February 2017, the Conservatives won Copeland, an area represented by Labour for more than eighty years, in a by-election.[14] Afterwards, several Cabinet ministers pushed for an early election. And the polls continued to look good. In April 2017, we had a poll lead over Labour of 21 percentage points.[15]

The coalition of support for an early election grew. Inside Number Ten, JoJo Penn and Chris Wilkins joined Fiona and me in arguing we needed to go back to the country. After Copeland, Stephen Gilbert and senior staff from CCHQ joined the chorus. In March, William Hague used his *Daily Telegraph* column to say an election would 'strengthen the Government's hand at home and abroad'.[16] And the pressure was not only political. Jeremy Heywood told Theresa he thought she needed a mandate and a majority to get Brexit done.

Theresa's attitude changed quite abruptly on 29 March. On that day, she sent her letter giving formal notification to the Council of

Ministers of Britain's intention to withdraw from the EU. When she made her statement in Parliament, the mood in the Commons was uneasy. She was interrupted repeatedly, and her statement prompted jeers and sarcastic laughter from the opposition benches. She did not decide to call an early election immediately after that statement, but I could tell her judgement changed that day. I sensed she was starting to believe an election was unavoidable.

Still, she took her time to decide. Ideally, the general election would have been held on 4 May, the same day as the local and mayoral elections, but the deadline to bring about an election that day came and went. Theresa finally announced her decision on 18 April. By that time, thanks to the timetable set out by the Fixed-Term Parliaments Act and the need to conclude parliamentary business, polling day could be no earlier than 8 June. The campaign was to last seven and a half weeks. We had sacrificed the advantage of surprise and made the first of many mistakes.

It is important to remember that at this point Theresa's leadership was still incredibly popular in the country. The political strategy we had established – framed in her original Downing Street speech and fleshed out at the party conference – was working well. She was determined to lead Britain out of the European Union, but she was just as determined to bring about lasting change to social and economic policy. She consciously put herself at the service of working- and middle-class families, and talked much more about using the power of government to change lives for the better. This was the strategy that had created her 21-point poll lead.

Yet none of us on the Downing Street staff, nor even among the senior CCHQ staff, had ever run a national election campaign. We had to bring in external support. So Stephen Gilbert returned to the fray, and so did Lynton Crosby, who had run the Tory election campaigns of 2005 and 2015. With Crosby came his business partner, Mark Textor, and the former Obama campaign adviser, Jim Messina.

Lynton was adamant we needed a completely different approach for an election campaign. Talking about workers' rights or public services, for example, would only increase the salience of issues that make people more likely to vote Labour. Just talking about policy was a bad thing, because policies are complicated. They prompt attacks from critics and opponents, and they muddy the message. It is much better, he said, to keep finding new devices to keep repeating the core message. And the opinion research, he said, showed swing voters did not want change. They wanted stability and continuity. Out went Theresa the changemaker, and in came the soundbite that would soon be mocked mercilessly: 'strong and stable government'. And so our answer to everything became strong and stable, strong and stable, strong and stable.

Before the campaign began, we had envisaged a campaigning style that would reflect Theresa's more traditional, unspun manner. We talked about holding daily press conferences, like in the elections of old, in which we would announce a new policy, or highlight a particular issue, or scrutinize our opponents. We expected to use different ministers, as well as Theresa, to front up each event. But this too was rejected. Press conferences would invite the media to cause all sorts of trouble, and we would lose control of the message. And the polling showed that while Theresa was tremendously popular, other ministers were not, and the Conservative brand itself was still badly tainted. And so we ended up with Theresa, introverted and shy, leading a campaign asking people not to vote for the Conservatives but 'Theresa May's team'.

We could have chosen to resist these changes. We were powerful enough to do so. But we didn't. Ironically, after being criticized as 'control freaks' in Number Ten, Fiona and I handed over control of the campaign to Lynton and the consultants. We knew we had never run a national campaign, and we put our trust in the people who had. Our roles would be subordinate to the consultants. Fiona took responsibility for communications. I took on policy. JoJo took on a sort of coordinating function. Chris, having been strategy director in Number Ten, was left kicking his heels as the new campaign strategists took over.

And the problems kept coming. Theresa was warm and natural when she met voters in person, on high streets, in markets and at country shows. But she was wooden on the stump and robotic in broadcast interviews. She seemed utterly terrified before her set-piece interviews and debates. And as the campaign went on, she grew increasingly tired and irritable. Interviews with print journalists were defensive and painful to watch.

The senior staff muttered and moaned about biased broadcast coverage. It is probably true that with the country expecting a Tory landslide, our plans were subjected to more scrutiny than Labour's. But we were not generating the stories to earn good broadcast coverage. Television and radio need a proposition to argue about: a policy that can be promoted by one side and criticized by another. But all we were offering was the same old shots of Theresa saying the same things at the same old rallies of activists. They say you campaign in poetry and govern in prose, but we were campaigning in sullen, monosyllabic grunts.

And we became the victims of what Harold Macmillan called, 'events, dear boy'. On 12 May, the NHS was struck by a massive cyber-attack, which dominated the news for days. And then, on 22 May, tragedy struck. Salman Ramadan Abedi, a suicide bomber originally from Libya, blew himself up at an Ariana Grande concert at the Manchester Arena. Twenty-two innocent victims were killed and hundreds, most of whom were children, were injured. On 3 June another attack came. Three Islamist terrorists rammed a van into pedestrians on London Bridge before stabbing people at random in bars and pubs in Borough Market. They killed eight people and injured forty-eight others. These were the second and third attacks on Britain in only three months, as they followed an earlier Islamist atrocity on Westminster Bridge, which had occurred in March.

Our response was flat-footed. Having spent years in the Home Office and Downing Street, we were used to responding to terrible crimes and terror plots. But yet again there was a split between the Downing Street team and the campaign consultants. The Australians wanted Theresa to take to Twitter and denounce what they called Islamic terror. We resisted kneejerk reactions on social media and took ourselves off to Cobra, the government emergency committee. By the time Theresa made her statements to the nation from behind the Downing Street lectern, with both Manchester and London Bridge, Labour's narratives were taking hold. Despite Jeremy Corbyn's long track record of appeasement and even support for terrorists, including Islamist terror groups, his claim that police cuts were to blame caught on. By the time Theresa adopted a tougher line after the second attack, we hadn't just lost control of the narrative, she appeared to have lost control of events. Things looked very far from strong and stable.

Then came the manifesto. I had spent most of the campaign to date working on the policies we would put to the country, along with Ben Gummer and the Downing Street policy team. The product, presented to the country on 18 May, was in many respects the next iteration of the vision Theresa had set out in her original Downing Street speech.

'Conservatism is not and never has been the philosophy described by caricaturists', the manifesto declared. 'We do not believe in untrammelled free markets. We reject the cult of selfish individualism. We abhor social division, injustice, unfairness and inequality. We see rigid dogma and ideology not just as needless but dangerous.' In government, the Conservatives would 'reject the ideological templates provided by the socialist left and the libertarian right and instead embrace the … good that government can do'.[17]

We sought to reconcile the conflicting judgements among the senior campaign team. Lynton hated making policy announcements, and accepted manifestos only as a grim necessity. And he maintained that the country wanted continuity, not change. But Theresa wanted an ambitious document that would give her a mandate to undertake reforms she believed were necessary. We struck on a way to emphasize both continuity and change, by making the manifesto about meeting the great long-term challenges facing the country. Mark Textor confirmed this was consistent with his understanding of voters' concerns, and so we settled on the economy, Britain's place in the world, social fairness, intergenerational fairness and the effects of new technologies.

In some respects, the policies lived up to the shift in values Theresa had promised in her early speeches and in the manifesto's opening chapter. We promised a raft of new workers' rights and changes to corporate governance laws, an industrial strategy and more research and development spending, and reduced energy prices for businesses and households. We promised a new regional development fund, reformed international aid spending, controlled immigration, and a clean Brexit. We wanted a technical education revolution, with new qualifications, institutes of technology and a promise to review tertiary education funding. We said we would reverse the bureaucratic elements of the NHS internal market and train more doctors. We promised domestic violence legislation, better mental health care, and action against various injustices. We pledged new housing, including a new generation of council houses, and more childcare support. We planned new protections for children online, a tougher approach to cyber security, and a legal framework to help Britain become a world leader in digital technologies.

There were plenty of positive stories to tell, but on the whole we did not tell them. Despite the constant worries of the consultants that we might not persuade traditional Labour voters that they could trust the Tories under Theresa's leadership, they did not want to show our values through policy. When Fiona briefed a story about new workers' rights, Lynton hit the roof. They wanted to reassure Labour waverers, but were never prepared to say why or how it was safe or appealing to vote for us.

The earlier failure to change fiscal policy also damaged us. In the policy team, we would have loved to announce the end of austerity. We could have gone further in increasing investment in the regional economy. We could have promised proper pay rises for public sector workers. We could have pledged increases in per pupil school spending. Instead, we promised to go on with austerity, and school funding in particular was an issue that hurt us across the country. Our intention to change pensioner benefits – in particular to means-test the winter fuel allowance – was further tough medicine, although, I would argue, still necessary regardless of the fiscal framework.

The biggest problem, however, was the manifesto's social care policy. Since 2010, as the Government had cut local authority budgets, councils had cut back on social care services. This meant increasing numbers of old people were living in confusion, pain and squalor, and the NHS was suffering as hospitals could not discharge older patients in need of social care that could not be provided. The problem was becoming more acute as the number of older citizens grew. And the consequences were – and remain – ruinous for many families. For residential care, the costs can deplete the patient's assets – including the value of their home – down to a floor of £23,250 and sometimes even less. Many thousands of people are forced to sell the family home to fund their care.

Our proposals were to include the value of the family home in the means test for domiciliary care – home visits and so on – as well as residential care. This would raise funds while also allowing decisions about care to be made according to the needs of the patient. But we would protect family assets by increasing the floor amount that would be protected from £23,250 to £100,000. And, of course, recovery of the costs from the value of the family home would be deferred until the end of the patient's lifetime. Nobody would have to sell their home during their own lifetimes to pay for their care.

At first the manifesto landed well. 'Mainstream May reaches out to Labour heartlands', said *The Times* front page.[18] 'May's manifesto for the mainstream', declared *The Daily Telegraph*.[19] Commentators described a 'new Toryism' and praised even its 'brave and necessary social care plan'.[20]

But quickly it all began to unravel. On the day the manifesto launched, a blogger on *The Spectator* website called the social care policy a 'dementia tax'.[21] Labour seized their opportunity, and Jeremy Corbyn and John McDonnell – Marxists both – took to the airwaves to defend inherited wealth. In the confusion, members of the CCHQ press team told journalists that the policy was to cap care costs at a maximum of £100,000. In fact, it was to create a floor of £100,000 below which people should not pay for their care costs. MPs and candidates struggled to explain the policy on the doorstep. Theresa herself failed to articulate it well: asked by the media how many people would have to sell their homes to pay for their care, she should have said, 'unlike now, nobody'. But she talked around the subject and failed to answer the question directly.

After failing to fight back, or even to explain the policy properly, we all accepted we needed to execute a U-turn. Just a few days after the manifesto was launched, Theresa confirmed at a press conference that a ceiling on costs would be added to the floor proposed in the manifesto. It was a clear change, and it was obvious that we needed to be up front about that. But under pressure from journalists, Theresa's patience – and pride – snapped. 'Nothing has changed!' she insisted, denying she was U-turning even as she was announcing the change in policy.[22]

What little credibility the 'strong and stable' mantra had left was now gone for good. We had triggered a snap election that lasted for weeks and weeks. We made the campaign all about a personality who hated the exposure. We had a Chancellor who the consultants insisted – correctly, in my view – must be hidden from the cameras. We ducked the leadership debates. We responded badly to the terror attacks. We made unforced errors, like Theresa's promise to hold a vote on overturning the ban on fox hunting. We eschewed policy announcements that might have conveyed positive and reassuring values. We screwed up the manifesto and its handling afterwards. We were talking continuity when much of the country wanted change. The campaign limped on towards 8 June.

All too human

Despite everything, when polling day came, the Conservatives won 2.3 million more votes than in 2015, and almost three million more than in 2010. We won more votes, over 13.6 million, than any party had managed in any British election other than 1992. Our vote share increased to 42.4 per cent, the best Tory performance since 1983.

The trouble was – unlike in the 2019 election – Labour surged too. We did too little to convince traditional Labour voters that they could trust us. Jeremy Corbyn managed to convince both Brexit voters and Remainers that he was on their side of the argument. And somehow he was able to unite previously fragmented left-wing voters. To the surprise of almost everybody – including Labour Party headquarters and Labour candidates up and down the country – Corbyn won 12.8 million votes, and a 40 per cent vote share. Theresa had called the election to win a mandate and improve her majority. She emerged from polling day a diminished figure with a disputed mandate and no majority at all.

For me personally, the consequences were dire. During the first year of Theresa's premiership, my role had been hugely prominent. Because Theresa had not previously said much about her views beyond the Home Office, journalists pored over columns I had written – and even my short biography of Joseph Chamberlain – to try to understand her likely priorities. I was, in the words of *The Economist*, 'the Sage of Birmingham' prescribing a new direction for the Conservative Party.[23] I was always uneasy about this kind of coverage, believing advisers, like Victorian children, should be seen but not heard. When I found my parents had kept news clippings of reports and columns that were kind about me, I told them that the higher my profile in the media, the harder my fall was likely to be.

I had no idea just how true that would turn out to be, nor how hard I would fall when the moment came. The briefing against me began as soon as the manifesto started to go wrong. The *Financial Times* reported that 'the [social care] policy was inserted by Mrs May into the Tory manifesto at the last minute on the advice of Nick Timothy … against the advice of John Godfrey, head of the Number 10 policy unit.' I alone, the paper said, had drawn up the manifesto in complete secrecy.[24] Whoever was doing the briefing was relentless and the narrative caught hold. A source told *The Sunday Times* that I had 'basically overruled everyone'.[25]

This was completely untrue. A Cabinet Office working group had been established almost a year before the election to develop proposals to fix the social care crisis. The result of that work was the policy that went into the manifesto. The proposition to include the family home in the means test for domiciliary as well as residential care originally came from the Department of Health. Other ministers and officials – including John Godfrey – had worked on the plans. I supported the policy, and defended its inclusion in the manifesto when Fiona wanted it dropped, but the idea that I alone was responsible for it was just wrong. Nor was it true that it had been kept from the campaign consultants. Mark Textor had tested it, along with other policies, in focus groups and polling weeks earlier, in late April.

I knew I was being scapegoated. Many people had their fingerprints on the social care policy. And many more mistakes – including the strategic framing of the whole election campaign – had been made. But I also knew that I had co-authored the manifesto, and the manifesto had blown up. That was why I offered my resignation on election night.

Walking out of CCHQ in the early hours of 9 June was a warning of what was about to happen. Fiona and I stepped onto the street and into hordes of cameramen and photographers. Eventually we cleared them and got back to St Ermine's hotel, where we had been staying. I packed a bag and headed to the country, far away from London, as fast as possible.

Messages from friends and loved ones came through in the hundreds. But the media barrage was intense. Cameramen gathered outside my flat. Some MPs went on television and radio to condemn Fiona and me. The newspapers were full of nasty and personal quotes about us, made on and off the record. By comparison, the consultants who had been in charge of the campaign got away lightly. The narrative had been spun during the campaign itself, and it had stuck. It was our fault, and only our fault. Theresa went to the 1922 Committee of Conservative MPs and, trying to save her job, reinforced the narrative. 'I'm listening', she said. 'I know changes in Number Ten needed to be made, and I've made them.' MPs texted us, saying: 'your boss has just thrown you under the bus.' I told them I thought she was doing what she needed to do.

Still, the attacks on our characters and our records serving the party and government continued. We were routinely described as 'disgraced', 'toxic', the 'terror twins' and the 'gruesome twosome'. I was even compared to the chicken pox virus, and a secondary infection.[26] Stories about us – so many of which were completely fictional – were briefed to the newspapers and to authors writing books about the election. Some were briefed by a source going through a very public mental breakdown. More were briefed by a former colleague we had sacked after she had done her job poorly. Some columnists and commentators did their best to defend us, but overall, we were on the receiving end of a brutal and uncompromising character assassination. We were attacked in the newspapers almost every day, every week for months.

Few people think about the human consequences of this kind of media onslaught. My father was still recovering from a heart procedure conducted the year before. My mother was diagnosed with cancer the next year. My relationship broke down. With no warning, I would sometimes experience a racing heart and shooting pains down my left arm. And there were other costs, which were too personal, too awful and too upsetting to others for me to write about now. Looking back, whole weeks and months are a blur, and today I realize that my mental wellbeing was on the precipice. I was never suicidal but there were times when I felt the people who loved me most would be better off if I was no longer around to cause them embarrassment or trouble.

No effort without error

I probably returned to work too soon. I took up a column in *The Daily Telegraph* in August following the election in June. But it took me many months to come to terms with what had happened and start to regain my confidence. And by writing a column, I was exposing myself to yet more online bullying and personal abuse.

On a few occasions, perfect strangers who had acquired my phone number texted insults and sarcastic abuse. Twitter, which I rejoined at about the same time as I joined the *Telegraph*, was even worse. Eventually, I decided to quit social media, and I deleted my Twitter account. Even this prompted yet more abuse, as hundreds of critics danced on my digital grave. I discovered that *Sky News* were reporting my departure from Twitter as 'breaking news' when friends got in touch to check I was okay. They thought I might be having a breakdown, and I sensed some worried I might have even harmed myself in some way.

Slowly, I started to collect my thoughts about what had happened. And I took myself outside the Westminster bubble. I started conversations with people in business. I visited schools and universities, and talked to young people about how they feel about the world. I talked to intellectuals and thinkers. I became a visiting fellow at Wadham College, Oxford, and a visiting professor at Sheffield University. I spent more time in my home city, Birmingham. I spent more time with my family. I became a father to a beautiful little girl. I met my incredible partner, Martina, who challenges and inspires me every day, and became a stepfather to her wonderful daughters.

Gradually, as I reflected on my time in politics and government, and on the huge challenges facing Britain and all other Western countries, the idea of writing this book began to form. It is consistent with many of my long-held beliefs, of course, but it is also based on what I have learned since leaving government. I remain convinced, for example, that the Conservative Party must become a truly 'One Nation' party, capable of speaking for people across the whole country, and across the divides of race, religion, gender, sexuality and social class. I am equally sure that to achieve these things, and to rise to the challenges of the future, conservatives need to become more sceptical about the perfection of the market and rediscover the importance of active government.

But, of course, I have learned a lot from my experiences in government, and through the work I have done since leaving Downing Street in 2017. My studies have allowed me to step back from day-to-day political trench warfare and to think more deeply about the philosophical assumptions behind politicians' beliefs and policies. I have reached new conclusions about the overreach of liberalism, and the reasons for its failures. I have realized – much more so than before – that the key question in our politics should not be about the balance between the state and the market, but how we reach a harmonious and healthy relationship between state, market and community. The decline of community and the failure of our political leaders to even notice – let alone produce a serious plan to revive it – is one of the great problems of our time. It is impossible to understand the economic and cultural crises we face without understanding how liberalism has grown ideological and overzealous.

Of course, over my years in politics I have made enemies, and I know my critics will mock me for even daring to write a book. But my mistakes do not delegitimize my arguments, just as my successes do not justify them. In fact, in many ways my mistakes inform the arguments I make. Throughout my time in Downing Street, for example, we neglected economic policy. In our defence, this was partly down to the personality of the Chancellor. Philip Hammond lacked an economic policy beyond the need to keep on cutting spending. Not for nothing did he relish being nicknamed 'Fiscal Phil'. But we should have had a stronger and more coherent economic policy. For her part, Theresa was always far too reluctant to devolve powers to the nations and regions of the United Kingdom. And too much of what we tried to do was done abruptly, without an electoral mandate, intellectual bridge building, or even attempts to communicate what we were doing to the country.

I have tried throughout this book to learn from these mistakes. As President Theodore Roosevelt said in one of my favourite speeches, 'there is no effort without error and shortcoming.'[27] But as he also said, we must still 'strive to do the deeds'. The botched election campaign does not invalidate the ideas I once promoted in government. This book is in large part an attempt to deepen the thinking behind those ideas, and where necessary to correct and go beyond them.

Inevitably, my perspective is shaped by my upbringing and background as much as my professional experience. Unusually for many people at the top of the Conservative Party, I grew up in a working-class family in a suburb of Birmingham. My parents were raised in Labour households, and only started voting Conservative in the 1980s. Dad worked in manufacturing, rising from the shop floor to sales positions that took him around the world. Mom worked at a school that served a nearby housing estate, first doing clerical work and later providing pastoral care for kids who needed additional support.

As I grew up myself, I needed little persuading that it was the Conservative Party, and not Labour, that shared my values and cared about people like me. Under Margaret Thatcher, the Conservatives were restoring Britain's competitiveness and prosperity, and helping working families like mine to get on. They were the party of law and order, controlled immigration and, during the Cold War, a strong defence. Perhaps the defining political moment for me came at the end of my first year at my secondary school, a grammar school full of working-class boys like me. That year, there was a general election in which Labour threatened to close down all remaining selective schools. The Conservatives, by then led by John Major, wanted me to go as far as I could. Labour seemed to want to keep me in my place.

With my background, I could never have been an ideological liberal or libertarian. Working in the Conservative Research Department after university, I was encouraged to read Ayn Rand, whose selfish individualism left me cold. Later, still in opposition but under the leadership of David Cameron, I remember making the case for firmer immigration policies. One of David's advisers dismissed my arguments, calling me 'a typical West Midlands Conservative'.

I suppose I was a fairly conventional conservative until my thirties. But then I started to reflect on the hostility many Conservatives feel towards the state. And I thought about my own experience. I knew I was doing fairly well. I had been the first person in my family to go to university. From my early twenties, I had been working closely with senior politicians and briefing the Leader of the Opposition. As my Mom often said, my grandparents would never have believed it. But I knew I had not made this journey on my own. I owed everything to my parents, who had given me love and security, and made so many sacrifices to give my brother and me the chances they had never had. I had been to one of the best state schools in the country. The NHS had saved my brother's life as a baby, and treated my grandparents as their health faltered in later life. Mom still worked in a school serving a deprived council estate. Not everything had gone right – Dad was made redundant and lost his entire pension savings as manufacturing declined, and my beloved Nan died after contracting MRSA in a dirty hospital – but even these experiences taught me about the power of political decisions and the importance of good government.

I listened to the way some politicians talk about social mobility – about 'escaping' the communities we grew up in and kids who were looking for 'something better' – and realized it did not reflect my own experience at all. I felt a sense of achievement, yes, but I also felt a sense of loss. I no longer lived in the community in which I had been proud to grow up, and which had given me so much. I lived further away from my parents and extended family. Far from feeling I had escaped from my old world, I missed it, and I realized that many people in positions of power rarely understood anything about the way families like mine lived their lives.

I started to apply these lessons to the lives of people who had had different experiences to mine. As I worked on policy, I made a conscious effort to seek out the views of people from different racial and religious backgrounds, and those who represent them. Working with the likes of Sir Simon Woolley, from Operation Black Vote, and Matilda MacAttram, from Black Mental Health UK, I led efforts in the Home Office to reduce deaths in police custody, handle mental health issues better in the criminal justice system, and make sure stop and search powers were only used in full compliance with the law. The latter issue was brought home to me in particular by the experiences of Alexander Paul, a brilliant young black student I mentored who later died tragically young after suffering brain cancer.

And the way I thought about policy became more unorthodox. Unorthodox, that is, to those modern Conservatives who have been enticed by liberal and libertarian ideology. In fact, my beliefs are entirely consistent with the long tradition of conservative philosophy. They are influenced by Burke, Hume, Smith, Disraeli, Oakeshott, Churchill, Macmillan and Thatcher. They are influenced by many others outside the conservative tradition, from my political hero Joseph Chamberlain to modern psychologists like Jonathan Haidt.

Few things matter more than political ideas. They have the power to change – for better or worse – the fates of individuals, families and nations. Yet it is striking how little political ideas are really debated and discussed. It is true, many politicians are ideological and zealous about their beliefs. But often this ideology is skin deep. For some, it is a handy signal to supporters, a means by which they can fill a political space, and a way of gaining political capital by leading a faction. For others, it is a useful template with which they can approach the decisions they have to make. Some believe in their ideology more than others, and some have read more widely and thought more deeply than others.

But many politicians – and almost all civil servants and technocratic experts called upon to shape policy – deny any kind of ideology. They say they believe in 'what works'. This is a nice line, but it is untrue. They are shaped and conditioned by the assumptions of liberal philosophy, and increasingly extreme forms of ultra-liberalism that span left and right. Some politicians understand these influences on their beliefs and attitudes, but for many the effects are less considered and more subconscious. We are governed by a political class that manages at once to be ideological yet uninterested in ideas.

This book is an attempt to trace the philosophical assumptions – and the evolution of ideas – that influence politics and policies today. It analyses the economic and cultural crises we are living through in Britain and across the West. And it makes a plea to conservatives in particular to look past liberalism: to respect not only personal freedom but also solidarity, to reform capitalism and rebuild community, and to reject selfish individualism while embracing our obligations towards others. We must take care not to throw the baby out with the bathwater. Individual rights and equality before the law are the foundations of our civilization. The essential liberalism that underpins market economies and free societies must be defended. But as liberalism grows more ideological and more dysfunctional, we need to look beyond the artificial limitations and choices it imposes upon us.

It is not the critic who counts; not the man who points out how the strong man stumbles, or where the doer of deeds could have done them better. The credit belongs to the man who is actually in the arena, whose face is marred by dust and sweat and blood; who strives valiantly; who errs, and comes short again and again, because there is no effort without error and shortcoming; but who does actually strive to do the deeds; who knows the great enthusiasms, the great devotions; who spends himself in a worthy cause; who at the best knows in the end the triumph of high achievement, and who at the worst, if he fails, at least fails while daring greatly, so that his place shall never be with those cold and timid souls who know neither victory nor defeat.

President Theodore Roosevelt, 23 April 1910

1

THE TYRANNY OF
THE MINORITY

Everywhere, liberal democracy is in crisis, and everywhere liberals look for something, and someone, to blame.

They have attacked the populists. They have attacked the voters. They have aped the populists. They have blamed Twitter bots. They have invented conspiracy theories. They have even questioned whether democracy is such a good idea after all.

Rarely, however, have they looked at themselves, assessed their records, or reconsidered their fundamental beliefs. Yet it is time for those of us who share essential liberal beliefs to do just that. For the overreach of liberalism risks the destruction of liberal democracy and the Western way of life.

Across the West, populists are surging and the institutions, laws and norms that make liberal democracy work are coming under pressure. Beyond the West, politicians look not to Europe and America for ideas, inspiration and investment but to authoritarian regimes of different stripes.

This ought not to be a surprise. Western workers have experienced a long-lasting squeeze caused by rapidly changing technology, globalization, our ageing societies, and the long-term effects of the financial crisis. At the same time, the rules of the game – the ways in which markets are governed and regulated – have changed and taken power away from ordinary people. These changes have made international finance and cross-border trade more efficient, but they have taken decision-making and democratic control further away from citizens and local communities. Many find themselves in increasingly precarious and poorly paid work.

These economic challenges have been accompanied by a serious cultural crisis. The West's largest demographic group – the white working class – finds itself in decline, and its members feel disrespected and left behind by the rich and successful. Solidarity between citizens is breaking down, and a rapidly developing culture war is already underway.

For all these reasons, we are experiencing a worrying decline in trust, between the people and the powerful and also between one another. This decline is accelerating thanks to social changes caused by new technologies, in particular the retreat of traditional media and the rise of social media, which polarizes and inflames political debate and is antithetical to nuance.

Some of these changes are unavoidable, even welcome, and we must resist the temptations of nostalgia. The reintegration of China into the world economy is an irreversible fact. The convergence of Eastern and Western economies, and of living standards in both hemispheres, is likely to continue. New technologies cannot be uninvented. The financial crash cannot be undone, and the policy remedies concocted in its wake, such as quantitative easing, have been implemented already. Demographic changes, such as longer life expectancy and lower birth rates will go on for the foreseeable future. The decline of white majorities will continue.

But policies matter. Many of the problems we face are the direct consequence of political decisions. Businesses can abuse broken markets because governments and regulators have failed to fix them. They can exploit their workers and customers in new markets because governments have failed to keep up with technological and commercial change. Wealth inequality will grow because housing, planning and pensions policies, and monetary and fiscal policies, have driven up the price of assets owned by the fortunate few.

Policies matter to the cultural crisis too. Governments have shown a consistent commitment to globalization and forms of international cooperation that rely on supranational government, despite domestic scepticism. They permit mass immigration despite public opposition. They pursue a policy of multiculturalism, in which minority communities are encouraged to live separately to protect their cultural traditions. And after spending decades promoting positive action for minority groups that suffer disadvantage and discrimination, they now deny the need for similar support for the struggling white working class.

These policies all reflect choices. And the choices reflect political – and philosophical – beliefs. Across the party divide, there is a commitment not only to liberalism but to different forms of ideological liberalism. Markets trump institutions, individualism trumps community, and group rights trump broader, national identities. Legal rights come before civic obligations, personal freedom beats commitment, and universalism erodes citizenship. We are experiencing a crisis of liberal democracy that is driven by the excesses of ideological ultra-liberals.

Ultra-liberalism

But what do we mean by ultra-liberalism? First, we must be clear that it is distinct from the moderate, essential liberalism required by liberal democracy. And we must also understand that there is no single ultra-liberal agenda. The ultra-liberalism of George Osborne may, despite party divides, be similar to the beliefs of Tony Blair and Nick Clegg. But it is very different to the form of ultra-liberalism pursued by the left-wingers who dominate the modern Labour Party.

We must also distinguish between the liberalism of theorists and philosophers and the liberalism and ultra-liberalism of politicians and other decision-makers. As we will see, the overreach of liberalism does have its roots in certain philosophical misconceptions, but ultra-liberalism is also a corrupted, mutated form of liberalism that ends up contradicting many of the insights and beliefs of the great liberal thinkers.

Of course, defining too precisely an intellectual tradition as rich and varied as liberalism is fraught with difficulty. As Michael Oakeshott once said, 'what may now be meant by the word "liberal" is anybody's guess.'[1] The same difficulties apply to attempts to define different forms of ultra-liberalism. But for the purposes of this book, definitions are vital. So let us imagine three concentric circles, each representing a different category of liberalism. Within the core circle, we have essential liberalism: the tenets that make liberal democracy, free societies and market economies function.

With the second circle, we have elite liberalism: the values that are shared by most members of the governing classes, but not necessarily the general public. In Britain, elite liberals believe in high immigration, multiculturalism, a lightly regulated labour market, limited support for the family, and the marketization of many public services.

With the third circle, we have the ultra-liberal ratchet: beliefs that are not shared across the party divide, but which keep propelling liberalism forward. On the right, market fundamentalists think mainly of the economy, while left-liberals pursue their agenda of cultural liberalism and militant identity politics. The two sides might attempt to reverse some changes made by the other, but generally speaking, most remain, and the atomizing social effects of both market fundamentalism and left-liberalism compound one another. Despite political differences, therefore, and the appearance of political choices in elections, economic and cultural liberalism have for many years proceeded apace.

Essential liberalism

Liberal democracy exists to allow for government 'by the people, for the people', but also to prevent the tyranny of the majority. Governments are elected, and power is transferred peacefully from one party to another. But there are also important checks and balances to protect minority interests. These include the separation of powers between government, parliament and the courts, a bicameral legislature, an independent judiciary, a neutral civil service, civilian control of the military, a free press, and laws and norms that guarantee individual rights.

In Britain these checks and balances, and individual rights, evolved over time. It is possible to track modern rights from Magna Carta, to the writ of *habeas corpus*, the abolition of torture, the Petition of Right, the Bill of Rights, and the Act of Settlement. It is also possible to track the development of Britain's parliamentary democracy over time. The electoral franchise was extended by successive Acts of Parliament, and the supremacy of the House of Commons over the Lords was established through the Parliament Acts of 1911 and 1949.

In the United States, on the other hand, both the structure of American democracy and its accompanying rights and checks and balances were debated and granted through the Constitution and Bill of Rights. Like America, and unlike Britain, most other states have codified constitutions that set out the balance between liberal rights and democracy. We should note that many of these rights – such as *habeas corpus* – originated in Antiquity and the Middle Ages before liberal philosophy developed. But liberals accepted these rights, and extended them and built institutions such as independent courts to guarantee them.

'Liberal democracy' is therefore the juxtaposition of two related but different concepts. Democracy gives the people their say, but its liberal prefix protects civil rights by putting constraints upon democracy. Without these constraints, democratic governments, often acting in the name of the people, can undermine the rule of law and the institutions that are vital to democracy's long-term health. Paradoxically the limitation of democracy is therefore necessary to save democracy from itself. The liberalism of liberal democracy is not only a constraint but also a vital component of a symbiotic relationship ensuring just and good government.

This essential liberalism is supported not only by laws and institutions but by norms of behaviour, including a willingness to compromise, to exercise restraint in power and to accept the outcome of democratic choices when defeated in elections. In sum, it requires a commitment to recognize pluralism and the inevitability of difference. Implicit in this recognition is the understanding that human values and interests are often in conflict. We need institutions, and a limited number of legal rights, to handle those conflicts. We need customs and traditions to maintain our shared identities and build up trust. Maintaining this fragile balance is a delicate and difficult job: when liberalism becomes ideological, as we will see, it undermines and sometimes attacks these institutions, customs and traditions. Essential liberalism, on the other hand, respects the vital roles they play, and does everything it can to defend them.

Essential liberalism also requires support for free markets. Lived experience as well as theory shows us that attempts to command and control complex economies lead to shortages, poverty and political corruption. They also deny citizens the ability to make elementary decisions for themselves and their families. Essential liberalism does not seek to turn every aspect of life into a market, however: it recognizes the possibility of market failure, and knows that laws are needed to prevent market abuses. But it understands the relationship between economic freedom and the human values we consider most important: personal freedom, yes, but other values including security, dignity, and recognition and respect from our fellow citizens.

This is why essential liberalism has been the basis for successful democratic government for many decades, and is accepted by all but the political extremes. It does not pretend to provide a general theory of rights or justice or an ideological framework that leads, inexorably, towards the harmonization of human interests and values or a single philosophical truth. It respects political diversity and allows for all manner of policy choices, from criminal justice to the tax system. It provides *modus vivendi*, which, as the philosopher John Gray argues, aims not to 'still the conflict of values', but to 'reconcile individuals and ways of life honouring conflicting values to a life in common'.[2]

This significant achievement is undermined, however, when liberalism abandons this limited and pluralistic understanding of the world, and becomes more ideological. It is not essential liberalism that is driving the crisis of liberal democracy, but the ultra-liberalism that has long dominated British politics.

Elite liberalism

The political consensus forged by elite liberals is normally dated back to the two liberal revolutions of the twentieth century: the social revolution of the 1960s and the economic revolution of the 1980s. And it is true that the liberal settlements left by those revolutions remain broadly untouched and, in certain respects, popular. But ultra-liberalism has a much longer gestation than a few decades. The real beginnings of elite liberalism lie with the thoughts – and errors – of liberal philosophers long gone.

From the start, liberalism was built on the premise that there are not only universal values but also natural and universal rights. Early liberals made this argument by imagining a 'state of nature': life without any kind of government at all. Life in the state of nature, according to Thomas Hobbes, was 'solitary, poore, nasty, brutish, and short', and to escape this hellish existence, humans agreed a 'social contract' to form a government.[3]

The content of that contract was disputed: Hobbes proposed a state so strong that few would consider him a liberal at all, but for John Locke the contract guaranteed personal safety and property rights. 'No one can be ... subjected to the political power of another without his own consent', Locke wrote, 'which is done by agreeing with other men, to join and unite into a community for their comfortable, safe and peaceable living, one among another, in a secure enjoyment of their properties.'[4]

From its earliest days, liberalism therefore had several features hard-wired into it. Citizens are autonomous and rational individuals. Their consent to liberal government is assumed. And rights are natural and universal. For this reason, many liberals fall into the trap of believing that the historical, cultural and institutional context of government is irrelevant. Institutions and traditions that impose obligations on us can simply be cast off. All that matters, as far as government is concerned, is the freedom of the individual and the preservation of their property. The relational essence of humanity – our dependence on others, our reliance on the institutions and norms of community life – is ignored. From its earliest days, liberalism has taken both community and nation for granted, and had little to say about the obligations as well as rights of citizenship.

This individualism remained at the heart of liberalism as it developed. In *On Liberty*, John Stuart Mill introduced the 'harm principle', in which the liberty of the individual should be restricted by the state or society only if his actions risk damaging the interests of others. Even in these circumstances, however, no encroachment on individual liberty should be made if it is disproportionate. Nor should the state or society fetter liberty in an attempt to prevent individuals from harming themselves. And nor should they restrict individual liberty in order to ensure conformity with the moral beliefs of the community. In his other works, Mill adopted a more nuanced view of rational autonomy but his individualism was a constant, and his arguments in *On Liberty* have proved much more influential with other thinkers and politicians to this day.

To a modern audience, some of Mill's proposals sound extreme. He argued that traditional rights should be removed from citizens if they undermine the liberty of others: his example of such an unjustified right was unrestricted procreation by inappropriate parents. While he argued for a universal franchise that included women, he proposed weighting votes to favour the educated and the knowledgeable.

We can see some of the principles established by early liberal thinkers in the beliefs of elite liberals today. Controversial human rights laws, for example, are the logical outcome of a belief in natural and universal rights. This same universalism lies behind elite liberal support for supranational government, historically high levels of immigration and new, transnational citizenship rights.

The liberal emphasis on individualism and disregard for our social and relational nature is evident in modern consumption culture, in which instant gratification often comes before commitment and responsibility. The logic of Mill's harm principle – which fails to acknowledge that all of our actions to some degree affect those around us – is evident in the elite's relaxed attitude to the use of hard drugs and its reluctance to encourage our obligations to family. Mill's argument that traditions that impede individual liberty should be abandoned can be seen in many politicians' disdain for the past and contempt for custom.

Mill and other liberal thinkers sometimes make the case for pluralism and tolerance on the basis that the trial and error they make possible leads to truth and an increasingly perfect society. It is this teleological fallacy that can lead liberalism towards illiberalism: its intolerance of supposedly backward traditional opinions, norms and institutions can quickly become intolerance of the people who remain loyal to those traditional ways of life. Think of how quickly, in America, the use of torture was justified in the name of pacifying Iraq, a country the United States had invaded in order to deliver democracy. Consider the frustration with which the elite responded to popular concern about mass immigration or Europe's recent migration crisis. Think of how politicians have described people who voted for Britain to leave the European Union as stupid, racist or too old to have a stake in the future.

If human rights are indivisible and universal in nature, and pluralism is only the route to a perfect society, then attachment to national cultures, identities and institutions are little more than a legacy from a more savage point in time. They are the irrational beliefs of an uninformed populace in need of direction from wise and rational leaders. They do not realize it, but elite liberals echo Auguste Comte, who once asked, 'if we do not allow free thinking in chemistry or biology, why should we allow it in morals or politics?'[5]

Elite liberals view economic policy in a similar way. Liberal economics are normally dated back to Adam Smith, author of *The Wealth of Nations* and the first writer to describe market economics, the division of labour, and what would become known as the theory of comparative advantage. But while many recall Smith's defence of the 'invisible hand' of the market, and use it to argue against market reforms and interventions of any kind, they often neglect to mention his warnings about market abuses and his emphasis on our interest in 'the fortune of others', which brings us happiness even though we derive 'nothing from it except the pleasure of seeing it'.[6] Smith was not simply a free market economist but a moral philosopher who understood our need for community.

Likewise, elite liberals accept the inevitability of Joseph Schumpeter's 'creative winds of destruction'. Schumpeter demonstrated how capitalism brings ceaseless innovation, but also causes permanent destruction as new products and new providers supplant those they have bettered. But even as Schumpeter lauded the market, he knew that capitalism relied on social institutions and capital. 'The capitalist order not only rests on props made of extra-capitalist material', he said, 'but also derives its energy from extra-capitalist patterns of behaviour which at the same time it is bound to destroy.'[7] This is why Schumpeter acknowledged that a mixed economy would 'conserve many human values that would perish' in a purely capitalist system.[8] These days, however, elite liberals simply marvel at Mark Zuckerberg's desire to 'move fast and break things' and breathlessly admire 'disruption' without contemplating its social consequences.

Elite liberals abhor any kind of market interference, forgetting of course that markets are not naturally occurring phenomena. They are man-made constructs consisting of laws, rules and codes of behaviour, backed by a strong state apparatus including the police, the military and courts and prisons. As chapter 2 will show, a number of market failures and abuses have been left to stand by successive governments of left and right. And even free markets rely on society to function: families to raise children, services to educate and train workers, norms and institutions to encourage trust. If capitalism destroys these vital public goods, it will also destroy the foundation upon which capitalism itself can function.

Elite liberals have little to say about these dangers, and here they are influenced not only by liberal theorists but their philosophical relatives, the utilitarians. The founding thinker of utilitarianism, Jeremy Bentham, rejected the notion of natural rights as 'nonsense upon stilts'.[9] And in this respect, unlike many other liberal thinkers, John Stuart Mill agreed with him. But like all liberals, Bentham argued that good government should depend upon reason. The test he set, called the 'felicific calculus', should be whether a decision brings about 'the greatest happiness to the greatest number'.

Bentham's approach lives on in two different ways. The first is in economic theory, which treats people as autonomous units, economically motivated, rational in decision-making and selfish in nature. Like Bentham's utilitarianism, economic theory aggregates the interests of individuals and, after running sophisticated models, tells us whether a particular course of action will, in aggregate, be beneficial or not.

We will return to the problems with this approach later, but it affects broader policy-making too. Government-by-impact-assessment leads politicians into the utilitarian trap: decision-making based on partial assumptions, ignorance of real life, and a crude calculation of net economic costs and benefits. So if a policy – such as large-scale immigration, for example – is believed to bring net benefits for society overall, however marginal, it tends to be implemented, regardless of its cost to particular regions, institutions or groups of people. Anybody who loses out from a policy, officials assume, can be compensated through other initiatives. This is why proponents of 'managed migration' simply argue that areas experiencing rapid immigration ought to receive greater public spending. Other examples abound: in 1980s Britain, many of those who lost their jobs as manufacturing declined were parked on disability benefits. In the 2000s, in-work benefits were extended to compensate those who were losing out in Britain's low-skill, low-wage economy.

And of course, utilitarian government inevitably tends towards centralization, because technocrats know better than local communities what is best for them. This would have come as no surprise to Bentham, who was so convinced of the rationality of his own theories, he once boasted he could legislate wisely for all of India from the comfort of his study in England.[10] For today's British technocrats, the distances between the rulers and the ruled are shorter, but many politicians and officials believe they can govern the many communities of the United Kingdom better from London than the people themselves.

The ultra-liberal ratchet

It would be a mistake, however, to believe that elite liberalism is the beginning and the end of the forward march of ultra-liberalism. There is also the ultra-liberal ratchet: beliefs that are not shared between the mainstream parties, but which still drive ideological liberalism onward.

Both left and right have their distinct ultra-liberal agendas. The right is attached to market fundamentalism, while the left favours cultural liberalism and militant identity politics. And once again, these agendas have not come from nowhere: they begin with philosophy.

On the right, support for the free market can quickly become libertarianism and an obsession with marketizing all public goods. Friedrich von Hayek, for example, brilliantly demolished the very idea of a planned, socialist economy by demonstrating the impossibility of price setting before sellers and buyers enter into free exchanges. The necessary information, he argued, was available only at the point at which it was used, and at that point it would be gone again forever.

But Hayek's philosophy, like that of many other liberals, is universal and ideological in nature. He argues that no political system, not even a democratic one, nor even a very small and local one, can accurately reflect collective choice in the way a market does. For his disciples, it follows, therefore, that the National Health Service cannot be the right way of delivering healthcare, since consumer choices and real pricing do not drive decision-making. It follows, too, that governments should not restrict housing developments except through pure market mechanisms. And those same market mechanisms ought to apply to other public services, from public transport to schooling.

For some policies and services, consumer choice might well be the best mechanism. But the assumption that choice is always the best mechanism reflects the assumption that personal freedom is the pre-eminent human value. If we accept that security or solidarity, for example, are values that rival personal freedom, it follows that individual consumer choice will not always be the most important principle for public services. Marketization therefore is an ideological policy.

Hayek also argued that attempts to deliver social justice were a 'mirage'.[11] This, he argued, is because with the spontaneous order brought about by the market, no agent determines specific economic outcomes for specific people. In fact, the outcomes set by the market are strictly impersonal and cannot judge what is socially 'just' for anybody. All governments can do, Hayek insisted, is set a legal framework governing the conduct of those participating in the market, and accept the results. It is difficult to hear this argument and not recall the failure of elite liberals and market fundamentalists to address Britain's regional economic and social disparities, and their dismissive attitude to the low skilled and the low paid.

Hayek considered himself to be a classical liberal, rather than a libertarian. But his thinking is clearly related to libertarians including Milton Friedman, Robert Nozick and even Ayn Rand, who continue to have an influence on politicians on the right. All believed that individual freedom is a universal and absolute value, and one that must come before all others. As the heroic character in Rand's novel *The Fountainhead* declares: 'I recognize no obligations toward men except one: to respect their freedom.'[12]

Ultra-liberalism on the right is matched by ultra-liberalism on the left. And here the intellectual influence comes from postmodernists such as Michel Foucault and the mainly American thinkers behind the rise of identity politics. Discourse, Foucault argued, is oppressive. It is controlled by the powerful and it exploits the weak. People are not in charge of their own destinies. Their social reality is imposed on them through language and customs and institutions, and even the victims of the powerful participate in their own oppression through their own language, stories and assumed social roles.

The result of this thinking is a vision of a society turned upside down. Because oppressive discourses work to favour those at the top of exploitative hierarchies, we should not simply remove the hierarchy but penalize those who subjugate others. Equal political rights are therefore not enough: because historically power lay with white men, today whiteness and masculinity must be attacked. Because we do not understand how our social roles are constructed, we do not understand the meaning of even our own words. Those who hear us – particularly if they are members of marginalized groups – understand better than us the true meaning of what we say. Because discourse is itself a form of violence, free speech is no longer sacrosanct, and it is legitimate to meet violent language with even violent direct action.

This is how left-liberals end up attacking the principles of essential liberalism and free societies. Customs, traditions and institutions are assaulted. Language is policed aggressively. And the nation is a source of shame and historical guilt. Because left-liberals sacralize their policy objectives, they punish opponents and anybody who gets in their way as atheists and heretics. Those who stand up to them – and even those who innocently use language deemed 'wrong' or 'unacceptable' – face excommunication in the form of reputational destruction and professional ostracism. Increasingly these almost religious wars are being fought not only through elected politics, but in the arts and media, in schools, on campuses and in the workplace.

Not every ultra-liberal on the left reaches these conclusions via postmodernist theories. Some attack notions like the nation because they believe in extreme individualism and universalism. Joseph Carens, for example, believes that borders should be completely abolished. 'Citizenship in Western liberal democracies', he argues, 'is the modern equivalent of feudal privilege – an inherited status that greatly enhances one's life chances. Like feudal birthright privileges, restrictive citizenship is hard to justify.'[13] But like others before him, Carens' individualism and universalism means he has no understanding of the significance to humans of family and community. His definition of community is so expansive it would – by destroying the common identity and solidarity that makes us meet our obligations to one another as citizens – destroy the privileges he wants to make available to everyone.

Not every politician on the left and right shares these beliefs, and not every element of these ultra-liberal approaches ends up implemented. Borders have not yet been abolished, nor are we living in a libertarian nirvana. But even these most extreme beliefs influence mainstream parties and push them towards ultra-liberal positions. And where the parties do pursue their own ultra-liberal agendas – market fundamentalism on the right, cultural liberalism on the left – only rarely does one side overturn the other's advances. Despite repeated changes in the political composition of governments, the marketization of public services survives, and cultural liberalism continues. And as they do so, the atomizing effects of both continue to erode social solidarity, community and the institutions and traditions that draw us together.

Sometimes, thanks to the elite liberalism of its leaders, even the left takes forward market-based reforms of their own. It was Tony Blair's Labour Party that introduced university tuition fees and extended the quasi-market within the National Health Service, for example. And the same is true on the right, which has proved itself as capable of advancing cultural liberalism as the left. In 2017, for example, it was Justine Greening, the Conservative equalities minister, who proposed allowing people to change their gender without a medical diagnosis of gender dysphoria.

This is how the liberal ratchet builds on elite liberalism. Just as a sergeant major marches his troops, so the liberal ratchet propels ultra-liberalism forward: left, right, left, right, left, right.

The motors of ultra-liberalism

Elected leaders are not the only motors of ultra-liberalism. Increasingly, laws and institutions are used not only to prevent the tyranny of the majority but to govern without proper democratic oversight.

This is appropriate for the rights and the checks and balances required by essential liberalism. Of course, these laws and institutions must by definition be kept out of reach of the powerful, including those who hold elected office, if they are to be meaningful. They must, therefore, be overseen by legal rather than political institutions.

But this is not appropriate for policies that go beyond the essential liberalism required by liberal democracy. Laws that take primacy over others are now commonplace. Britain's membership of the European Union has meant British law has been subordinate to EU law and the judgments of the European Court of Justice for decades. Similarly, since the incorporation of the European Convention on Human Rights into British law through the Human Rights Act, the rights in the Convention – which are guaranteed ultimately by the European Court of Human Rights in Strasbourg – are of a higher order than other laws.

But these are not the only ways in which laws have been passed to bind future parliaments and make some laws and policies subordinate to others. The Government is, for example, legally bound to spend 0.7 per cent of GDP on international development spending each year. The legislation not only determines the amount that must be spent, but what the money can be spent on: the budget has to comply with the OECD definition of Overseas Development Assistance. Since 2008, the Climate Change Act has required the Government to set binding carbon budgets, which are recommended by the Committee on Climate Change, an independent quango, to comply with the legally-binding target to reduce carbon emissions by 80 per cent from 1990 levels by 2050. In 2019, following another report by the Committee on Climate Change, and with remarkably little debate, the Government legislated to change the target to 'net zero': a 100 per cent reduction in carbon emissions by 2050.

The deliberate effect of these laws is to tie the hands of ministers and prevent Parliament changing the direction of policy in future. Because they create rights, obligations on the state, and legal checks and balances, the Government's actions can be tested in the courts. Interest groups – rarely accountable and often publicly funded – make sure this happens, by bringing test cases that attempt to broaden the scope of the legislation. And legitimate policy options – for example about the rights of terrorism suspects, the use of international development budgets, or the rate of reduction in carbon emissions – are closed down.

This anti-democratic legalism has suited ultra-liberal politicians who do not want the bother of making and winning the case for policy changes. They can rely on quasi-constitutional laws like the European Convention on Human Rights and liberal judges to shape policies and laws in ways that Parliament would never permit. And in certain members of the judiciary, they have found willing allies. In countless immigration and deportation cases, judges have extended the meaning of the Convention's right to a family life, for example. European judges have extended the legal definition of EU free movement rules.

Lord Bingham, the former Lord Chief Justice and Senior Law Lord, always maintained that parliamentary sovereignty remains the cornerstone of the British constitution. 'Then, as now', he wrote, 'the Crown in Parliament was unconstrained by any entrenched or codified constitution. It could make or unmake any law it wished. Statutes, formally enacted as Acts of Parliament, properly interpreted, enjoyed the highest legal authority.'[14] But other senior judges have disagreed with him. Lord Hope argues, 'parliamentary sovereignty is no longer, if it ever was, absolute.'[15] Lord Steyn says the supremacy of Parliament is 'out of place in the modern United Kingdom'.[16] Claiming parliamentary sovereignty was 'a construct of the common law', he argued; 'the judges created this principle' and therefore 'it is not unthinkable that circumstances could arise where the courts may have to qualify a principle established on a different hypothesis of constitutionalism.'[17] Baroness Hale has argued that judges can overrule the decisions not only of government but Parliament. She has warned, 'the courts will treat with particular suspicion (and might even reject) any attempt to subvert the rule of law by removing government action affecting the rights of the individual from all judicial scrutiny.'[18]

But the judges are wrong to believe they can upend the principle of parliamentary sovereignty. Lord Bingham argued, 'parliamentary sovereignty has been recognized as fundamental in this country … because it has for centuries been accepted as such by judges and others officially concerned in the operation of our constitutional system. The judges did not by themselves establish the principle and they cannot, by themselves, change it.'[19]

Another former Supreme Court judge, Lord Sumption, has pointed out the dangers of anti-democratic legalism. Paraphrasing General von Clausewitz, Sumption says 'law is now the continuation of politics by other means'.[20] But this is, as Sumption says, profoundly undemocratic: unlike politicians, judges are not accountable to anybody but themselves. Worse than that, because litigation is a process designed to create binary outcomes, and winners and losers, it is, unlike politics, incapable of accommodating the public's divergent values and interests.

Anti-democratic legalism is therefore hastening social division and the culture wars that emerge from it.

The rise of the liberal technocrats – unelected experts and bureaucrats – is another motor of ultra-liberalism. In Britain, we have not had the technocratic government that has been imposed at different points on countries like Italy and Greece, but as a member state of the European Union, we have been subject to the powers of the European Commission. We have more than one thousand unelected and barely accountable technocratic quangos. And we have an independent central bank, which since the financial crisis has created half a trillion pounds of new money through quantitative easing. Immediately after the crash, this was vital emergency medicine, but as we will see later, the social and economic consequences of the asset bubble it created have been profound. Yet the policy was implemented and extended with remarkably little debate, scrutiny or accountability.

It has become commonplace for politicians to declare that they are 'taking the politics out' of an issue, and commission an independent and technocratic report about what to do. These reports, almost always carried out by elite liberals, produce recommendations that are then implemented in full by ministers. Examples include the Browne Review, carried out by the former chief executive of BP, which recommended increasing university tuition fees, and the Stern Report into the economic effects of climate change, overseen by a former Treasury and World Bank official, which informed the subsequent Climate Change Act.

Elite liberals have promoted a policy programme that is purportedly non-ideological and based instead on 'evidence-based policy making' and, in the words of Tony Blair, 'what works'. In reality, its policies reflect choices based on ultra-liberal ideology, but its technocratic guise means that legitimate policy alternatives are denied. Like other ideologists who believed in the perfection of their system, the ultra-liberals believe they can replace 'the government of persons' with 'the administration of things'.[21] But they are destined to fail just as surely as Friedrich Engels, who first made this promise more than 140 years ago.

These motors of ultra-liberalism – elected politicians, anti-democratic legalism and the liberal technocrats – are reinforced by one final motor.

And that is elite institutional liberalism. For while it is untrue that the senior civil service, the BBC and academia have a party political bias, it is undeniable that each has an elite liberal bias.

David Goodhart tells the story of a conversation he had over dinner at an Oxford college in 2011. Gus O'Donnell, then the Cabinet Secretary, the head of the British civil service, remarked to him, 'when I was at the Treasury I argued for the most open door possible to immigration ... I think it's my job to maximize global welfare not national welfare.' Sitting next to O'Donnell was Mark Thompson, the director general of the BBC. According to Goodhart, 'he defended O'Donnell and said he too believed global welfare was paramount.'[22]

This is a single anecdote, but it reflects a state of mind shared across elite society. In 2007, a report commissioned by the BBC Trust found 'support', among those consulted, 'for the idea that some sort of liberal consensus existed' at the BBC.[23] This was not a conspiracy, the report found, but cultural groupthink: BBC producers and journalists exercise 'a largely unconscious self-censorship out of a misguided attempt to be "correct" in their thinking'.[24] In 2013, in another report, the BBC's former head of news, Helen Boaden, said there was a 'deep liberal bias' in the way the BBC reported news about immigration.[25] Several BBC journalists admit that the conclusions of these reports are correct. Andrew Marr says, 'the BBC is not impartial or neutral ... It has ... not so much a party-political bias. It is better expressed as a cultural liberal bias.'[26]

The same cultural groupthink exists in the senior civil service. Several months after the Brexit referendum, one permanent secretary sidled up to a colleague and declared, 'do you know, I've come to the conclusion we're going to have to do this.'[27] Refusing to implement the referendum result was clearly an option the mandarin had entertained. Others were less subtle: one ambassador told a friend with a wink, 'don't worry, we'll put a stop to it.'[28]

And similar attitudes prevail in academia. Robert Tombs and Graham Gudgin, two respected Cambridge academics, have reported that 'a considerable number of scholars, especially in fairly junior positions, feel that if they are intellectually honest and express views favouring Brexit, their careers will suffer. We are sorry to say that we think they are right to be worried.'[29] Since the election of President Trump and the Brexit referendum, some academics have been open in arguing that democracy, government by the people, should be replaced by epistocracy, government by experts.[30]

In any case, government by the people has increasingly become government by certain kinds of people. While Parliament and government have over recent years become more diverse in terms of gender, race and religion, the political classes have become less diverse from the perspective of social class. As the academics Roger Eatwell and Matthew Goodwin have noted, after the 2017 general election, the percentage of MPs who had had blue-collar jobs fell to 3 per cent, an all-time low and half the number who had previously been lawyers. Similar trends are evident in US and European politics, as well as in the media. Half the leading newspaper columnists in Britain attended private schools, while only one in ten was working class. And this matters: as many studies have shown, highly educated elites have very different views compared to ordinary members of the public.[31]

The cynical centre

One of the attractions of democracy is its ability to self-correct, and change direction when policies are not working. The obvious reason is that governments formed by different parties feel no reluctance to overturn the mistakes of their predecessors.

This advantage is lost, however, when the mainstream parties do not disagree. And as we have seen, ultra-liberalism relies on a consensus of elite liberals from across the party divide, the liberal ratchet, and the motors that propel it forward regardless of the effects of democratic politics. The result is that ultra-liberalism struggles to correct its own failures. Yet thanks to the narrative of the cynical centre, the cycle of failure is allowed to continue.

The language of the 'centre' is used with abandon by politicians, political commentators and the members of elite society who support ultra-liberalism. Those who belong to the centre, they say, stand for moderation. Conversely, those who 'abandon' the centre-ground, they argue, are giving in to extremists and ideologues and forfeit their right to hold power. But what they mean by the 'centre' is rarely defined, and there are in fact three different meanings for the term.

First, just as the 'right' is used to refer to conservatism, and 'left' refers to socialism, the 'centre' is used to refer to liberalism, which is an ideology in its own right. Second, the 'centre' is often used to imply political moderation: those occupying the centre-ground offer a compromise between right and left and pursue non-ideological, evidence-based policies. And third, the 'centre' is often used to describe majority, or mainstream, public opinion.

It is easy to see why ultra-liberals are happy to elide all three meanings of the term. At once, their beliefs are deemed to be moderate, rejecting, as they say they do, more ideological alternatives, and popular, representing, as they claim, the beliefs of most voters.

This might suit the ultra-liberals, but it is, however, nonsense. As Sir Keith Joseph established in a celebrated speech in 1976, the political centre, defined as the centre-ground between the parties, does not mean political moderation at all. In fact, defined in this way, the centre is 'unrelated to the aspirations of the people', and, given the state of politics at the time of Sir Keith's speech, 'a guarantee ... of a left-wing ratchet'.[32] Given the state of Western politics today, defining the political centre in this way would be a recipe for sharp movements towards the extremes of both right and left.

Neither can the centre be treated as a useful means of identifying majority or mainstream opinion. This is because, as many academic studies have established, the beliefs of the public cannot be plotted on a simple, single axis from left to right. If they could, then the centre would be easy to identify and political compromises would be simple to strike.

In reality, public opinion is far more complex and dynamic, and any models that are produced to understand it are inevitably oversimplistic. But they can still be useful. In trying to understand how far-removed the liberal centre is from mainstream public opinion, it is helpful to borrow a model devised by two academics who studied American politics.

In *The Two Majorities*, Byron Shafer and William Claggett argue that public opinion is organized around two clusters of issues.[33] In the US, they identified an economic/welfare factor, comprising social welfare, social insurance and civil rights, and which is associated with the Democrats, and a cultural/national factor, comprising cultural values, civil liberties and foreign relations, which is associated with the Republicans.

A growing volume of research suggests two similar sets of issue clusters exist in Britain. According to polling by Lord Ashcroft, when British voters are presented with choices between not only the Conservatives and Labour but a culturally liberal party and a culturally conservative party, more voters choose the two new parties than the established two, and the cultural conservatives come first.[34] And on the basis of its own research, Onward, the centre-right think tank, reports: 'the centre ground [is not where] many centrists imagine: it is where the centre of public opinion sits – marginally to the left on the economy, and marginally to the right on cultural and national issues.'[35]

One study by YouGov examined political opinions that were both held by large numbers of voters and which they believed were unrepresented by mainstream political parties. The results were not elite liberal policies of the 'centre' but, consistent with the Shafer and Claggett proposition, slightly more left-wing on public spending and regulation, and slightly more right-wing on matters of security and culture. Popular responses included 'government should regulate big business more' and 'there should be more government intervention in house building', as well as 'the justice system is not harsh enough' and 'immigration restrictions should be tighter.' People who voted for Britain to leave the EU, meanwhile, were more likely to feel unrepresented than those who had voted to remain.[36]

The evidence is clear. The cynical centre does not represent political moderation, and it does not represent mainstream public opinion. It represents nothing more than the views of elite liberals: the tyranny of the minority.

Overreach

What is behind this ultra-liberal overreach? As John Gray has argued, liberalism has for several centuries had 'two faces'. In one, he explains, 'toleration is valued as a condition of peace, and divergent ways of living are welcomed as marks of diversity in the good life.' But in the other, 'toleration is justified as a means to truth. In this view, toleration is an instrument of rational consensus, and a diversity of ways of life is endured [only] in the faith that it is destined to disappear.'[37]

In other words, liberalism can mean pluralism, the means by which diversity, tensions and conflicts can be peaceably managed in a complex world. Or as Gray puts it, 'an ideal of *modus vivendi*'.[38] But liberalism's other face is ideological. And like all other ideologies, that means liberalism can be teleological and, paradoxically, illiberal. Herein lies an important difference between essential liberalism and ideological ultra-liberalism.

Yet it is not quite so simple as that. As we have seen, ultra-liberalism comes in different guises. And both essential liberalism and ultra-liberalism have their roots in similar intellectual traditions. What those traditions have in common is a commitment to the extension of personal liberty, and a belief that the individual – rational, autonomous and determined to be free – can overcome the restrictions placed upon him by nature, society and his own ignorance, superstitions and passions. Even left-liberalism, which ends up subordinating individual interests to those of identity-based groups, draws from these traditions.

There are many ways of conceptualizing these liberal traditions, but one stands out better than the rest. In *Two Concepts of Liberty*, Isaiah Berlin stated that there is a negative conception of liberty and a positive one. He said the negative conception asked, 'what is the area within which the subject – a person or group of persons – is or should be left to do or be what he is able to do or be, without interference by other persons?'[39] The positive conception asked, 'what, or who, is the source of control of interference that can determine someone to do, or be, this rather than that?'[40]

Negative freedom is at its heart a simple concept. We are free to do as we wish, until or unless another prevents us from doing so. Our inability to do what we wish, perhaps because of a lack of physical or mental prowess, or our incapacity to do so, perhaps because of a lack of education or spending power, does not constitute a restriction of freedom. All that matters is that we are left to our own devices: we are free as long as nobody else tries to frustrate our desires and wishes.

But how broadly should this rule apply? The greater the area of non-interference, the greater our freedom. But the greater my freedom, the greater is my ability to encroach on the freedom of others. And the stronger, wealthier and more powerful I am, the greater is my ability to interfere with the freedom of my weaker, poorer and less powerful neighbours. Clearly, a balance needs to be struck. Liberal thinkers agree, therefore, that there is a core to individual freedom that must never be disturbed, but they also agree that our freedom must be restricted in some ways if we are to be prevented from violating the rights of others.

Where we draw the line depends on our view of human nature and of human values and interests, and here liberal thinkers differ. Those who believe that values and interests will always conflict argue that our core, inviolable freedoms must be limited. Those who believe that human interests can be harmonized – or indeed are essentially the same – argue that the core can be far larger. Where precisely the line should be drawn has been, and will continue to be, a matter of argument and controversy among liberals.

Two things, however, will always remain true. First, liberal thinkers will agree that there are core freedoms that cannot be disturbed, even if they differ on the size of the core. To surrender that core – in the name of security, equality or any other value – would be to surrender to despotism. Second, if the core is defined too broadly – if the list of freedoms that cannot be disturbed grows too long – one person's freedom will end up denying others of theirs. And in particular, the freedom of the powerful will disturb the freedom and the wider interests of the less powerful. 'Freedom for the pike', said the socialist critic, R. H. Tawney, 'is death for the minnow.'[41]

Yet for some thinkers – liberals and others – this negative conception of liberty is not enough. The positive conception, therefore, begins with the desire to take control of one's own destiny: not to be free 'from' others, but to be free 'to' live their lives in the manner they choose.

Negative liberty does not, after all, require democracy or self-government. An autocrat such as a dictator or an absolute monarch might allow his people a very broad area of personal freedom. He might still govern in an unjust manner, or preside over vast inequality, public disorder and poor health for his subjects. On the other hand, a democracy can very easily disrupt or remove the liberties of its citizens that might be unfettered in non-democratic states. Supporters of positive freedom are as concerned about who determines our personal liberties as much as what those liberties are.

This can bring about a more enlightened attitude towards the pursuit of liberty and other values. Rather than restrict the objectives of government to dictating the parameters of individual liberty, practitioners of positive freedom can be credited with significant achievements, such as universal education and healthcare, welfare and workplace protections. These achievements have freed millions to lead fulfilled lives, and not simply freed them from the interference and interventions of others.

But the risks of this conception of freedom are plain. It can, of course, encroach on the personal liberty of citizens through excessive regulation, taxation and nannying. But its consequences can also be more dramatic, violent and tragic. When we are asked to think of ourselves as simply part of a larger entity – such as tribes, nations, races, faiths, churches and totalitarian parties – it need not take many steps before governments subordinate individual freedom to a supposedly superior, higher freedom. In the wrong political hands, positive liberty can be used as a justification for the state to coerce its citizens in the name of their own freedom. It can sometimes mark the beginning of a dangerous journey towards tyranny.

Essential liberalism recognizes that we need both concepts of liberty – negative and positive – for a just society. We need negative freedom because it protects a core set of freedoms that defend us 'from' despotism. We need positive freedom because it provides the dignity of self-government and the means by which we become free 'to' lead fulfilled lives.

At their extremes, the two concepts of liberty conflict with one another, but there is no great logical distance between them. If both are necessary for a society to be just, both need sensible boundaries to be drawn around them and between them. The trouble with ultra-liberalism is its tendency to draw those boundaries too wide. On the right, market fundamentalists define negative liberty too broadly, allowing the freedom of the powerful to damage the welfare and interests of others. Correspondingly, left-liberals define positive liberty too broadly, restricting our personal freedom, and undermining democracy and self-government. Elite liberals manage to achieve both things at once.

Fatal flaws

So the dangers of ultra-liberalism lie in its overreach. But the roots of this overreach lie in some of the flawed assumptions of philosophical liberalism itself.

The first problem is that liberalism overstates the importance of freedom. Of course freedom matters, and any form of government that consciously or systematically denies its people their core liberties is not just. But personal freedom is only one human value, along with many others. We place great importance on wealth, health, happiness, justice, security, dignity and many other values. Often these values coincide with the pursuit of liberty. A free society may be the best place to establish a family with somebody one truly loves, for example, regardless of race, religion, class or sexuality. But often these values clash, rather than coincide. A liberal state that cannot maintain security cannot uphold the laws that are supposed to grant its citizens freedom. A liberal society that upholds negative freedom, and defines it broadly, may be incapable of limiting the growth of inequality. Conversely, an illiberal state might be very effective at establishing order, generating economic growth or minimizing inequality.

Of course, many liberal thinkers recognize the significance of other values, but what distinguishes liberals from others is their belief that personal freedom is the supreme human value. And this stems from the liberal assumption that we are naturally autonomous, rational and individualistic, an assumption for which there is remarkably little evidence.

Liberal thinkers acknowledge that we are interdependent, which is why they accept that personal freedom does need to be curtailed at least in certain ways. But they imagine humans connecting with one another like colliding snooker balls, one disturbing another's place and forcing him to move. Human relations are in reality far more complex. We are not born in a state of nature, rational individuals who decide to form a society based on rights. We are born into families, communities and nations. We inherit, at the start of our lives, rights and obligations that last until death and are passed on to future generations. We participate in, and are shaped by, human institutions that existed before we were born and endure far beyond us. We are social animals.

This is not so simply because of our need to cooperate with others. It is that we are incapable of even understanding ourselves without reference to others. If I were alone on a desert island, what would I understand myself to be? If I were in the company of others, I would think of myself as a man, a father, a writer, concerned about how others perceive me. If I were in the company of others and in England, I might feel my identity as somebody who lives in London and was born in Birmingham. If I were in France, I might feel my identity as an Englishman. If I were in Asia, I might feel my identity as a European. What I realize I am, and consider myself to be, depends on my relationships with other people.

The status we seek is not only the freedom to do as we wish, but recognition from others. 'I may not be seeking for a rational plan of social life, the self-perfection of a dispassionate sage', Berlin argued. 'What I may seek to avoid is simply being ignored, or patronized or despised, or being taken too much for granted – in short, not being treated as an individual, having my uniqueness insufficiently recognized, being classed as a member of some featureless amalgam, a statistical unit without identifiable, specifically human features and purposes of my own.'[42] This is not the personal freedom described by many liberal thinkers, but a different value: dignity and acknowledgement from one's fellow citizens. Liberals might argue that personal freedom is the means by which we earn this dignity and recognition, but a society concerned by personal freedom alone will undermine solidarity and our sympathy towards others.

Equally problematic is the liberal belief in the power of reason. John Stuart Mill argued that freedom was necessary so that man could discover truth. Indeed, he believed that truth could only be discovered when man is free. Not only is this a dubious claim – intellectual enterprise and discoveries have been known in unfree, autocratic and even repressive societies – it also generates a contradiction within liberalism. Liberal pluralists believe difference and diversity are natural, many and inevitable, and therefore need to be managed. If difference and diversity are only to be tolerated as a means by which society discovers truth, what happens to those who dissent against those who believe they have discovered that truth? If those who have discovered truth are rational individuals, surely those who dispute that truth or do not understand it are irrational? Mill might have argued that we should not suppress dissenters, but on a whole host of topics this is precisely what many modern liberals do. Its belief in the power of reason means liberalism can sometimes turn quickly to illiberalism.

Essential liberalism – and its commitment to pluralism – does not make this error. But as liberalism becomes more ideological, it tolerates dissent and diversity only as a means of discovering truth, and accepts different perspectives and traditions only in the expectation that they will soon disappear. This defies the essential liberal insight that human values and interests will always conflict, and reveals a belief in inevitable progress towards truth. But this is, of course, fallacious. While it is possible to agree that there are universal human values – we can agree, across cultures and polities, that to take a human life is wrong, or to degrade another human is unethical, for example – it is a leap of logic to assert that human values, and human interests, never conflict.

A state reserves the right to take the life of enemy combatants at times of war, for example. An individual may reserve the right to practise his religion, but if in so doing he evangelizes aggressively, he may undermine the rights of others to practise their religion or go about their lives. A transsexual may assert her rights as a woman, but in so doing she might undermine the privacy or security of women born as women. The right to privacy might have meant one thing in the mid-twentieth century, but another altogether in an age of big data, social media and artificial intelligence.

It is as great a leap of logic to assert, therefore, that there are timeless, universal and indivisible human rights and workable theories of justice. Yet this is what ultra-liberalism does. It seeks to achieve the impossible, by providing a single, coherent, universal theory of life. But, like every other ideology, it is bound to fail because it cannot cater for conflicts of values and interests, and the changing contexts of time and place.

The unravelling

The liberal conception of the individual, and the belief that freedom is a value more important than any other, would have surprised the philosophers and thinkers who came before the earliest liberals. Individual rights as we know them today were absent from ancient civilizations.

In Greece and Rome, Benjamin Constant noted, the individual was 'sovereign in public affairs but a slave in all his private relations'.[43] Pre-Enlightenment Christian thinkers believed, like Aristotle, that man is a social animal. Thomas Aquinas argued that reason can lead us to virtues such as prudence, temperance, justice and fortitude, but Christian belief must lead us to the 'perfect' virtues of faith, hope and charity.[44]

Of course, few liberal thinkers argued that individual autonomy ought to lead inevitably to licentiousness. In one recently published history of liberalism, Helena Rosenblatt has gone to great lengths, citing mainly French thinkers, to argue that liberalism does not need to mean selfishness.[45] But there is no escaping the fact that, unlike philosophical traditions before it, liberalism begins with a concept of the individual as autonomous, rational and capable of standing above or apart from others. As Mill argued, 'Pagan self-assertion is as worthy as Christian self-denial.'[46]

The excessive individualism of liberalism was not only contradicted by philosophers who came before it, but by those who came afterwards too. Thinkers like Hegel, Herder, Marx and Freud all believed that humans are shaped by external or internal forces, in ways that cannot be recognized by liberal thinking. Hegel argued that individuals were affected by change and the onward march of history. Herder rejected individualism and instead imagined a world of organic communities living in peaceful co-existence. Marx believed we are controlled by apparently independent forces, laws and institutions that perpetuate the dominance of one class over another. Freud maintained that our rationality and independence are constrained by psychological forces within us.

The empiricist and sceptic David Hume insisted that people accepted government and felt allegiance to a community not because of some social contract but out of 'habit and custom'. If citizens wonder why they must accept allegiance to their government, he said, 'as soon as they learn, that they themselves and their ancestors have, for several ages, or from time immemorial, been subject to such a government … they immediately acquiesce, and acknowledge their obligation to allegiance.'[47] Hume explained that we obey the law – and approve of others who also obey the law – because we understand that doing so brings benefits to wider society. Self-interest may be the fundamental motive for the establishment of justice, he said, but a sympathy with the public interest lies behind our approval of the good behaviour of others.

Edmund Burke also dismissed the social contract invented by the state of nature theorists. 'Government', he said, 'is not made in virtue of natural rights, which may and do exist in total independence of it; and exist in much greater clearness, and in a much greater degree of abstract perfection: but their abstract perfection is their practical defect.' Instead, he argued, 'the restraints on men, as well as their liberties, are to be reckoned among their rights. But as the liberties and the restrictions vary with times and circumstances, and admit of infinite modifications, they cannot be settled upon any abstract rule; and nothing is so foolish as to discuss them upon that principle.'[48]

This was more than a disagreement about the state of nature as a conceptual device. It was a disagreement about life as it is lived in practice. Because liberals tend to divorce social and political organization from its historical, cultural and institutional context, they fall into the twin traps of impractical individualism and unrealistic universalism. Because the more zealous among them believe in the possibility of the discovery of truth, they are hopelessly ideological. It is not enough to claim – as many defenders of liberalism now argue – that the state of nature and its variants are simply a model that is not intended to replicate real life. Liberal thinkers created this model to understand the world, and their theories reflect the flaws in their model.

Modern discovery has reinforced old arguments. Ground-breaking psychological research vindicates many criticisms of liberal theory. The behavioural economist Richard Thaler has distinguished between humans, real people living their real lives, and 'econs', the supposedly rational, autonomous units created by economists for their Benthamite modelling. Using behavioural economics and psychological experiments, Thaler demonstrates the absurdity of the 'econ', the modern descendant of the rational man who formed the social contract, and the subject happy to be governed in accordance with the felicific calculus.[49]

The Nobel Prize winner Daniel Kahneman has drawn similar conclusions. 'The assumption that humans are rational', Kahneman has written, 'provides the intellectual foundation for the libertarian approach to public policy: do not interfere with the individual's right to choose, unless the choice harms others.' Kahneman, it should be said, is using American terminology: he is talking not only about libertarianism but also about liberalism as defined by thinkers like Mill. 'Although humans are not irrational,' he says, 'they often need help to make more accurate judgments and better decisions, and ... policies and institutions can provide that help.'[50]

More recently, the moral psychologist Jonathan Haidt has weighed in, arguing against the 'rationalist delusion'. Haidt compares the human mind to a small rider on a very large elephant. The rider is our conscious reasoning, while the elephant is the other 99 per cent of our mental processes. The elephant makes most of our decisions, and the rider ends up justifying them using often ridiculous, *post-hoc* arguments.[51]

Haidt also warns us against moral monists: those who argue that 'there is one true morality for all people, time and places.' While secular, Western thinkers tend to focus on harm and fairness as the only moral tests, Haidt says they neglect other powerful, moral intuitions, such as liberty, loyalty, authority and sanctity. Anybody who asserts that 'all societies, in all eras, should be using one particular moral matrix, resting on one particular configuration of moral foundations', he says, 'is a fundamentalist of one sort or another.'[52] This is, of course, exactly what ultra-liberals do.

So we are not entirely rational and personal freedom is not the pre-eminent human value. Nor is it true, concludes Haidt, that we are inherently selfish either. We are a strange combination of 'selfish and groupish'. Our evolutionary history has taught us to compete with other individuals within communities, but also to cooperate and come together within our communities to defend ourselves and defeat others. The most cohesive and cooperative groups tended to overcome the more selfish and individualistic groups, so cooperation gave us an evolutionary advantage. As Haidt shows, this means we have it within us to be 'profoundly altruistic, but that altruism is mostly aimed at members of our own groups'.[53]

This conclusion is clearly problematic for both the individualism and the universalism of philosophical liberalism. And Haidt is not the only one to expose the difficulty. Many academic papers have established what David Willetts, the Conservative politician, calls the 'progressive dilemma': the problem that diversity and solidarity are negatively correlated.[54] Studies from across Europe, for example, have shown that support for redistributive taxation falls as immigration increases.[55] Studies in the United States, Canada, Britain, Europe and Australasia have shown that communities that become more diverse experience a reduction in trust in strangers and even between neighbours and among residents of the same ethnicity.[56] While social scientists like Robert Putnam argue that these trends can be overcome with time and effort, 'in the short to medium run', he accepts, 'immigration and ethnic diversity challenge social solidarity and inhibit social capital.'[57]

It should be no surprise, therefore, that ultra-liberalism is coming unstuck. Old philosophical thought and modern scientific evidence teach us that it is flawed, ideological and destined to fail. Like other ideologies, however, ultra-liberalism is blind to its failures and will go on boasting of its achievements and condemning its critics. Yet sure enough, ultra-liberalism is unravelling, and as it does so, it risks the destruction of the essential liberalism that is the foundation of our civilization's strength and success.

2

DESTRUCTIVE CREATION

In the final year of his presidency, on 8 March 2000, Bill Clinton made a speech at Johns Hopkins University. Earlier that day he had submitted legislation to Congress that would ratify a trade agreement between the United States and China, and pave the way for China to join the World Trade Organization. Amid the jokes and folksy charm, he made a serious promise: the US would 'export products [to China] without exporting jobs'.[1]

Clinton predicted that trade would make China more law-abiding at home and abroad, more tolerant of human rights, and more likely to become a free and open society. In words that matched the hubris of those who believed that liberal democracy reigned supreme and history had ended, he declared: 'China is not simply agreeing to import more of our products; it is agreeing to import one of democracy's most cherished values: economic freedom.'[2] Economic freedom, he predicted, would inevitably bring personal and political freedom to the people of China.

As Clinton poked fun at the Chinese government for 'trying to crack down on the internet', the laughter from the audience sounds foolish now.[3] China is not only adept at internet censorship, it is using big data and internet technologies to create a social credit system to assess the civic worth of individuals and businesses, punishing and rewarding them as the state sees fit. It uses technology to steal secrets from Western companies and infiltrate servers including those belonging to Western militaries and security services.[4] It can do these things because Western countries often allow Chinese companies to operate within their critical national infrastructure, and because Western businesses use Chinese firms in their transnational production networks.

Today, China remains a developing economy. Its per capita income is still far lower than Western economies, and in 2015 there were still 55 million people living in poverty in its rural regions.[5] But its transformation since 2000 is unprecedented and extraordinary. Between 1980 and 2000, the Chinese economy grew from $191 billion to more than $1.2 trillion. Between 2000 and 2017, it grew again to more than $12.2 trillion, and it is forecast to keep growing by more than 6 per cent a year into the future.[6]

The positive effects of its reintegration into the world economy are clear for China. The number of Chinese people living in poverty has fallen from 17.2 per cent in 2000 to 3.1 per cent in 2017.[7] Already the largest trading nation in the world, some predict the Chinese economy will be bigger than the American economy by 2030.[8] But the advantages for Western workers are not obvious. Since China joined the WTO, almost 60,000 American manufacturing companies have closed and 4.7 million manufacturing jobs have been lost.[9] David Autor, an economist at the Massachusetts Institute of Technology, says, 'it's certainly not the case that all of US manufacturing job loss after 2001 is due to China's WTO accession. But conservatively, 40 per cent of the decline between 2001 and 2007 can be attributed to that source.'[10]

The great stagnation

Whatever the role of China, Western workers have certainly experienced a long stagnation in pay. This great stagnation is evident in a chart created in 2012 by a then-obscure World Bank staffer named Branko Milanovic. The Elephant Chart (figure 1) quickly attracted attention – and criticism – around the world. As the British people voted for Brexit, the Americans for Donald Trump, and voters around the West for populists of different kinds, commentators began to point to Milanovic's research as an explanation.

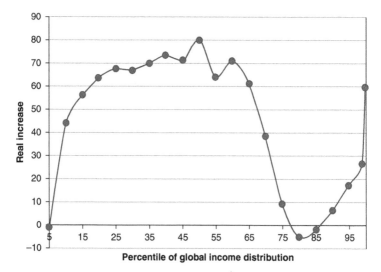

Figure 1 *The Elephant Chart: Change in real income between 1988 and 2008 at various percentiles of global income distribution (calculated in 2005 international dollars).*

Source: Milanovic, Branko. 2013. Global income inequality by the numbers: in history and now – an overview. Policy Research working paper 6259. Washington, DC: World Bank. http://documents.worldbank.org/curated/en/959251468176687085/ Global-income-inequality-by-the-numbers-in-history-and-now-an-overview

The Elephant Chart shows the distribution of global economic growth between 1988 and 2008, broken down by percentiles of the world economy.[11] The chart is likened to an elephant because its shape conveys the sharp increases in income growth for the world's poorest people (40 to 70 per cent), the emerging middle classes in countries like China and India (70 to 80 per cent), and the super rich (more than 60 per cent). But it also shows a dramatic decline for people occupying the 75th and 90th percentiles of global income distribution, which include the West's working and middle classes. The increase in their income, the chart showed, was 'essentially nil'.[12]

Milanovic declared the change in global income distribution over this period as 'probably the profoundest global shuffle of people's economic positions since the Industrial Revolution'.[13] He was referring to the change in the global share of income growth, but the change he showed was as great within the West as it was between the West and the rest: the significant gains of Western elites, juxtaposed with the stagnating incomes of the working and middle classes, demonstrated a polarization between the winners and losers of globalization.

Since 2012, several predators have taken aim at the Elephant Chart. It does not track the same people, they pointed out, but compares people in one percentile in 1988 with other people in the same percentile in 2008. Faster population growth in the lower percentiles distorts the data, they argued, pushing the shape of the graph rightwards. Not all of the occupants of the 75th to 90th percentiles are Westerners, they showed: in 1988 many were Latin American and by 2008 many were Chinese.[14]

Much of the criticism was fair, and indeed related to claims made not by Milanovic about his work, but by others who drew over-simplistic conclusions from it. What is noteworthy about the critical analyses, however, is that while they argue that 'the elephant shape itself may be an overburdened and inaccurate depiction', they cannot demolish its key finding.[15] Even rival models produced by critics find 'slow growth' rather than 'stagnation' for people around the 80th percentile.[16]

The problem is confirmed by national data in Britain and elsewhere. In the United States, while productivity increased by 77 per cent between 1973 and 2017, hourly pay rose by only 12.4 per cent.[17] In Britain, between 1983 and 2014, productivity increased by 60 per cent, while median pay increased by 40 per cent.[18] Since the financial crash, both productivity and pay have stalled: in real terms, average pay in Britain continues to be lower than it was more than a decade ago.[19]

Some critics deny that globalization has anything to do with these trends.[20] Others, such as Britain's Resolution Foundation, accept that it probably has 'played a structural role in driving lower income growth for some groups and higher growth for others', but argue that variation between countries suggests 'the distribution of gains is susceptible to domestic policy choices as much as global pressures.'[21]

This argument is corroborated by studies showing that the breakdown between productivity and pay is not internationally uniform. In some countries, like the US and Canada, it is longstanding and 'chronic'. In others, such as Britain and Germany, it is more recent, yet still acute. In others, such as Denmark and Sweden, it is recent but mild.[22] This suggests that global forces are indeed having an effect, but the structure of national economies, and the policies pursued by national governments, matter too.

The effects of globalization

The most recent wave of globalization has completely transformed the world economy, and in ways that are not commonly understood.

The first wave of globalization began in the early 1800s, when the cost and ease of transporting goods fell. This caused what the economist Richard Baldwin calls a 'great divergence', in which the industrial countries of the West became far richer and more powerful than the rest. Today, we are experiencing a 'great convergence', as technology allows companies to create international production networks, in which they move their goods and intellectual property around the world with ease.[23] The result is not a general levelling up across the world but dramatic growth in what Baldwin calls the 'Industrializing Six' – China, Korea, India, Indonesia, Thailand and Poland – and a severe reduction of manufacturing production in the West.

This reduction was slow before 1990 but accelerated suddenly and rapidly afterwards. The G7's share of global manufacturing output fell from two-thirds to under a half between 1990 and 2010.[24] During this period, almost a fifth of the world's manufacturing moved from the G7 to the Industrializing Six.[25]

This has had a dramatic effect on Western workers. A generation ago, when British technology improved, and British companies became more competitive, British workers shared in the success of the company. Now, as functions like research and development and product design remain in the West, production and assembly is often completed in lower-cost countries. The wealth created by the company is distributed between its shareholders, its executives and its high-skilled designers and technicians. Lower and medium-skilled workers in Britain do not just get a smaller share in the company's success: many are no longer employed by the company at all.

As Baldwin observes, this change has increased rewards for high-skilled workers in developed countries and encouraged developing countries to make more goods that require low-skilled labour. Baldwin concludes, similarly to Milanovic: 'High-skill workers in rich nations won, while low-skill workers in rich nations lost.'[26]

Britain's experience has been particularly severe, and the decline of its manufacturing sector began earlier than elsewhere in the West. As a share of the UK's total economic output, manufacturing fell from 27 per cent in 1970, and 17.4 per cent in 1990, to 10 per cent in 2017.[27] Some of this reduction can be explained by globalization, but manufacturing accounts for a smaller share of the British economy than in most developed countries. At 20 per cent, the share of German GDP generated by manufacturing is unusually large, but in France it is 11 per cent, in the United States it is 12 per cent, and in Italy it is 16 per cent.[28] Domestic policies have also played a role: the failure of post-war corporatism, ultra-liberal 'shock therapy' during the 1980s, and, more recently, ruinously expensive energy prices have contributed to the decline of manufacturing.

And the effect on jobs has been marked. Between 1981 and 2017, the British manufacturing workforce halved. There were 5.7 million manufacturing jobs in 1981, 4.4 million in 1991, and 2.7 million in 2017.[29] Manufacturing accounted for 16 per cent of all jobs in 1991. Now it accounts for just 8 per cent.[30]

As Baldwin explains, 'the contours of industrial competitiveness are now increasingly defined by the outlines of international production networks rather than the boundaries of nations.'[31] As supply chains have become multinational, and knowledge transfers have become cross-border, comparative advantage has narrowed even further, and international economic competition has become more individual. As a result, elite liberal assumptions about free trade – traditionally, that the more free trade we have, the richer we all become – are increasingly disputed.

The rise of the robots

As with previous waves of globalization, the changing nature and growth of international trade is made possible by changing technology. It was steam power in the early nineteenth century and the development of information and communications technology in the late twentieth century that drove earlier waves of globalization. Now it is the turn of digital technologies.

These technologies are changing the way we work. As the work of the past moves eastward, like the West's lost manufacturing jobs, or is rendered obsolete by machines, like the work done by supermarket cashiers, banking clerks and others, many find themselves in jobs that are lower-skilled, lower-paid and more precarious.

This is demonstrated by academic analyses that show that while low-skilled and high-skilled employment has grown since the early 1990s, mid-skilled employment has fallen sharply. In Britain, the growth in low-skilled work began during the 1990s, declined in the 2000s, but then increased again after the financial crash. When self-employed workers are included in the data, the change is even more pronounced: mid-skilled employment falls more sharply, and low-skilled employment rises faster. Mid-skilled jobs that have disappeared tend to be manual trades, such as machine operatives and skilled electrical workers, and office workers, such as sales staff, secretaries and administrative workers. These jobs are most at risk because technology cannot replace less routine, higher-skilled, higher-paid work, and it is less profitable to automate very routine, low-skilled, low-paid work.[32]

This means that while technology has rendered some jobs obsolete, it has not reduced overall employment. But for many people it has changed the nature of work and the pay and job security workers can expect to enjoy. According to the Chartered Institute of Personnel and Development (CIPD), around 1.3 million people in Britain now work in the gig economy, the equivalent of 4 per cent of all employment. Their statistics suggest that more than half of these workers are already in full-time work, but use the gig economy to supplement their income. The CIPD expects the number of people employed in this way – effectively as self-employed or contract workers – to grow in the coming years.[33]

International research confirms that technology has not, so far, reduced employment but it has reduced pay. In a study for the Brookings Institution in the United States, two academics found that automation does not reduce the number of jobs available. If anything, it appears to increase employment due to productivity improvements and increased consumer spending. But these effects do not offset the impact automation has on workers' wages: the effect on overall wages is negative.[34]

As David Autor, one of the report's authors, says:

the concern should not be about the number of jobs but whether those are jobs that can support a reasonable standard of living. We have more great jobs in the world than we've ever had, but we also have a lot of low-skilled jobs that are not well paid, are not stable and don't offer a very good standard of living. And that latter category is growing really rapidly.[35]

In Britain, the effects of changes in the labour market on pay have not been straightforward. Average pay, in real terms, is still lower than it was before the financial crash.[36] But the National Minimum Wage and the National Living Wage have increased the lowest wages relative to the median and eradicated the most extreme low pay in Britain. And as low-skilled European immigration has fallen since the vote to leave the European Union, average wage growth has started to rise, albeit gently.[37] Research conducted by the Resolution Foundation suggests that where hollowing out has taken place in relation to pay, it is driven by the number of men working part-time and the reduced numbers of hours worked by men overall. These changes mean that, between 1997 and 2016, the number of men earning about the typical weekly male wage fell by 15 per cent, the number of men earning more than twice the male median increased by 15 per cent, and the number earning only about a third of the median increased by 70 per cent.[38]

Unsurprisingly, involuntary part-time work occurs mainly with low-paid workers, and the growth in self-employment occurs mainly among the low-skilled, in care, construction and taxi driving, for example, and the high-skilled, such as lawyers and accountants. The increase in self-employed workers – who now constitute 15 per cent of everybody in work – is hastening the hollowing out of work and pay.[39]

These are the effects of technology as it is already applied in the workplace. But rapid advances in technology suggest we have seen nothing yet. In March 2016, DeepMind, a British company acquired by Google two years earlier, developed a program called AlphaGo. This program had been trained to play Go, the complex board game invented in China more than 2,500 years ago, using thirty million moves made by expert human players. Unlike other artificial intelligence programs before it, AlphaGo defeated the human world champion.

Eighteen months later, DeepMind produced a second program, called AlphaZero, which did not use any moves from humans to train. Instead, it learned by playing against itself. AlphaZero defeated AlphaGo as well as the world's best chess and shogi computers. Ian Hogarth, a tech entrepreneur and expert in artificial intelligence, says AlphaZero created 'a simpler algorithm that used zero human data' which was 'more competent and exhibiting more transferable intelligence'.[40]

We are still a significant distance from machines reaching human cognitive ability, or what is known as artificial general intelligence. But machine learning is already used commercially, and at scale, for search engines, advertising targeting and warehouse automation. It already supports sophisticated tasks such as pharmaceutical research, recruitment and city trading. Its use will soon be extended to many other economic activities.

This should still not mean the end of work as we know it. In one study, McKinsey found that around half of the activities humans are paid to do have the potential to be automated based on existing technologies. However, they conclude that less than 5 per cent of occupations can be automated entirely. Instead, they say that 30 per cent of the constituent activities of 60 per cent of jobs could be automated. 'More occupations will change', McKinsey predict, 'than will be automated away'.[41] Nonetheless, the hollowing out of the labour market will continue, and with it, the share of productivity improvements enjoyed by workers is likely to continue to fall. New technology will continue to drive the great stagnation. Yet in response the silence of elite liberals and market fundamentalists is deafening.

New World Disorder

These big, international, structural changes are contributing towards perhaps the most important fact of the modern era: the return of international competition and rivalry and the breakdown of the rules-based system of global governance.

When the Cold War ended, President George H. W. Bush proclaimed a 'new world order'. Fascism had been defeated, communism had collapsed, Islamism was not yet understood, and liberal democracy reigned supreme.

This ideological hubris might have appeared absurd, but it coincided, from a Western point of view, with a period of unusual peace and calm, and a sustained economic expansion. Between the collapse of the Berlin Wall and the 9/11 attacks on New York City, the West felt secure, and its military action was limited to elective wars of liberation or humanitarian intervention. Britain's Prime Minister Tony Blair promised a foreign policy based on liberal interventionism and the installation of democracies around the world.

Meanwhile, the long economic boom that lasted through the 1990s and early 2000s led many to speculate that the business cycle had been abolished. Britain's Chancellor Gordon Brown boasted that he had ended 'boom and bust'. It was not just liberal democracy but liberal economics that had triumphed.

Neither Blair nor Brown – nor US Presidents Bill Clinton and George W. Bush, nor European leaders such as Gerhard Schröder, Angela Merkel and Nicolas Sarkozy – realized that the basis of Western stability during this period would become one of the causes of its current crisis. The globalizing forces that kept Western inflation low and stock prices high during the 1990s were the same forces that internationalized production networks and squeezed the incomes of Western workers. Blair's liberal interventionism, allied with US neoconservatism, caused a disastrous war in Iraq that weakened the West's geopolitical strength. Clinton's assumption that free trade would liberalize China's society and government has proved hopelessly misplaced.

Liberal democracy did not, for very long at least, reign supreme. In fact, the international system it built is now under attack from all sides. A unipolar world has given way to a multipolar world, in which American leadership is challenged by China, Russia, Iran, North Korea and even the European Union. Making the case for a 'real European army', the French President Emmanuel Macron explains, 'We have to protect ourselves with respect to China, Russia and even the United States of America.'[42]

The conflict between values and interests around the world is on open display. Under President Trump, the United States has said it will always put 'America first'. A trade war between the US and China is underway. China is asserting its security rights in the South China Sea and the Western Pacific Ocean. Russia has annexed Crimea, sovereign territory in Ukraine, which borders the European Union. North Korea continues to flaunt its defiance of international law. India has tense relationships with Pakistan to its West and China to its east. The conflict in Syria became a proxy sectarian war between Middle Eastern powers, and an opportunity for Russia to humiliate the West. Iran seeks nuclear weapons and threatens Israel. Saudi Arabia seeks nuclear weapons of its own.

At the same time as states play out these rivalries, new technologies and methods of warfare mean weaker states – and non-state actors such as terrorists – can attack the interests of others from distance and with impunity. So-called hybrid warfare involves combinations of conventional warfare and unconventional methods, which include the use of terrorism, criminality and interference in another country's diplomacy, media and politics. Weapons and equipment that were once the exclusive property of powerful states, such as drones, thermal night-vision devices and guided missiles are now in the hands of smaller states and terrorist groups.

Cyber capabilities are an important part of the new threat. The British government has attributed state-sponsored cyber-attacks against Britain to Russia, China, North Korea and Iran. There continues to be a serious threat from organized cybercrime, which often has links to hostile foreign states. One major London listed company, reported to be Rio Tinto, lost £800 million as a result of a single hostile state cyber-attack believed to have come from China.[43] Nonetheless, Britain has allowed Huawei, the Chinese telecommunications company, to play a crucial role in providing transmission and access equipment, including routers, in its telecommunications infrastructure.[44] At the time of writing, it is not yet clear whether Britain will permit Huawei to play a role in the development of its 5G infrastructure, even though the United States has banned the company from playing any such role in its systems.

Trade and economic relations are driving and reinforcing security and military tensions. China's Belt and Road Initiative, launched in 2013, spans 65 countries, covers more than 60 per cent of the world's population, and involves investment plans reportedly worth $900 billion.[45] Many analysts agree that the initiative is about extending China's military and political reach as much as its trading relationships.[46] Whether this is true or not, the Belt and Road Initiative is causing other countries, like India and Japan, to form new alliances, as they respond to the perceived threat. Meanwhile, as the European Union refuses to countenance fiscal transfers from richer to poorer member states, a policy required by the logic of its single currency, China is investing heavily in Eastern Europe and gaining diplomatic leverage.[47] Even in the US, China owns more than $1 trillion of public debt.[48]

Climate change and mass migration are also driving changes in geopolitical relations. Europe is still struggling to deal with the migration crisis that began in 2015. In that single year, more than 1.8 million people were detected crossing Europe's borders illegally.[49] Germany received 1.1 million asylum applications alone.[50] Thousands of migrants are still reaching Europe's southern borders every week.[51] And as the migration crisis raged, thousands of European Muslims travelled across the Continent's porous borders to Syria to fight for ISIS or live in the so-called Caliphate, only to return to Europe later, further radicalized, unimpeded and unprosecuted.[52]

This mass migration and poor border security has quickened the populist advance across Europe, prompting politicians on the right to vilify immigrants and ethnic minorities. As Italy's Deputy Prime Minister, Matteo Salvini proposed a census of Romany gypsies.[53] For the first time since the Second World War, Nazis sit in Germany's Reichstag. And even in the supposedly great liberal victory won by Emmanuel Macron, one third of the electorate voted for the French National Front. In a panic, the EU's Council of Ministers has instructed the Commission to establish 'regional disembarkation platforms', where asylum claims are processed outside the EU, although there is as yet little sign of the new policy.[54]

As the balance of global power changes, the world's institutions are not changing with it, and many are in decline. The United Nations was powerless to prevent the war in Syria or Russia's annexation of Crimea. NATO – the alliance that protected the West throughout the Cold War – faces an uncertain future and constant criticism from the United States. The World Trade Organization has also come under attack from President Trump. The Chinese have established the Asian

Infrastructure Investment Bank in a bid to rival the World Bank. And the European Union seems incapable of resolving the contradictions and tensions caused by its single currency and state-building ambitions.

Across the West, elite liberals seem incapable of responding to this changing world. They cling to their belief in open borders. They refuse to question free trade even with countries like China that openly abuse international markets. They have failed to invest in their defence and security capabilities. They go on attending summits hosted by international institutions oblivious of the need to reform them. They mix in privileged and gilded circles, remote from the reality of ordinary, everyday life, and blame everybody but themselves for the rise of populism.

The baby boomer bubble

With a troubled global future ahead of them, younger people feel the pinch at home too. Despite enjoying a far higher employment rate than the baby boomers had in their late twenties, millennials are the first modern generation not to experience higher earnings than those who came before them. They face higher housing costs than previous generations, and are more likely to find themselves – thanks to globalization and the effects of new technology – in precarious self-employment.

They also find themselves on the wrong side of a demographic bulge, as the baby boomers age and life expectancy continues to rise. In 1997, 15.9 per cent of the UK population was aged 65 or older. This increased to 18.2 per cent in 2017, and will reach 24 per cent by 2037 and 26.5 per cent by 2066. As people live longer, the old-age dependency ratio – the number of people of state pension age for every thousand of the working-age population – increases. In 2017, the dependency ratio was 289, up from 244 a decade before. In 2041, without the planned increase in the state pension age, it will reach 419. And the increasing dependency ratio is combining with low fertility rates, which have declined from 1.87 children per woman in 2007 to 1.79 in 2016.[55] The UK, like other Western countries, is an increasingly old society.

Demographic bulges are not new, of course, and neither are they limited to Western countries. But this is the first time that a demographic bulge has occurred on such a scale and at a time of state pensions and free healthcare: we are experiencing the early stages of the bursting of the baby boomer bubble. The post-war welfare state will only survive if it is cut back, impoverishing pensioners, or funded through extra borrowing or higher taxes, which will transfer the burden to younger generations.

The numbers are stark. Benefits and services for older people are due to cause spending to increase rapidly. Health and social care spending is forecast to go up from 7.3 per cent of GDP in 2016–17 to 12.6 per cent of GDP in 2066. Welfare spending, mainly in the form of pensions and pensioner benefits, will increase by a further 2 per cent of GDP. In today's prices, this additional spending pressure amounts to £24 billion per year by 2030 and £63 billion per year 2040.[56]

The Resolution Foundation has calculated that if the additional spending pressure is met through borrowing, it will push the national debt above 100 per cent of GDP by 2040 and above 230 per cent of GDP by 2066. This would mean debt interest payments alone would reach an unsustainable 9 per cent of GDP, and place an impossible burden on future generations.[57]

But if the burden of higher spending on ageing baby boomers is met by taxation, the younger generation will still feel the pain. The Resolution Foundation's calculations suggest that those born in the late 1980s would face a cumulative additional tax bill of around £14,000 over the 2020s and 2030s. The extra £63 billion needed annually by 2040, they say, is the equivalent of a 15p increase in the basic rate of income tax today.[58]

So not only are young people facing precarious employment and low pay, they face a higher tax burden through their working lives too. And they are unlikely to experience some of the advantages experienced by baby boomers. Already, the days of free university tuition are over. Defined benefit pensions have given way to less secure defined contribution schemes. And millennial families are only half as likely to own their home by the age of thirty than the baby boomers were.[59] When wealth is passed down to younger people, through inheritance from their parents, prosperous millennials stand to gain by four times as much as those with no property wealth.[60]

No wonder, then, that a clear majority of British people – in common with all other Western populations polled – consistently say they expect to be worse off than their parents' generation.[61]

The British disease

This is not Britain's inevitable fate. Policies matter, and Britain's ultra-liberal policies have created a low-productivity, low-skill, low-wage economy.

Measuring productivity and comparing it across different countries can be difficult, but according to official estimates, labour productivity is on average 16.3 per cent higher in the other G7 countries than in Britain. It is 22.6 per cent higher in the United States, 22.8 per cent higher in France and 26.2 per cent higher in Germany.[62] In other words, if our economy produced the same goods and services as efficiently as Germany, British workers would be able to take off one week in four without our economy getting any smaller.

And the problem is getting worse. Productivity is lower in all the G7 countries than it would have been if trends before the financial crash had continued. But Britain has the largest so-called 'productivity puzzle' of all the developed economies. The difference between Britain's post-crash productivity performance and the pre-crash trend is 15.6 per cent, almost twice as bad as the G7 average of 8.7 per cent.[63] According to the Office for National Statistics, 'had the pre-2008 trend continued, productivity would have been 20 per cent higher than it actually was at the end of 2017.'[64]

This does not necessarily mean that each British worker would be 20 per cent better off. There is no guaranteed link between rising productivity and higher wages: as we have already seen, there is evidence that new technology is causing labour's share of the spoils to reduce. But if we want wages to rise, productivity also needs to rise. This is because better productivity is how workers – and capital investments in things like infrastructure, machinery and technology – can add greater value. It is also the main way of increasing economic demand without increasing inflation. Better productivity is therefore an important way of improving economic stability, contributing in another way to lower prices and higher wages.

It is no surprise, then, that British workers earn less than their counterparts in more productive countries such as Germany and the United States. According to the OECD, the average American wage in 2017 was $60,558, while in Germany it was $47,585. In the UK it was $43,732.[65]

But even this does not tell the full story, because Britain's regional performance, when it comes to both productivity and pay, divides sharply. Labour productivity in London is 33.3 per cent above the UK average and in the South East of England it is 6.1 per cent above average. Every other region and nation of the United Kingdom is below average. Performance is especially poor in Northern Ireland, Wales, Yorkshire and the Humber, the North East and the East and West Midlands. In these nations and regions, productivity is between 11 and 17 per cent lower than average.[66] It should be no surprise, therefore, that the average wage in London is more than 25 per cent higher than the UK average, and more than 40 per cent higher than in the country's lowest paid region, the North East of England. There, wages are almost 11 per cent below the average for the rest of the UK.[67]

Some analysts question whether the problem is really as stark as it appears, and doubt we are measuring productivity properly and fairly. But even studies that seek to ensure consistency between international statistics show significant UK underperformance. In 2018, for example, the OECD used a more generous methodology but still concluded that Britain underperforms the United States by 10.4 per cent, and lags behind other G7 countries including Italy, France and Germany.[68]

The problem comes down to policy. There is a lack of long-term investment in the British economy: in infrastructure, research and development, and people.

Britain spent 2.2 per cent of GDP on infrastructure between 2008 and 2013, behind rapidly growing economies like China and India, but also behind developed economies including Australia, Canada, Italy, Japan and the United States. According to the McKinsey Global Institute, we face an infrastructure funding gap: Britain needs to spend an extra 0.4 per cent of GDP every year until 2030 to meet its infrastructure needs.[69]

Britain has tended to rely far more on private investment, or public/private partnerships, to deliver infrastructure projects than other countries. This brings some advantages, but there are widely-held concerns that the British approach leads to systemic over-rewards for investors, and an ultra-liberal aversion to the use of public debt financing, even though this can be acquired at cheaper rates than private sector investment. After the formation of the coalition government in 2010, for example, capital spending was cut, even though it could have been financed cheaply and many economists, including those who supported austerity, argued that such spending would have delivered a return on investment and better economic growth.[70]

Investment is not the only barrier to building Britain's infrastructure. Other barriers include poor planning laws, poor productivity in the construction sector, and political indecision about big infrastructure projects.

No new airport runway has been built in the South East of England since the 1940s, for example, and Heathrow Airport has been running at full capacity for years. Yet it took a debate lasting half a century, and multiple commissions and consultations, before the Government approved a third runway at Heathrow in 2018. Even now, there are questions about whether construction will go ahead. If it does, the new runway will still not be operational until at least 2026.[71]

Aviation capacity is not the only problem. Thanks to delays in infrastructure projects, and elite liberal environmental policies that have deliberately increased costs, Britain's industrial electricity prices have gone up by more than 160 per cent since 2004.[72] They are the sixth highest of the 28 mainly Western member countries of the International Energy Agency. They are 83 per cent more expensive than in America. And they have been getting increasingly uncompetitive. In 2010 our industrial electricity prices were in line with the IEA average; now they are 28 per cent more expensive.[73]

The North of England is home to five of the UK's largest ten cities, yet its transport connectivity compares terribly to London. Around half a million people travel thirty kilometres or more to work in London, yet only half as many people travel the same distance to work across the major city regions in the North.[74] Only 3 per cent of the UK has full-fibre internet connectivity, compared with 70 per cent or higher in countries including Spain, Portugal, Japan and South Korea.[75] Britain's well-documented housing problems – in which supply has failed to meet increasing demand and prices have risen accordingly – severely constrains labour mobility, limits the benefits of agglomeration in successful cities, and restricts saving and investment.

There are similar problems with research and development too. Britain invests less in R&D than most of our competitors. According to government figures, we spend 1.7 per cent of GDP compared to 2.8 per cent in the United States and 2.9 per cent in Germany.[76] The OECD confirms that both public and private investment in R&D is below the average of its member countries and below Britain's principal competitors.[77]

But even this masks the true performance in different regions and sectors of the economy. According to the Government, just 400 businesses account for more than three-quarters of all private R&D spending in Britain. Fewer small and medium-sized businesses introduce new products and processes compared to European firms. 'We are good at low-cost innovation and flexible start-ups', admits the Government's Industrial Strategy, 'but the long and patient process of getting a new technology to market is difficult.' In general, it says, 'British businesses' R&D tends to favour quick routes to market, rather than long development times, and selling businesses to growing them.'[78]

Unsurprisingly, R&D spending is lowest in Britain's less productive regions. Public investment in R&D is higher in London, the South East and East of England than it is in struggling regions like the North East and the West Midlands, which has the lowest level of public investment in the UK.[79] According to government figures, London, Oxford and Cambridge receive almost half – 46.1 per cent – of all public R&D investment in England.[80]

Consider this alongside the fact that London gets more than a third of English transport spending, more than twice as much per head than any other region, and more local and national government spending per head than anywhere else, including on schools, and it is no surprise that Britain has the greatest regional productivity divides of any OECD country.[81] London is further ahead than Britain's second-best performing region, the average region and the worst performing region than is the case in any other country surveyed.[82] And this is bad for everyone: comparative studies suggest that regionally unbalanced economies are less productive and less prosperous overall.[83]

It is not just infrastructure and R&D that drives better productivity, but people too. There is a strong positive relationship between productivity and educational attainment across the nations and regions of the UK. Predictably, there are more people educated to secondary level and more graduates in London than anywhere else, and there are fewer in places where productivity is poor, such as Northern Ireland.[84]

While Britain boasts world-class universities, it has a very poor skills record. More than a quarter of adults in England have low basic skills, and this is not something that is getting better with time: young people are as likely to have weak basic skills as people approaching retirement age. In other developed economies, report international studies, younger people are better educated than older people, but this is not the case in Britain.[85]

Low-skilled workers in the UK also earn less than low-skilled workers in the other G7 countries. And in the UK family background matters more: young people whose parents have poor educational qualifications have the lowest level of basic skills than in all other developed countries. The OECD explains that 'the provision of post-secondary [vocational education and training] is much more limited than compared to most other ... countries. As a result, the percentage of adults who have short-cycle ... vocational education and training as their highest qualification is one of the lowest in the OECD.'[86]

The resulting skills shortages may explain why the British economy is so dependent on immigration. But immigration does not only fill skills gaps: a considerable proportion is low-skilled in nature. Official statistics show that 44 per cent of the UK-born workforce is in low or lower- to middle-skilled employment. Yet 69 per cent of workers from the A8 countries – those such as Poland who joined the EU in 2004 – work in low or lower-skilled jobs. For the A2 countries, Hungary and Bulgaria, it is 61 per cent.[87] In 2016, there were around two million workers from these countries in Britain, the vast majority doing low-skilled work.[88]

Elite liberal politicians and campaigners claim that all immigration makes the economy more competitive. But Professor Alan Manning, the Chairman of the Government's independent Migration Advisory Committee, makes clear this is a myth. 'Lower-skilled migrants', he told Parliament towards the end of 2018, 'have been fiscally negative ... they make the UK a slightly lower wages, lower productivity kind of economy ... if you say, "what has been the benefit of this lower-skilled migration?" there is not very much on the positive side of the ledger.'[89]

Britain's skills problem is not limited to low-paid workers. Several studies have shown that British management skills are poorer than in competitor countries such as the United States, and there is a much longer tail of companies with poor management scores in Britain than in other developed countries. According to Andrew Haldane, the chief economist at the Bank of England, there are about twice as many badly run companies in Britain as there are in Germany and America.[90]

Haldane points out that the problem is not only on the shop floor and the managers' offices. It goes right to the top, all the way to the boardroom. Bank of England research shows that the UK has only a small number of companies with directors who are 'hyper-connected' to board members of other firms. Instead, most have directors who are poorly connected, and as Haldane observes, 'for companies' productivity, connectivity counts'.[91]

This is compounded by what academics call Britain's 'agency problem'. In 50 per cent of corporations in Austria, Germany and Italy, a single investor or group of investors controls more than 50 per cent of the voting shares. In 50 per cent of Dutch, Spanish and Swedish corporations, a single shareholder controls more than 30 per cent of the voting shares. In Britain, they control less than 10 per cent. 'Long, persistent holdings, frequently in the hands of families, dominate on the Continent', notes Professor Colin Mayer, but in Britain 'they died out rapidly, giving rise to the phenomenon of the dispersed ownership corporation'. As a result, businesses are run by executive teams on behalf of shareholders, none of whom have holdings big enough to properly oversee what the executives are doing.[92] Yet elite liberals and market fundamentalists see nothing wrong with this staggering lack of accountability.

Back to the original sin

These failings are directly related to the flaws and contradictions in ultra-liberal thinking described in chapter 1. It is the belief in the sanctity of the market, the assumption that markets are always best left to themselves, that private investment is always better than public spending, and spending must always be low, that means politicians have failed to address the structural weaknesses in the British economy.

Hayek, as we have seen, explained the superiority of the market above the planned, socialist economy. The price of goods and services cannot be set before sellers and buyers trade. The information they need to determine the price is available only at that instant, and subsequently disappears forever. A centralized command and control economy is therefore doomed to fail. But this only tells us so much. Simply because the free market is superior to the planned economy does not mean that the pure, unregulated market is always right. And just because the market usually is the most efficient way of allocating resources does not mean it is the fairest way of doing so.

Sellers and buyers do not always have the information they need to determine the correct value of a product, for example. They might not understand its complexity, just as the City traders who brought about the financial crash trading Collateralized Debt Obligations did not understand the worthlessness of those bundles of subprime mortgages. Businesses might not understand or care about the negative externalities, or the costs to others, of their trading, which is why, for example, we have planning laws to prevent over-development and inappropriate construction work. Companies might be able to exploit the absence of competition in a market to drive up the prices of their goods and services, or drive down the prices of their suppliers unfairly. And with international trade, a price established by the market might not take into account subsidies and state support enjoyed by some companies over others, such as Chinese steel producers over their Western competitors.

Even Adam Smith, the great free market economist, warned against unethical business practices such as price-fixing. 'People of the same trade seldom meet together', he said, 'even for merriment and diversion, but the conversation ends in a conspiracy against the public, or in some contrivance to raise prices.' In the same work, *The Wealth of Nations*, Smith also cautioned against the exploitation of workers: 'Masters are always and everywhere in a sort of tacit, but constant and uniform combination, not to raise the wages of labour above their actual rate.' And he warned against government policies that put the interests of producers ahead of consumers. 'Consumption is the sole end and purpose of all production; and the interest of the producer ought to be attended to, only so far as it may be necessary for promoting that of the customer.'[93]

Yet despite these warnings from a thinker they often lionize, ultra-liberals cling to their belief in the perfection of the market. Where market failure stares them straight in the face, they claim that the causes of these failures originate with government interventions in the market. So it is not right to complain that the construction industry is over-consolidated and builds too few homes: if the supply of land was not restricted by planning law, the market would provide enough houses. But whatever the shortcomings of planning law, and however much it might need to be reformed, it cannot simply be removed or radically pared back, because people value the conservation of the natural environment and the sensible regulation of their local, built environment. In other words, liberty – expressed in the ability to build whatever developers like on land they own – is not accepted as the most important human value. It is balanced against other values.

This is proved time and again. As we saw in chapter 1, according to Hayek, social justice is a 'mirage' that must not be pursued, and the only rational way to set prices and determine collective choices is to trust the market. Yet no country in the world relies only on the market to deliver healthcare for its citizens. Some systems may be more market-based than others, but practically all countries provide free healthcare for those who cannot pay. This is because human values such as dignity and solidarity influence health policies at least as much as, and probably more so, than personal freedom. The same is true of education policies, and taxation and public spending. We do not believe that justice means, in some crude calculation, that we should all receive precisely what we earned, or be treated in accordance with our ability to pay. Values like solidarity rival personal freedom and shape policy just as much.

Yet elite liberal politicians and right-wing market fundamentalists routinely ignore this insight. Their attempts to reform public services invariably require their marketization. No politician dares to propose the privatization or explicit marketization of the National Health Service, for example, but the creation and extension of the NHS internal market went ahead anyway, at the cost of enormous bureaucracy. No politician ever promised to introduce university tuition fees or increase them in a general election campaign, but all three parties – Labour, Conservatives and Liberal Democrats – have done just that.

And their economic policies remain as dry as dust. Public investment in R&D remains low. Public investment in infrastructure remains insufficient. There is only a limited role for government in regenerating struggling regional economies. There is barely a role for government in reforming dysfunctional markets, such as housing, the railways or the utilities. And there is next to no role for government in regulating emerging markets created by new technologies, like the big platform companies such as Facebook and Uber. Ultra-liberals have forgotten that markets do not and cannot exist in a state of nature. Once upon a time, liberal thinkers like Adam Smith knew that markets were constructs of contracts, rules and laws that relied on social goods like trust and virtue. Yet ultra-liberals now forget that it is up to government to create and change market rules in response to changing circumstances.

And the ultra-liberal economic agenda marches on. As rapid deindustrialization has shorn many communities of their traditional sources of employment, the 'invisible hand' of the market has not replaced lost prosperity. The regions have fallen further behind London and the booming South East, in investment, productivity, jobs, wages and wealth. And as this has happened, public investment has followed private investment: rather than seek to rebalance the economy, public spending is higher per head in London than anywhere else in the country.

Where deindustrialization has occurred, many communities have lost important local institutions, including not only the big local employers, but others such as smaller businesses in the supply chain, trades unions, workers' clubs, and services such as local hospitals, post offices and transport connections. Gone too are the skills in which working men and women once took enormous pride. As we have already seen, a hollowing out in both employment and pay is underway, with mid-skilled work declining, and men in particular bearing the brunt. And Britain's poor provision of technical education and skills training means those who do not make it to university are more likely to be left behind. Those who do attend university are more likely to come from the prosperous South East, but those who come from poorer communities are unlikely, after graduating, to return home. A deskilling crisis is thus compounded by a brain drain.

The point of capitalism's 'creative winds of destruction', described by Joseph Schumpeter, was that innovators and entrepreneurs destroy the old and the inefficient as they produce new and better goods and services. But for many communities, capitalism's creativity has brought only destruction. The fruits of its creations have been enjoyed by people elsewhere, while the destruction has not been limited to old and inefficient firms, but applied equally to the institutions, civic confidence and social capital of whole communities.

Since personal freedom trumps other values, and since the market knows best, elite liberals and market fundamentalists believe, not much can be done for these poor benighted places. In fact, they feel not only resignation about the plight of their fellow citizens, but scorn. In the words of Janan Ganesh, a *Financial Times* columnist, ultra-liberal Londoners, like those living in other prosperous communities around the West, 'look at their domestic stragglers and feel … shackled to a corpse.'[94] The best response, he says, is to simply ignore these stragglers altogether: 'a seething minority is still a minority'.[95]

No wonder, then, that the ultra-liberals have done so little to resuscitate the communities and people they dismiss as corpses. Of course, on occasion their utilitarianism means they have been prepared to throw a few breadcrumbs to less prosperous parts of the country. In the 1990s, tax credits were introduced to top up the incomes of low-paid workers, while tax revenues generated mainly in London and the South East were used to fund public sector jobs. Between 1998 and 2007, for example, 69 per cent of the 1.2 million net additional jobs in UK cities were in the public sector.[96] But government has done little to invest in people and places to get Britain's regional economies firing in a sustainable way.

The teleological tendency of liberalism means the ultra-liberals feel only impatience towards the 'stragglers', who are holding back progress. They need to work harder, and expect less support, if Britain is to prosper in what David Cameron used to call 'the global race'. After all, according to market fundamentalists, as global competition becomes more intense, the state needs to become leaner and leaner if Britain is to survive. Never mind the fact that Britain is failing to give its workers the skills they need to compete. And never mind that for many of Britain's economic rivals, and many of the rapidly developing economies, government intervention and industrial strategy is an important pillar of their prosperity. For the elite liberals and market fundamentalists, there should be little or no role for government in the economy at all.

Neither is there any question about the desirability, inevitability or nature of globalization. As Tony Blair once said, 'you might as well debate whether autumn should follow summer.'[97] The universalism of ideological liberalism – and its belief in inevitable progress – leads to a common belief among ultra-liberals in internationalism and the possibilities of supranational and ultimately even world government. For ultra-liberals, opposition to mass immigration is backward and often racist. Scepticism about supranationalism is narrow-minded and xenophobic. Concern for local traditions, institutions and one's fellow citizens is unnecessarily parochial. An unholy alliance between market fundamentalists and left-liberals, who support mass immigration and supranationalism but for different reasons, ensures continuity in policy and shuts down dissent.

These ultra-liberal policy positions are all related to the original sin of liberalism. Personal liberty is the most important human value of all. And individuals are rational, autonomous and self-interested. But on economic policy, ultra-liberalism is proving the impossibility of its own assumptions. Like other ideologies, it is creaking under the weight of its own contradictions. As it destroys communities, institutions and solidarity between citizens, it is destroying the foundations upon which capitalism itself depends. And as that happens, elite liberals are stacking the cards in favour of the rich and successful at the expense of ordinary working people.

Redistributing to the rich

Inequality is nothing new, of course. Income inequality has fallen, slightly, over the last ten years. But it remains far higher than it was in the 1970s, and the effects of the sharp rise in income inequality experienced in the 1980s have not been reversed.[98] Britain is one of the most unequal developed countries in the world: of the G7 countries only the United States has a worse record. Across Europe, only Lithuania is more divided.[99]

Elite liberals and market fundamentalists insist this does not matter. Famously, Margaret Thatcher dismissed attacks on her government's record on inequality, claiming her critics 'would rather that the poor were poorer, provided that the rich were less rich. That way one will never create the wealth for better social services, as we have.'[100] But it is not the case – if indeed it ever was – that the rich are simply getting richer at a faster rate while the rest of us also get richer more slowly. As we have already seen, average wages in Britain are no higher than before the financial crash, and British workers earn less than their counterparts in other developed economies.

Neither is it true that our economic model is funding better public services. Britain's decade of austerity caused the longest squeeze in the history of the National Health Service.[101] School spending per pupil fell by 8 per cent in real terms between 2010 and 2018.[102] Spending per person on services provided by local government fell by 24 per cent.[103]

But even if this were not the case, the vision of a society comprising a super-wealthy elite funding better social services for the rest of us, taken to its logical conclusion, feels darkly dystopian. It might be compatible with a society that cares only about individual freedom, but not one that values recognition or solidarity in equal measure.

Britain not only suffers extreme income inequality; it is also deeply unequal when it comes to accumulated wealth. The wealth held by the richest 10 per cent of households in Britain is around five times greater than the wealth of the bottom half of all households combined. This is, in fact, in line with the average for developed countries.[104] But there are several reasons to worry that the picture is getting worse.

The main components of the country's wealth are pensions savings and housing. While automatic enrolment for pensions has increased the number of workers contributing to a workplace pension by a quarter since the policy was introduced in 2012, the amounts saved have tended to cluster around the minimum contributions set out in statute.[105] The growing number of self-employed workers will not be covered by the automatic enrolment legislation. And while savings for average income groups remain insufficient, tax relief on pensions savings has for years disproportionately benefited higher earners. Pensions savings attract 100 per cent tax relief, and until recently were subject only to generous annual and lifetime maximum caps. A new taper should reduce the benefits for rich savers, but as recently as 2015–16, the top 11 per cent of income tax payers accounted for 52 per cent of pension tax relief.

The top 1 per cent, with incomes of more than £150,000 and more, accounted for 15 per cent. Yet those earning less than £20,000 per year – 40 per cent of taxpayers – accounted for just 7 per cent of pension savings attracting tax relief. And the cost to Treasury revenues is considerable: total pension tax relief is worth an estimated £38.6 billion per year.[106]

So for the biggest component of the country's wealth – pensions savings – government policy has been helping the rich to get richer. And the same is true for housing, the second biggest component of wealth in Britain.

And international studies show that countries with low home ownership rates, such as the United States and the Netherlands, tend to be those with the highest levels of wealth inequality.[107] Yet this is the direction in which Britain is heading. Home ownership in England has been falling since 2003, long before the financial crash.[108] Young people are increasingly likely to find themselves trapped for years in rented accommodation.[109] And more people now own their home outright than pay a mortgage, demonstrating not only the difficulties faced by the hard-pressed and the young, but the consolidation of wealth by the affluent and the elderly.[110]

And policy is not fixing the problem, but fuelling it. The Government concedes England needs between 225,000 and 275,000 new homes to be built every year to keep up with rising demand. But since the 1970s, just 160,000 new homes have been built each year.[111] Partly as a result, the average house now costs almost eight times average earnings, the worst ratio on record. The proportion of people living in the private rented sector has doubled since 2000, and more than 2.2 million working households with below-average incomes spend more than a third or more of their disposable income on housing.[112] It should be no surprise, then, that British households are among the most indebted in the developed world.[113]

Elite liberal politicians talk about fixing Britain's housing crisis, but their ideology prevents them from taking the measures that would achieve that. Immigration, for example, is behind 37 per cent of new demand for housing in England, yet no ultra-liberal – of any persuasion at all – shows any intention of reducing or controlling the numbers of people coming to Britain.[114]

Neither has government addressed the market failures that mean far too few houses are being built. Britain has not built the number of houses it needs since the state, in the form of local authorities, built significant numbers itself, often totalling more than 100,000 per year.[115] In particular, not enough affordable housing is built, with some estimates suggesting an additional 78,000 to 145,000 affordable new homes need to be built every year.[116] Successive governments have failed to address the over-consolidation of the construction sector, which allow firms to land bank, build out slowly and profiteer.

But the problem is not only one of supply. It is also about the financialization of housing. When the normal means of buying a home – through mortgage borrowing, savings, inheritance, and gifts and loans from the 'bank of mum and dad' – are supplemented by government finance schemes, house prices will inevitably rise.

'Help to Buy', the government scheme set up in 2013, lends people up to 20 per cent of the cost of their new home, if they have a 5 per cent deposit and a mortgage for the remaining 75 per cent of the value of the house. In London, the government loan increases to 40 per cent and applies to homes worth up to £600,000. No interest is charged on the government loan for five years, and the home must be newly constructed.[117] Unsurprisingly, the scheme has significant deadweight costs. Thirty-five per cent of recipients could have afforded a home without the government subsidy. Forty per cent of the loans have gone to people with annual incomes above £50,000. And it is expensive: a National Audit Office analysis shows it took up 45 per cent of the government's housing budget in 2016/17.[118] But perhaps more alarmingly, Help to Buy has increased house prices even further, because property developers have baked the government subsidy into their prices. The valuation of new-build homes leapt suddenly after Help to Buy was introduced and has increased faster than older homes since.[119]

True, ministers have removed the tax incentives for buy-to-let investors and increased stamp duty for second home purchases, but they have failed to take action on other ways in which the property market is warped. Foreign investment in British housing, often by anonymous companies operating from tax havens, is estimated to have increased prices by 28 per cent in just fifteen years.[120] And the explosion of short-term letting, through Airbnb in particular, is behind the phenomenon of 'disappearing homes'. In 2016, around 25,000 homes in London were listed on Airbnb, reducing the number of homes available on stable, long-term rents.[121] This is about as many as the total number of new homes constructed in London that year.[122]

In multiple ways, then, government policy is inflating the price of housing assets, redistributing to the rich and making it harder for those without wealth, or worse, those with debts, to catch up. And yet there is one further way, which is what George Osborne used to call 'monetary activism'. Super-low interest rates and quantitative easing, in the form of half a trillion pounds of newly created money, have not caused rampant inflation as some predicted, but a narrower and hidden form of inflation instead, in the form of higher prices for housing and financial assets including pensions savings.

The Bank of England has defended monetary activism robustly, saying 'the overall effect of monetary policy on standard relative measures of income and wealth inequality has been small.'[123] And it is certainly true that following the financial crash, monetary policy supported the incomes of younger workers and those with less wealth.

The immediate effects of monetary activism were to rescue the financial system and keep the real economy going. The Bank's estimate is that, without monetary easing, the economy would have been around 8 per cent smaller and unemployment four percentage points higher.[124] Because younger people are more likely to work than older people, and their employment tends to be more pro-cyclical, there were obvious short-term advantages for them.

The Bank insists that, relative to the income and wealth enjoyed by different households before monetary activism, the effects of the policy have been similar for rich and poor alike. But this is a strange way to look at things because, as the Bank admits, 'the marginal gains from … changes in monetary policy for wealthier groups are estimated to have been much larger in cash terms than for less wealthy households, with the main contributions coming from higher housing wealth and pension wealth.' In the years following monetary activism, the poorest 10 per cent of households experienced only a marginal increase in their measured real wealth of around £3,000, compared to £350,000 for the wealthiest 10 per cent.[125]

Several academic studies show that the policy has made the rich richer. One study, by Haroon Mumtaz and Angeliki Theophilopoulou, found that monetary activism has caused 'an increase in earnings, income and consumption inequality' and has had 'a larger negative effect on low income households ... compared to those at the top of the distribution.' Its conclusion was that 'quantitative easing may have contributed to the increase in inequality over the Great Recession.'[126]

According to the OECD, 'wealth inequality increased in both the United States and the United Kingdom since the Great Recession.' And they were clear about one of the principal causes: 'These changes are associated with ... higher prices of financial assets in the recovery benefiting those at the top of the distribution.'[127] In other words, monetary policy has made the rich richer.

Unhelpfully for the Bank of England, its own chief economist, Andrew Haldane, has observed that in the time since quantitative easing began, the rich have got richer. 'Those in the bottom two-fifths of the income distribution have seen virtually no gains in their wealth since 2010', he says. 'Indeed, those in the bottom 20% have seen their wealth *fall* over this period. By contrast, those in the top quintile have seen their wealth increase by almost 20%.' To a significant degree, Haldane says, the recovery since the financial crash belongs to 'those already asset-rich'.[128]

But even if the Bank is correct and monetary activism has not yet caused an increase in inequality – a claim refuted by many studies – the end effect will in all likelihood be a redistribution to the rich. It was the deliberate aim of monetary activism to increase the value of financial assets and to maintain the value of overpriced housing assets. These are the main components of wealth in Britain, and monetary activism means they will end up further from the reach of those who do not already possess them.

The decline of civic capitalism

These are not the only ways in which ultra-liberal economic policies are making life harder for ordinary people. Quietly, slowly, imperceptibly, the laws and regulations that govern markets have been changed in ways that suit big business, investors and the executive classes, but which work against the interests of ordinary workers and citizens.

Yet ultra-liberals behave as though markets are naturally occurring phenomena. Proposals to change the rules to make markets work fairly are routinely rejected, because to do so would be 'anti-market' and therefore 'anti-business' and bad for economic growth. But as we have seen, the ultra-liberal market addiction is based on the misconception that personal freedom is the pre-eminent human value. Yet the freedom to make money, and lots of it, is not more important than our obligations to one another. The market addiction also fails to account for market failures, caused by imperfect information, a lack of competition, or unfair competition, often from companies backed by foreign governments. And it also fails to learn the essential liberal lesson that markets are man-made constructs – contracts, perhaps – that can be reformed and made to work better.

The laws that underpin markets are there to ensure that trades are conducted fairly and to increase confidence that contractual commitments will be met. These laws are not, and should not be, limited to trades between businesses selling to one another. They should include, too, trades between employers and employees and sellers of goods and services and their customers. This is why, as capitalist economies developed, and as Western countries became more democratic, governments regulated markets to create a more civic capitalism that protected the interests of workers and consumers and wider society too.

Many changes were resisted by the vested interests of their day, but far from being a drag on growth, many made further growth possible. Factories were made safer, children were educated and housing was improved. There was compensation for workplace injuries, pensions and support for people who found themselves out of work. The environment was protected. Trades unions were recognized, their roles confirmed in legislation and collective bargaining was permitted. Later, a minimum wage was introduced and individual rights, covering maternity pay, paternity leave and other protections in other circumstances, were introduced and extended.

This civic capitalism was not only about complying with the law. By paying their taxes, contributing philanthropically, and educating and training local people, many companies not only met their legal obligations but also became important community institutions. In doing so, they made sure that the foundations of capitalism – a skilled and healthy workforce, a prosperous consumer society, civic confidence and social capital, infrastructure and institutions – grew stronger.

But this civic capitalism is now in dangerous decline. In particular, the relationship between labour and capital has become precariously unbalanced. In part, this is because of the structural issues discussed above. Globalization and changing technology are squeezing Western workers. And Britain's low-skill, low-productivity, low-wage, high-immigration economic model puts its workers on a weaker footing. But the imbalance between labour and capital has also been brought about deliberately through ultra-liberal policies.

Today, fewer than one in seven private sector workers is a member of a trade union. The total number of unionized workers has fallen from 13 million in 1979 to 6.2 million in 2017.[129] Nine in ten workers were subject to collective bargaining in the 1970s, while today fewer than three in ten negotiate their pay collectively.[130] Over the same period, labour's share of national income has fallen from two-thirds to just over one half. While Britain has a history of poor labour relations and irresponsible trade union leadership, studies prove what many trades union members know: organized labour can increase wages for its members through collective bargaining.[131] But government policy has sought to limit the role of trades unions and decentralize pay bargaining as far as possible.

Instead of emphasizing collective rights, British governments since Margaret Thatcher have prioritized individual workplace rights. But these rights are only of use to workers who are legally entitled to them: many workers are not because they are made to work as self-employed contractors or because their employment is casual, meaning that they never reach the qualifying period. More than 15 per cent of British workers are self-employed, and more than 6 per cent are in temporary work. Around 3 per cent are on 'zero hours' contracts, which offer only limited rights and protections.[132] Studies suggest 'hidden employment' is common, where employers evade their legal responsibilities by deliberately recruiting agency workers rather than full-time employees. Prominent complaints about employers' conduct include the unauthorized deduction of wages, unfair dismissal and exploitative terms and conditions.[133]

And these rights are only of use to people if they are applied to those who are entitled to them: there is plenty of evidence that rights are simply not enforced for many workers. According to official figures, there are 342,000 jobs that pay below the National Living Wage, notably in hospitality, retail and childcare. Another prominent form of 'wage theft' is unpaid holiday pay, worth at least £1.8 billion, and affecting an estimated one in twenty workers. Similarly, temporary workers are often encouraged to opt out of their right to receive the same wage as permanent workers, which begins after twelve weeks of work, in return for 'pay between assignments'. But pay between assignments is then often withheld, costing workers an estimated unpaid wage of around £1 billion each year.[134]

The decline of 'countervailing power', as Robert Reich, the former US Labor Secretary, calls it, has consequences not only for pay and conditions but for the protection of jobs. Manufacturing jobs have been exposed brutally to the reality of global competition, while other jobs have not. Professionals who provide services have been shielded from globalization through non-tariff barriers to trade including, for example, the need to have specific qualifications and licences to practice. Meanwhile, low-skilled and unskilled workers in both manufacturing and service sectors have faced competition for work and lower wages caused by mass immigration.

As Britain's labour market changes, and more people find themselves in self-employment and temporary work, this countervailing power will decline further, and more people will become exposed to the risk of exploitation. Yet the ultra-liberal policy response has not been to try to protect workers, but to celebrate the rise of the gig economy. It is confirmation, for some market fundamentalists, that 'in the industrial towns and port cities ... the call of freedom rings loudest', because 'this generation are [sic] Uber-riding, Airbnb-ing, Deliveroo-eating, freedom fighters.'[135] Never mind that the reality of the gig economy already means the loss of rights and protections for many workers, never mind the fact that the relationship between these tech companies and their workers amounts to a form of neo-feudalism, individual freedom – and the untouched market – is all that matters.

While workers throughout Britain's labour market struggle, those at the top have never had it so good. Britain's broken corporate governance renders shareholders, workers and consumers powerless and leaves the executive classes largely unaccountable and very well paid. In the last twenty years, executive pay has more than quadrupled. In 1998 the average FTSE100 chief executive earned £1 million. By 2015 it had increased to £4.3 million. In 1998 chief executives were paid on average 47 times what their employees earned. Today, the ratio is 128 to 1. Over the same period, the value of the companies they run has hardly increased at all.[136] Yet any attempts to reform corporate governance are attacked by ultra-liberals for being 'anti-market' and blocked or watered down.

Dysfunctional markets

It is not just the labour market that is changing dramatically, and it is not just corporate governance that is broken. Many markets have become completely dysfunctional. We have already seen how the housing market has helped to redistribute to the rich and widen inequality. And we have also seen how the marketization of higher education has undermined social justice. Not only are English graduates now saddled with the highest student debts in the world, at an average of £50,000, and not only do many university degrees fail to provide any kind of salary premium for graduates, the effect of government policy on technical education has been deleterious.[137] One study shows that just 4,900 learners in further education colleges achieved post-secondary technical qualifications in 2014–15. In the same year, higher education recorded 745,000 undergraduate and postgraduate degrees, of which 395,580 were full first degrees.[138] That means there were almost 81 undergraduates awarded degrees for every person awarded a post-secondary technical qualification by a college. Yet the recently constructed higher education market remains untouched.

Britain's railways were privatized in the 1990s. Since then public subsidies have fallen, services are more reliable, safety has improved, and the number of rail passengers has doubled.[139] But public frustration with the service is considerable, and there are consistent calls to either renationalize the railways or reform the operating model root and branch.

Ninety-nine per cent of passenger miles are delivered by the franchised train operating companies, the vast majority of which run a monopoly service.[140] The government, when it awards the franchises, tends to favour over-inflated bids from the train companies, which causes many companies to struggle financially or abandon their contracts altogether. Poor labour relations mean services are often disrupted by strikes: official figures show the transport sector accounted for 68 per cent of all working days lost to strikes in 2017.[141]

The pricing system is so complex that there are an estimated 55 million different fares, often causing passengers to buy needlessly expensive tickets.[142] Some fares on inter-city lines have increased by three times the rate of inflation since privatization.[143] Fares are estimated to be the highest in Europe.[144] It is often more than twice as expensive – and far more time consuming – to take the train than it is to take domestic flights for longer journeys.[145]

Energy is another problem. The retail market is supposed to be founded on competition, with consumers switching between companies and tariffs. In practice, however, the 'Big Six' dominate the market, supplying 75 per cent of electricity and 74 per cent of gas in Britain.[146] Only a quarter of households have ever switched tariff with the same provider, and only 44 per cent have ever switched supplier.[147] The result is that the Big Six ruthlessly rip off their loyal customers who do not switch. Two-thirds of households – 18.5 million of them – are on expensive default contracts. These Standard Variable Tariffs, or SVTs, can be on average £130 per year dearer than the cheapest tariffs, and up to £380 more expensive.[148] And those who lose most in this broken market are, predictably, the poorest households. For them, energy costs form 10 per cent of annual expenditure. According to Citizens Advice, a quarter of households on low and middle incomes struggle to pay their energy bills.[149] The energy price cap, introduced at the start of 2019, has helped a little by limiting what firms can charge customers on SVTs. As the *Financial Times* has noted, 'charges are lower than they would be without the price caps' yet 'the overall number of [customers] switching is nonetheless on the rise.'[150] But the market still needs fundamental reform.

Britain has a problem with a lack of meaningful choice and competition in many markets. In banking, it is estimated that 90 per cent of customers would be better off if they switched to a better account. In telecoms, one million mobile phone customers have their handset included in the price of their service after their minimum contract period ends. Average broadband prices can jump by as much as 43 per cent at the end of fixed-term contracts.[151]

Just as big a problem is the way Britain systematically over-rewards investors. At first, the rush to buy Britain's privatized utilities was because the efficiency gains made possible by market forces and price controls had been underestimated. This explains why much of the 40 per cent increase in profit in the water industry since privatization took place between 1990 and 1995, and prompted Labour's early 'windfall taxes'.[152]

But since then, poor regulation has meant that for many utility companies – water, energy and airports, for example – ownership has been a licence to print money, with little incentive to serve customers well. This has been allowed to happen because regulators have consistently underestimated the borrowing capacity of utility companies, and this causes two big problems.

First, regulators must decide appropriate returns for shareholders, or what they call 'the cost of capital'. Always motivated to keep the investment flowing, they tend to be naturally cautious and cap shareholder returns generously. This means regulated companies have an incentive to seek ever more capital, which of course comes at a cost, which in turn is met by customers in the form of higher prices. This is why so many big infrastructure projects have been so expensive. The Thames Tideway Scheme, for example, known as the London Super Sewer, is estimated to cost £4.2 billion and, according to Sir Ian Byatt, the former water regulator, its scale and cost make it 'a complete disaster'.[153]

Second, utilities can make more profit, in the words of Michael Gove, from 'financial engineering just as much as real engineering'.[154] Energy and water companies are required, for example, to maintain a ratio of 60:40 between debt, which is cheaper to finance, and equity, which is more expensive. In truth, using complex financial structures to increase their reliance on cheaper debt funding, their debt to equity ratios are much higher. This allows them to fund generous payouts to shareholders, while ignoring customers and taxpayers and exposing them to greater risk. One study shows the Big Six energy companies used debt financing to make excess profits of up to £11.1 billion in an eight-year period.[155] In the water industry, between 2007 and 2016, the nine big English companies made £18.8 billion in profit, much of it thanks to debt financing. Very little was reinvested in the companies or their infrastructure: 95 per cent went straight to shareholders.[156]

Unregulated markets

As older markets have become dysfunctional, new markets are emerging and growing fast. Yet they are, to a large degree, unregulated, and the big companies that dominate them are hardly taxed at all. Concerns about the use of data and the abuse of privacy are ignored, blatant anti-competitive practices are tolerated, and a refusal to behave responsibly – when it comes to child abuse, hate crime, terrorism and fake news – is simply accepted. Some politicians struggle to work out how to tax and regulate these modern robber barons, but many ultra-liberals simply do not want to act.

Big tech is creating mammoth companies. In 2000, the world's top four firms by market value were General Electric, ExxonMobil, Pfizer and Citigroup. By 2018, the top four were all tech companies: Apple, Alphabet/Google, Microsoft and Amazon. Of the top ten companies in 2000, only one remained in the top ten by 2018, and that was Microsoft.[157] And these mammoths are making a small number of people super-wealthy. As the tech writer Jamie Bartlett says, 'the world's richest eight men own more than the bottom half of the world's population – and four of them are founders of technology companies.'[158]

These changes will not be limited to companies that provide internet communications and social media services. Big tech – data analytics, machine learning, robotics and artificial intelligence – is disrupting every conceivable industry. Car manufacturers – and others, including Google – are racing to design the first safe, mass-manufactured self-driving vehicles. As the BBC's media editor Amol Rajan has written, online streaming is causing television to bifurcate between high-end entertainment on the one hand and live, event-based news and sport on the other, which is driving mega-mergers between the likes of Disney and 21st Century Fox. The advertising industry is in crisis, as

Facebook and Google dominate the online market. Only one company seems capable of challenging them, and that, unsurprisingly, is Amazon.

This disruptive change is coming to every sector of our economy. And tech firms are changing the way we think about the economy itself. Competition law designed for the pre-digital age cannot cope. Companies like Facebook and Google provide services for free. Amazon and Uber have not increased prices but reduced them. And technology is changing the very nature of the economy. Our understanding of productivity, the ways we raise taxes and the nature of work are changing beyond all recognition. And so, inevitably, will our policy responses. The traditional response to monopolies, for example, will not necessarily work for many of these firms: the very point of a successful network is its scale. Mandate the reduction of the network and you destroy its value to its users.

Nonetheless, national governments – acting alone or in concert – will need to update their policy and legal frameworks to deal with disruptive technology. Workers and consumers need to be protected. Intellectual property laws need to be updated. Taxes need to be levied and collected. Journalism needs to be rigorous and independent. Political debate needs to be informed and unimpeded by big business and foreign interests. Wealth and power cannot be allowed to accumulate in the hands of a small elite.

And as technology develops even further, some of the questions we need to ask ourselves will become more profound. If and when future knowledge and discovery is generated not by people but by machines, for example, to whom should the fruits of that discovery belong? The original inventors and investors who made the machines possible – and their heirs – or society as a whole?

These are undoubtedly enormous questions, and since they span complex technology, ethics and national and international law, they are difficult to answer. But ultra-liberal ideology – with its reluctance to intervene in the market, and its distaste for challenging the freedom of the rich and the powerful – undoubtedly makes the task harder. New markets need to be regulated, and the modern robber barons who dominate these markets need to be confronted. It will take the power of states to do so.

Citizens of nowhere

Until political leaders take action, and until they return order to older markets too, the rich and the powerful will be free to abuse their privileged status. Of course, not every chief executive or investment banker wants to exploit people. Many pay their taxes and are generous in their philanthropy. Almost all of them are trying to run their businesses, and make investment decisions, in ways that provide a good return for their shareholders and clients.

But as Barack Obama has said, globalization has created the conditions in which 'many titans of industry and finance are increasingly detached from any single locale or nation-state, and they live lives more and more insulated from the struggles of ordinary people in their countries of origin.' Unburdened by parochialism, Obama says, 'they are equally comfortable in New York or London or Shanghai or Nairobi or Buenos Aires, or Johannesburg', but rarely live among the men and women who buy their goods and services or work for them.[159] This distance from their fellow citizens – a social, economic and cultural distance as well as a literal geographical distance – is undermining their sense of solidarity.

Sometimes the decisions they take are not consciously cruel, but simply rational and in line with their economic interests. Decisions to relocate factories, or to award contracts to one supplier or another, will on the whole be taken for commercial reasons, but that can often be scant consolation for the affected workers. On other occasions, the decisions feel straightforwardly unethical. When Kraft bought Cadbury in 2010, for example, they promised to keep open the Cadbury plant in Somerdale, Bristol. As soon as the deal went through, they announced its closure.

In 2015, Sir Philip Green sold BHS for £1, after taking an estimated £580 million from the company in dividends, rental payments and interest on loans.[160] The next year, the company collapsed, at the cost of 11,000 jobs and leaving a pension fund deficit of £571 million. As many as 20,000 past and present BHS employees suffered cuts in their pensions, and for some this was as significant as 77 per cent.[161] As his former workers digested the news, Green awaited the delivery of *Lionheart*: his new £100 million super-yacht.[162]

In 2016, a Parliamentary inquiry found that Sports Direct, a company employing more than 3,000 people, treated its employees in a manner 'closer to that of a Victorian workhouse', rather than 'a modern, reputable high street retailer'.[163] Workers were being paid below the National Minimum Wage, and were penalized for taking short breaks to drink water and taking time off work while they were ill. Health and safety breaches were common, with ambulances called to the Sports Direct distribution centre 76 times in only two years. Some workers said they were promised contracts in exchange for sex.[164] The company's billionaire owner, Mike Ashley, eventually accepted the need to change, but for some time dismissed the inquiry as 'a joke' and refused to engage with it.[165]

In 2018, Jeff Fairburn, then chief executive of the construction company Persimmon, was awarded a record-breaking performance bonus of £110 million, on top of his basic £2.12 million annual salary. While Persimmon did increase its sales and profits that year, whether the company's improved performance was down to Fairburn's brilliance is doubtful. About half of the homes Persimmon sold over the period were subsidized by the taxpayer through the Government's Help To Buy scheme.[166] Despite the public outcry, Fairburn refused to pay back a penny, insisting he deserved the bonus because he had 'worked very hard'.[167] The bonus was almost three and a half thousand times the annual wage of the average construction worker at the time.[168]

These examples cannot be written off as a few bad apples. In 2017, Anglian, Southern and Thames Water companies paid no corporation tax at all, despite making huge profits, while Thames has paid no corporation tax for a decade.[169] According to the Director of Labour Market Enforcement, there are 'serious gaps' in the application of workers' rights and protections across the whole economy.[170]

And the problem is not limited to British businesses. Before the terrorist murder of Lee Rigby in 2013, his killer, Michael Adebowale, had his Facebook account taken down because the company believed it was 'associated with terrorism'. Yet they refused to warn the authorities.[171] Volkswagen, the German car manufacturer, has admitted it systematically cheated emissions testing for its diesel cars while marketing its vehicles on the basis of their environmentally-friendly, low-emission credentials. Amazon has exploited loopholes to pay only £61.7 million in corporation tax in Britain in the last twenty years – less than Marks and Spencer pays in a single year – despite turning over more than £7 billion of sales during that time.[172] Firms including Apple, Google and Starbucks have all been exposed for avoiding British taxes.

International business leaders may believe, from their corporate headquarters and their international conferences and summits, that they owe little to the people whom their decisions affect. But they are wrong. Just as much as individuals, businesses need to respect the obligations of citizenship. If they do not, these self-styled corporate citizens of the world are nothing more and nothing better than citizens of nowhere. Their irresponsibility will continue to undermine popular support for capitalism and the essential liberalism which capitalism relies upon to function.

And yet ultra-liberalism does not require these privileged elites to show solidarity with their fellow citizens. It does not insist that they pay their fair share of tax. It does not demand that they train up local young people before hiring cheaper labour from overseas. It does not seek a voice for workers in the future direction of their companies. All it asks is that we should respect individual freedom, and in particular the freedom of the rich and the powerful, even as they neglect and exploit the poor and the weak.

E PLURIBUS NIHIL

I + E = M. In *The Rise of the Meritocracy*, published in 1958, Michael Young foresaw a society in which 'intelligence and effort together make up merit', and merit would be the sole determinant of success and prosperity.[1] Afterwards, as politicians picked up the mantle of social mobility and declared themselves meritocrats, Young despaired, for his vision of a meritocracy was not a hopeful one: it was a dystopia he was warning us against.

Before the meritocracy, Young said, 'educational injustice enabled people to preserve their illusions', because, 'inequality of opportunity fostered the myth of human equality.' But with the meritocracy, Young imagined, things changed. 'The upper classes are, on the one hand, no longer weakened by self-doubt and self-criticism. Today the eminent know that success is just reward for their own capacity, for their own efforts, and for their own undeniable achievement. They deserve to belong to a superior class.'[2] But on the other hand, 'all persons, however humble, know they have had every chance ... Are they not bound to recognize that they have an inferior status ... because they are inferior?'[3]

More than sixty years on from Young's warning, *The Rise of the Meritocracy* feels uncomfortably prescient. Unlike the meritocratic society Young describes in his book, we are not on the brink of a violent revolution. But the bonds of solidarity are breaking. The rich and successful believe they have earned their wealth through talent and hard work alone, and many look down their noses at their less fortunate fellow citizens.

We have already seen how Janan Ganesh of the *Financial Times* says prosperous Londoners look at the rest of Britain and believe they are 'shackled to a corpse'. His attitude is not unusual. In 2014, Emily Thornberry, a London MP and Labour shadow minister, was sacked after she sneeringly tweeted a picture of a resident's house, which was adorned with the English flag, while she was campaigning in the working-class city of Rochester.[4]

The same year, Matthew Parris, a former Conservative MP and *Times* columnist, wrote in excoriating terms about the working-class people of Clacton, Essex. 'Only in Asmara after Eritrea's bloody war', he wrote, 'have I encountered a greater proportion of citizens on crutches or in wheelchairs'. Continuing, he declared, 'this is Britain on crutches. This is tracksuit-and-trainers Britain, tattoo-parlour Britain, all-our-yesterdays Britain ... I am not arguing that we should be care-less of the needs of struggling people and places such as Clacton. But I am arguing – if I am honest – that we should be careless of their opinions.'[5]

The same disdain is directed towards the many working-class voters who chose to leave the European Union. Nick Cohen, writing in the *Observer*, complained, 'it is as if the sewers have burst', describing Leave voters as 'a know-nothing movement of loud mouths and closed minds'.[6] Sir Vince Cable, the leader of the Liberal Democrats, said the Brexit vote was 'driven by a nostalgia for a world where passports were blue, faces were white, and the map was coloured imperial pink.'[7] And angry Remainers have been unable to resist pointing out that Leave voters were on average less educated than Remain voters, as though formal academic qualifications were indisputable evidence of superior intellect and judgement.[8]

As Professor David Runciman, from Cambridge University, argues, education is becoming a fundamental divide in our democracy. 'It points to a deep alienation that cuts both ways', he says. 'The less educated fear they are being governed by intellectual snobs who know nothing of their lives and experiences. The educated fear their fate may be decided by know-nothings who are ignorant of how the world really works.'[9] In this divide lie the seeds of a dangerous culture war.

The mirage of meritocracy

However uncanny it seems, Michael Young's prophecy is turning out to be only partially correct. While Britain is suffering all the downsides of a country that believes its citizens stand or fall on their own merits, there is scant evidence that we really are a meritocratic society.

The Sutton Trust, an independent charity dedicated to improving the life chances of poorer children, says social mobility in Britain is stalling. Using cohort studies that compare the experiences of sons born in 1958 with those born in 1970, they concluded that, 'in just one decade, Britain had become less mobile'.[10]

The Government's own Social Mobility Commission agrees. Five million workers, mainly women, are 'in a low pay trap from which few find escape'. Only one in six workers who were low paid in 2006 had found a permanent route out of low pay a decade later.[11] Meanwhile, at the top end of the labour market, the professions are still out of reach for many working-class people. Only 6 per cent of doctors, 12 per cent of company chief executives, and 12 per cent of journalists come from working-class families.[12]

This sounds a lot like the outcome Young feared. 'By 1990 or thereabouts', he foresaw, 'all adults with IQs of more than 125 belonged to the meritocracy. A high proportion of the children with IQs over 125 were the children of these same adults. The top of today are breeding the top of tomorrow to a greater extent than at any time in the past. The elite is on the way to becoming hereditary; the principles of heredity and merit are coming together.'[13]

But while many members of the elite do tend to believe they got to the top through their own talents and efforts, universal education until the age of eighteen and the expansion of higher education have created only the appearance of a meritocratic society.

In reality, disadvantage for poorer children begins immediately. A child's learning and development in the first few years of their lives are crucial to their future development. And children from poorer backgrounds are far less likely to have reached the expected level of development in their early years – in communication and language, physical development, personal, social and emotional development, literacy and mathematics – than children from more affluent families.[14] This means the fate of many poor children is decided by the age of five: they can expect worse educational, social and economic outcomes throughout their later lives.

And the pattern continues as children get older. Government figures show how children from affluent families dominate intakes at the best-performing state schools.[15] House prices near the 10 per cent best-performing primary schools are estimated to be 8 per cent higher than in the surrounding area. Near the 10 per cent best-performing non-selective secondary schools, they are 6.8 per cent higher. This is the equivalent of a £18,600 premium for living near a good primary school, and £15,800 for living near a good secondary school.[16]

For those with deeper pockets still, there are even greater advantages. Analysis of university admissions data shows pupils from independent schools are more than twice as likely to attend a Russell Group university than pupils from comprehensive schools, and seven times as likely to attend Oxford and Cambridge. Between 2015 and 2017, just eight top schools and colleges sent as many pupils to Oxford and Cambridge as three-quarters – 2,900 – of all schools and colleges across the UK.[17]

Despite accounting for 7 per cent of the population, the alumni of private schools dominate the bar (74 per cent), the judiciary (71 per cent), the military (71 per cent), medicine (61 per cent), journalism (51 per cent) and the civil service (48 per cent).[18] And there is an increasing pay premium for those who attend private schools. In 1991, privately educated 33–34-year-olds were earning 25 per cent more than their peers who had attended state schools. In 2004, the pay premium had increased to 41 per cent more.[19]

And this is not all. The consolidation of wealth by a privileged few is making matters worse. We have already seen how the broken housing market is putting the possibility of home ownership – the foundation of higher levels of social mobility – out of reach for many families. We have seen, too, that wealth inequality will get worse as government policies cause financial and housing asset prices to rise artificially. And when it comes to income, Britain is one of the most unequal countries in the developed world.[20]

The great disparities in Britain's regional economy are also making matters worse. As the Social Mobility Commission says, 'there is no simple north/south divide in opportunity. If anything, the major divide that exists in England today is between London (and its commuter belt) and the rest of the country.'[21]

The communities that struggle the most can be found in remote rural or coastal areas and in the former industrial towns, particularly in the Midlands. 'Many of these places', reports the Commission, 'combine poor educational outcomes for young people from disadvantaged backgrounds with weak labour markets that have a greater share of low-skilled, low-paid employment than elsewhere in England.' While Britain's regional cities are no longer the worst performing places for social mobility, 'they are not yet the engines of social mobility they have the potential to be' and 'punch substantially below their weight.'[22]

This is not happening, as Young worried, because 'heredity and merit are coming together'. Of course, we are learning more about how intelligence and character traits are passed on from parents to children. But the absence of clear demographic and geographic patterns confirms that we are not simply living out our genetic destinies. If the decline of social mobility, and the concentration of success, were simply down to genetic advantage, we would expect to see the same pattern in other countries. But according to an international study by the OECD, 'higher mobility … is associated with lower inequality within countries when measured over several years.' This is why countries like Denmark, Norway, Sweden and Finland have far better social mobility than Britain.[23]

Within Britain, the Social Mobility Commission confirms that some of the country's poorest communities, such as Slough, are social mobility 'hotspots'. Conversely, some of the richest communities, like the Cotswolds or West Berkshire, are among the worst places to live for disadvantaged residents. And some places can divide sharply: half the population of St Albans, for example, works in a well-paid and professional job, but a quarter earn below the living wage.[24]

The lesson is that policy matters, but ultra-liberal policies are failing to make social mobility a reality. They are allowing great income inequality, growing disparities in wealth, and great divides in education and opportunity. And ultra-liberals are doing remarkably little to close the gaps. According to Paul Johnson, the director of the Institute for Fiscal Studies, 'inheritance is increasingly contributing to life wealth, which in turn has consequences for social mobility ... inheritance is probably the most crucial factor in determining a person's overall wealth since Victorian times.'[25]

Forgotten places

Even if social mobility was a reality for more people, that would not alone make for a socially just country. This is because values like fairness and solidarity dictate that we should care about the welfare of our fellow citizens regardless of their ability to climb up the social ladder.

This is something ultra-liberals often overlook. Shortly after Margaret Thatcher died, Channel Four produced a documentary about her life. Charlie Mullins, the millionaire founder of Pimlico Plumbers, was interviewed about how she had inspired him to become a Conservative supporter. Mullins stood in front of the council flat he lived in as a child, and pointed towards its windows. Pointing into what is still somebody's home, he said: 'I was brought up in that shithole there, absolute khazi ... I voted for Tories because this ain't what I wanted for the rest of my life.'[26]

Mullins is not alone. In 2017, the then Education Secretary Justine Greening made a speech about social mobility. Telling her own life story, Greening recalled 'all the years I spent growing up in Rotherham where I was aiming for something better.' Her choice of words was not a mistake. A little later she reiterated, 'I knew there was something better out there.'[27]

The examples continue. In 2018, Angela Rayner, the Labour MP, gave an interview to *The Spectator*. Explaining why she is not a Conservative, she told the story of how a Tory MP had once approached her, saying: 'You should be one of us, Ange, this is why we're Conservatives! You've done well, you've climbed out!' Describing her appalled reaction, she said: 'They don't get it. My mates, who are struggling now, are no different to me. My brother and sister are smarter than me. But I'm the most successful because I've been given opportunities they never had.'[28]

Rayner is right, and the ultra-liberals are wrong. Nobody, however successful they might be, has succeeded alone. They might have relied on their families to give them love and security. They might have a school, college or university to thank. They might have benefited from the kindness or wisdom of a mentor or employer. They might have been supported by the state, through the welfare system or, in Rayner's own story, the childcare provided by a Sure Start centre. Precisely because nobody has succeeded alone, we all have a debt to others.

Disparaging the working-class communities they grew up in, talking about how they 'knew something better was out there', and celebrating the people who 'climbed out' of a culture they dislike is plainly insulting. Yet when ultra-liberals talk about social mobility, they talk about 'escape'. They talk of 'escaping' the families people love, the homes they lived in as children, and the communities that supported them. Only the most obnoxious people who experience social mobility want to give up the social bonds with which they grew up. But even if the apparently lucky few did think like that, the majority of people do not get to 'escape'. They stay in the places like Rotherham that Greening was inadvertently, yet revealingly, so rude about.

Three in five of us live within twenty miles of where we lived at the age of fourteen.[29] And many of these places are badly neglected. We have already seen how London and the South East of England are far ahead of the rest of the country when it comes to productivity, pay and opportunity. The problem, however, is even worse than these statistics suggest.

Analysis by the Bank of England shows that outside London and the South East of England, there has been no economic recovery since the financial crash. In Northern Ireland, GDP per head is still 11 per cent below its peak before the crash, and in Yorkshire and Humberside it is 6 per cent lower. Outside London and the South East, there has been no recovery in families' disposable incomes at all. According to Andrew Haldane, both regional income inequality and regional wealth inequality are widening.[30]

London's economic dominance is causing a brain drain from other parts of the country. While the capital has 19 per cent of British jobs, it attracts 38 per cent of Russell Group university graduates with good degrees.[31] This matters to everybody because proximity to highly-educated workers increases the wages of lower-educated workers.[32] Research by the Centre for Cities shows that the majority of British cities have fewer high-skilled workers and more low-skilled workers than their European counterparts. The proportion of low-skilled workers in British cities is more than twice the proportion in Germany and almost three times the proportion in Swedish cities.[33] According to the Joseph Rowntree Foundation, 'young adult migration to London and the south is ... detrimental to the growth of many provincial cities.'[34]

Of the cities the Foundation calculates are in relative decline, all are in the North of England or Scotland. Rochdale, Burnley, Bolton, Blackburn, Hull, Grimsby, Dundee, Middlesbrough, Bradford, Blackpool, Stoke and Wigan all struggle. And cities from all four nations of the UK and the Midlands and North of England are not far behind them. They include Nottingham, Huddersfield, Sunderland, Glasgow, Belfast, Birkenhead, Liverpool, Newport, Sheffield, Barnsley, Telford and Birmingham. Nowhere in the South of England makes the list of declining cities, but two-thirds of Northern cities do.[35] And the future looks even more threatening: many of these struggling cities have the highest percentages of people working in declining industries and doing jobs most at risk from automation.[36]

A similar, but slightly more complicated, story is evident with Britain's towns. A significant number of towns are prosperous and outperform the national average when it comes to employment and pay. But many are in severe difficulties. Towns in the South of England, like Winchester and Maidenhead, are economically strong, while towns in the North, like Hartlepool and Scunthorpe, continue to struggle.[37]

Regardless of the North/South divide, however, towns near cities, like Solihull near Birmingham, are more successful than towns that are geographically isolated, like Grimsby. But not all towns near cities prosper. Hartlepool is near Middlesbrough and Llanelli is near Swansea, but both have poor employment records. Sometimes, towns near struggling cities can succeed, like Beverley near Hull, as they attract the few higher-skilled and higher-paid workers with jobs in the nearby city.[38]

Many analyses of forgotten places are rich in data and statistics that convey the extent of the problem and the failure of public policy. Behind those statistics, however, are human stories. And in these struggling communities, people still feel a sense of solidarity among themselves, and a hope that life can be better in future. There are public servants, social entrepreneurs and volunteers – often from faith groups – who are striving to deal with local problems. But in many places the scale of the problem is too great, the social capital of the community too depleted, support from government and elsewhere too limited, for them to make the difference they would like. And so the social and economic problems of these forgotten places continue.

Some communities find themselves in severe crisis. Blackpool, for example, is one of the most deprived places in England. As its tourism industry declined, so did its economy, and today unemployment is higher, pay is lower and poverty far more prevalent than elsewhere. Family breakdown and teenage pregnancy are common. Drug and alcohol abuse is widespread. An abundance of cheap housing means the state uses Blackpool, in the words of the Centre for Social Justice, as 'a dumping ground for people facing problems such as unemployment, social exclusion and substance abuse'. In some schools, the annual turnover of pupils can be as high as 30 per cent, and new children often arrive with complex problems.[39] Incredibly, Blackpool has twice the rate of early deaths than more prosperous parts of the country.[40]

Forgotten people

Blackpool is an extreme example, but it is one of Britain's many forgotten places. Yet geography can only tell us so much, because Britain has forgotten people living across the country as a whole. They might be more concentrated in particular places, but they can also be found in prosperous towns and cities too, living near, but not quite side-by-side, the rich and comfortable.

These forgotten people are not always especially poor. They might earn as much as £30,000 per year, approximately the median British annual income.[41] They might own their home. They might be able to afford a foreign holiday. But they often feel insecure. Their employment might sometimes be precarious, and they are vulnerable to increases in taxation and mortgage interest rates. They rely on public services, and cannot opt for private sector alternatives when local schools, childcare, or health and social care are not good enough.

They are the 'Somewheres' in David Goodhart's dichotomous description of the divide between the liberal, progressive and prosperous 'Anywheres' and the more rooted working and lower middle classes.

They see the world from the perspective of their home, their somewhere, while Anywheres see the world from the perspective of their 'portable, achieved identities, based on educational and career success which makes them generally comfortable with new places and people.'[42]

The success of Goodhart's analysis of Somewheres and Anywheres was his recognition that social class is still relevant to modern life, but that class structures are changing as the economy and our society change around us. Other writers agree with him. Professor Vernon Bogdanor talks about a divide between the 'exam-passing classes' and the rest of the country.[43] Claire Ainsley describes the emergence of an entirely new working class. All three agree that the divide is not only economic, but cultural.

'The working class as a relatively clear group of people in society, with a common economic experience and cultural identity, has been fractured by the changes of the past few decades', Ainsley has written. 'A new working class is emerging, as sizable as its historical predecessor, and as in need of political and workforce representation, but it is more disparate, more atomised, and occupies multiple social identities that make collective identity less possible.'[44]

Many of the changes described in chapter 2 are behind this shift. Fewer people work in manufacturing, and more work in services. More people change jobs over the course of their working lives. There is more part-time work, contract work and self-employment. Trades unions are weaker and workplace rights and protections are not available to everybody. There has been a decline in mid-skilled employment and pay. There are more women and older people in work. Income inequality is persistently high. Inequality in wealth is profoundly entrenched. Younger people are finding it harder than generations before them to get onto the property ladder and build up their own wealth.

According to official estimates, which are based on occupational definitions of class, the working class is shrinking and now accounts for around a quarter of the British population.[45] But as Ainsley says, this does not reflect the reality of modern Britain. Significant numbers of people live on low to middle incomes and while some low earners live with a partner or spouse on a higher wage, as a family they might still feel economically insecure. Sixty per cent of people still identify as working class.[46]

Based on the Great British Class Survey, conducted by the London School of Economics, Ainsley suggests that the new working class consists of the traditional working class (approximately 14 per cent of the population), emerging service workers (19 per cent), and what Guy Standing terms 'the precariat' (15 per cent). Beyond the new working class, there is the elite (6 per cent), the established middle class (25 per cent), the technical middle class (6 per cent) and new affluent workers (15 per cent).[47]

The profile and interests of each part of the new working class differ. The traditional working class has an average age of 66, is largely white, and has a very low average annual income of £13,000. Their accumulated wealth, however, is greater than new affluent workers, thanks to lifetime savings and the value of their home. They are likely to have plenty of social contact with other people, but do not typically know people beyond their social class.[48]

Emerging service workers are younger, with an average age of 32. They are more likely to be educated, and one in five is from a minority ethnic background, which is about the same as the overall population. They tend to enjoy modern culture, exercise regularly, and enjoy significant social networks, online and in person.[49]

Finally, there is the precariat, which has very low household income and little or no savings. This group is likely to be in rented housing, and has a narrower social circle, knowing fewer people in higher-status jobs and enjoying far less high-end cultural capital. Not all the precariat have jobs, and those who do are likely to cycle in and out of badly paid and insecure work, claiming benefits between periods of employment.[50]

Whether Ainsley's precise definitions are correct or not, they articulate a truth about the insecurity with which millions of people live in Britain today. Yet the interests of the new working class are neglected by ultra-liberal politicians, who often find discussing class distasteful and uncomfortable. But class is a relevant fact of life, and while other identities such as ethnicity, age or sex matter too, class helps us to understand the challenges many people face, and what we can do to help and support them.

It is impossible to fully address Britain's housing crisis, for example, without understanding the class context of the problem. As the last chapter revealed, 45 per cent of the money that the Government spends on housing goes to Help to Buy, the scheme that subsidizes homes worth up to £600,000 and pushes up the price of housing. Meanwhile, not nearly enough new housing is built, to rent or buy, that is affordable for people on low incomes.

In education, policy and resources are in some respects focused on the most disadvantaged children. But the Government's measure of disadvantage identifies children who receive free school meals, which are available for pupils whose parents receive primarily out-of-work benefits, or have been in receipt of free school meals within the last six years. This means officials are unable to distinguish between children from ordinary and low-income families on the one hand and wealthier families on the other. As the Government has admitted, 'this means we have very limited understanding of the experiences of children in families with modest incomes compared to the experiences of children in the wealthiest 10 per cent of families.'[51]

In 2017, the Department for Education quietly published a one-off study which showed that about a third of schoolchildren are from families whose incomes are below the national median but are not eligible for the pupil premium. The study found that these working-class children have lower attainment, make less progress and attend poorer schools than better-off children. They are also more likely to live in parts of the country where school funding is lower.[52] Yet neither funding nor policy is directed at them, and the report continues to gather dust inside the Department for Education.

Minority interests

Solidarity dictates that we should be concerned about the fortunes of the working class as a whole. As we have seen, inequality is entrenched, wealth is concentrated among a fortunate few, and social mobility is in decline.

But to understand the full picture, we also need to look at the fortunes of specific groups. And here, official statistics show wildly different experiences for people of different ethnic backgrounds. These statistics, it should be said, do not prove rampant racism or direct discrimination. But they do reveal significant discrepancies in the experiences of different ethnic groups. Black men are more likely to be stopped and searched by the police, for example, and three and a half times more likely to be arrested than white people. White people found guilty of crimes receive shorter sentences than all other ethnic groups.[53]

Children in black, Asian and minority ethnic families are more likely to live in persistent poverty than white children. And their parents are less likely to work. While adults with Indian heritage are as likely to have a job as white people, people from a black, Pakistani or Bangladeshi background are more than twice as likely to be out of work. People from Pakistani and Bangladeshi backgrounds are also more likely to find themselves in low-skilled, low-paid jobs than other ethnic groups, and more likely to be self-employed.[54]

Academic research by Eva Zschirnt and Didier Ruedin suggests that ethnic minority jobseekers have to send out 50 per cent more job applications than their white counterparts to get invited to the same number of interviews, even when they have the same qualifications. Other studies have found that 40 per cent of African graduates and 39 per cent of Bangladeshi graduates end up in jobs where they are over-qualified for the work they do.[55]

Ethnic minority families are more likely to live in rented accommodation than white families, spend a higher proportion of their income on rent, and live in lower quality and overcrowded conditions. Again, this is more likely for families with Pakistani and Bangladeshi backgrounds, who the statistics suggest are less well integrated than others. Only a little more than half of people with Pakistani and Bangladeshi backgrounds were born in Britain, and one in five speak English poorly or not at all.[56]

If we want to address inequality and improve social mobility – and offer recognition and solidarity to our fellow citizens – we need to take targeted action to help people out of these established social problems. And to do that, we need to understand that different communities often tend to face different kinds of problems for different reasons. One explanation for the struggles faced by Pakistani communities, for example, is that so often even third- or fourth-generation babies are born to a parent who was born in Pakistan. According to a study by academics from Bristol University, half of British Pakistanis marry in Pakistan, and most of these marriages are between cousins or other members of extended kin groups.[57] The 'first generation in every generation' problem, as David Goodhart calls it, makes it far harder for families to participate in wider society.

The crisis of the white working class

By and large, elite liberals and left-liberals are comfortable talking about the needs of specific minority groups. They are less comfortable, however, talking about the needs of a larger group that finds itself in crisis: the white working class.

Even those on the radical left who believe in positive action for minorities reject the idea that specific action is needed for the white working class. Kenan Malik, for example, calls the argument 'dangerous' because it 'legitimises racist attitudes'. He says, 'It pitches the interests of working-class whites against those of minority ethnic groups and imagines that too great a focus on black and Asian children has undermined white working-class culture.'[58]

But it should do no such thing. Just as there should be action taken to support minority communities with their specific problems and challenges, so there should be action taken to support the white working class where help is needed. This should in no way neglect the experience of ethnic minority members of the working class – who also need targeted support – and neither should it divide people. It is about responding to a very real, and growing, crisis.

White working-class children are struggling badly at school. Even by the end of their first year in primary school, white British children have fallen behind several other ethnic groups, including black Africans, Indian and Chinese children in their phonics tests. White working-class boys struggle more than anybody else: less than two in three white boys on free school meals meet the expected standard of reading aged six.[59]

This pattern continues throughout the school years. By the age of sixteen, official statistics show, white pupils have made less academic progress than children from any other ethnic group. They are less likely to enter the English Baccalaureate – the core of traditional subjects most likely to lead to further study and future work – than any other group. Along with black pupils they are outperformed by Asian, Chinese and mixed-race pupils in English and mathematics and important subjects including the sciences, history and foreign languages. And again, it is working-class white children who are struggling most. 'White pupils who are eligible for free school meals', noted the Department for Education, 'have significantly lower attainment compared to pupils from other backgrounds who are eligible.'[60]

What is true in schools is true in universities. Only 29.5 per cent of white students go on to university aged eighteen, compared to more than 41.2 per cent of black students, 46.7 per cent of Asian students, and 66.3 per cent of Chinese students.[61] For white boys, and white working-class boys in particular, the numbers are even worse. Some studies show black and Asian girls on free school meals are more than three times as likely to go to university as white boys on free school meals.[62]

Amanda Spielman, England's Chief Inspector of Schools, says, 'we can't pretend that [school inspection] judgements are not lower in certain areas – many of them with a high proportion of white working class children … We are having to grapple with the unhappy fact that many local working class communities have felt the full brunt of economic dislocation in recent years, and, perhaps as a result, can lack the aspiration and drive seen in many migrant communities.'[63]

We have already seen how the regional economy lags behind London and the South East, and how many communities have been simply forgotten by the rich and powerful. And we have seen how economic change is hollowing out work and pay, with men in particular increasingly working for fewer hours and for less pay. These changes have a particular effect on the white, working class and, especially, white working-class boys and men.

Just 10.1 per cent of England and Wales's white population lives in London. A further 16.2 per cent lives in the South East. The vast majority of whites live in Britain's neglected regions. By comparison, 35.9 per cent of Asians, and 58.4 per cent of black people, live in the capital.[64] There, housing might be overcrowded and expensive, but school performance and social mobility are superior to other parts of the country. Twice as many disadvantaged pupils go on to university from London schools than in the rest of the country. While 10 per cent of disadvantaged young people go to university from places like Hastings and Barnsley, in some London boroughs 50 per cent make it.[65]

It is not only a question of economic dislocation, however, because the problem is also cultural. Family breakdown, for example, is much more common in white working-class families than in Asian families and in more prosperous white families. Thirteen per cent of white parents are lone parents, compared to only 7 per cent of British Asian parents.[66] And lone parents are disproportionately likely to come from poorer backgrounds. One study suggests half of pre-school children from low-income families live with only one parent.[67] The decline of the family – and its contrast with strong families in many minority communities – is central to the crisis of the white working class.

Ultra-liberal debates in politics and the media simply ignore the reality of the working-class experience. Government policies aimed at achieving female equality, for example, tend to focus almost exclusively on highly educated and successful women. Ministers try to increase the number of women on company boards, rather than improving the availability of childcare for mothers on low wages. Of course there should be action to tackle the gender pay gap and workplace discrimination against women, but these exclusively elite equality debates alienate working-class men and women alike.

Closely associated with the crisis of the white, working class is a crisis of masculinity. Not only is it true that other pupils outperform white working-class pupils at school, girls outperform boys and are more likely to go on to higher education. In the workplace, it is men more than women whose jobs and pay are coming under threat. Unlike generations in the past, working-class boys grow up, often with few male role models around them, without the confidence that they will learn skills, get a trade or stay in a steady job for any length of time. Increasingly, academic and economic defeatism, accompanied by anti-intellectual norms, has become widespread in white working-class culture.

Meanwhile, society places an ever-greater premium on a university education, and as mid-skilled work declines, the prospects for non-graduates grow worse. As the economically and socially successful enjoy their achieved identities, those with fewer achievements stick resolutely to their 'ascribed' identities based on home town, class and nationality. As they do so, ultra-liberals view them with bewilderment: increasingly they see this attachment to community, culture and tradition as backward and parochial.

The constitution of a crisis

Like with the economic crisis discussed in chapter 2, the cultural crisis can be traced back to ultra-liberal ideology and policy and, in some cases, flawed assumptions in liberal philosophy itself.

In *On Liberty*, John Stuart Mill set out not a contract or a constitution of rights but a single principle. 'The object of this essay', he wrote, 'is to assert one very simple principle ... that the sole end for which mankind are warranted, individually or collectively, in interfering with the liberty of action of any of their number, is self-protection. That the only purpose for which power can be rightfully exercised over any member of a civilised community, against his will, is to prevent harm to others.'[68]

Mill's harm principle is strict. There should be no interference in the freedom of the individual even if it benefits that individual. 'His own good, either physical or moral, is not a sufficient warrant. He cannot rightfully be compelled to do or forbear because it will be better for him to do so, because it will make him happier, because, in the opinion of others, to do so would be wise, or even right.'[69] On matters of personal freedom, argued Mill, 'his independence is, of right, absolute. Over himself, over his own body and mind, the individual is sovereign.'[70]

On first hearing, this might sound sensible. But our individual actions harm people all the time. For example, an elite liberal might, knowingly or unknowingly, echo the harm principle and assert that neither the state nor society has any business interfering with an individual's use of hard drugs. But the risk of drug abuse and addiction lies not only with an individual. His actions might have consequences for his family, friends, employer, employees, colleagues or neighbours. The cost of treating his addiction will likely fall to wider society. The cost of the criminality involved in supplying the drugs will have consequences for communities across many different countries.

Our inaction can sometimes be just as damaging. Non-interference might feel like an attractive principle if you live in a rich and success-ful part of the country, like London, or if you can afford to live in a community that has a successful school for your children to attend. But non-interference, translated as non-intervention in the economy, or passive acceptance of grave inequality in the provision of public services, can mean abandonment for the less fortunate. Freedom for the rich, successful and powerful can come at the expense of the interests of others.

The problems with the harm principle are legion. There is no clear consensus in society on what constitutes harm, for example. If we have different views on what is a good life, we will have different views on what is harmful to us. We will have different perspectives on the facts of particular cases. We will judge the severity of harm differently. And we will differ on the solutions. 'No more than any other', writes John Gray, a critic of the harm principle, 'can Mill's principle of liberty avoid running aground on conflicts of value.'[71] Different moral outlooks, and different views on the importance of one human value versus another, mean we will inevitably have different accounts of social problems and the harm we can do to one another.

A successful City trader in London, for example, might not believe that his prosperity has come at the expense of others. He might not believe he has many obligations to people living in struggling towns and cities beyond the South East of England. But others might argue that the success of financial services in London has come at the expense of other sectors and regions of Britain's economy. They might argue he should pay more in taxes, or that other parts of the country should receive similar spending on infrastructure and services as London. Our understanding of human values and interests mean we will always differ in our understanding of harm and the solutions put in place to prevent or mitigate it.

Ultra-liberal politicians often behave as though they believe there are no trade-offs in public policy, insisting time and again that their proposals bring only benefits and no costs. This is partly because they never want to admit the downsides of their policies to voters, but it is also because they accept the ideological liberal belief in the possibility of a single truth. They believe it is possible to reconcile and bring into harmony the almost infinite array of human interests. And they believe rational decision-making can get us there. Pluralism is not simply a means of managing conflict in diverse societies: they believe it is a process of trial and error leading progressively to a more perfect society.

This returns us to the teleological fallacy discussed in chapter 1: the means by which liberalism can lead to illiberalism. If our rationality leads us always towards a better future, then disagreement about the desirability of that future path must be irrational. If it is possible to establish a single truth, dissenting voices must be speaking untruths. This is how ultra-liberalism can quickly become a byword for intolerance.

Some of these same flaws are evident in the work of a second thinker influential among ultra-liberals. Friedrich von Hayek is a hero to many Conservatives in particular: legend has it that Margaret Thatcher used to pull *The Constitution of Liberty* from her handbag and declare, 'this is what we believe'.[72] Yet Hayek was a liberal: he ended *The Constitution of Liberty* with a postscript entitled, 'Why I am not a conservative'.[73]

'The believer in freedom cannot but conflict with the conservative', Hayek insisted.[74] This is because liberals 'regard the advance of knowledge as one of the chief aims of human effort and expect from it the gradual solution of such problems and difficulties as we can hope to solve'.[75] Unlike conservatives, Hayek was admitting, liberals believe in the capacity of rational individuals to discover universal truths. And the best way to resolve the problems and difficulties confronting human society is through the market.

Hayek argues that the free market is an example of a spontaneous order, a concept similar to Adam Smith's invisible hand. The market has not been planned or organized by the state, but comes about instead through the free association of individuals, solving problems through innovation and ensuring the fair exchange of goods through competition. In successful communities, this might appear to be true, but lived experience suggests there are problems with Hayek's analysis. In some communities, like those forgotten places we have discussed already, there is no spontaneous and virtuous order that brings greater opportunity and prosperity to local people.

This is because market forces can sometimes cause a cycle of decline for particular places. Competition does not need to give way to monopoly for communities to suffer. Competition can lead to the destruction of older and more inefficient firms, which give way to newer and more efficient rivals, which might be based elsewhere. It is not inevitable that new employers emerge where old businesses have gone bust. And when this happens, companies that form supply chains disappear, and retailers and service providers who relied on the spending power of local customers close their doors. The young and talented move away, important local institutions wither, and communities lose their self-confidence and civic capital.

This is a story familiar to many towns and cities across the Midlands and North of England, and to communities in other parts of Britain too. If the invisible hand, or spontaneous order, of the market always worked as Hayek seems to have believed, new businesses – with each generation more efficient, more productive and better paying than the last – would emerge. But in many places, this is simply not the case. In many places, the invisible hand has proved to be invisible because it did not exist.

Perhaps in a world that worked more like that imagined by elite liberals and market fundamentalists, things would work differently. Entirely rational individuals, motivated by material gain, would be prepared to move to different parts of the country for work. In those more prosperous places, an abundant supply of housing would mean they could move quickly and affordably. Back in the original town or city, as property prices fall and as the supply of labour rises, new investment would give rise to new businesses and more employment.

The problem is that this is not how the world we live in works. People are not purely rational individuals, motivated only by material gain. They form families, groups of friends, and communities. Some will leave, but many will not want to abandon their homes and lives as they have known them.

Ultra-liberals fail to understand the social, and relational, essence of people. They fail to properly consider the role of many non-market relationships and institutions. Markets rely on a strong society: on families to raise children, public services to educate and train workers, and traditions and institutions to encourage trust. Yet ultra-liberals have little to say on these matters, and take for granted almost every non-market institution, from the family to the nation state. When market forces undermine or destroy these public goods, they destroy the foundation of capitalism itself.

A further problem for Hayek is in his warning that governments that attempt to regulate prices and incomes become intrusive in other ways. Intervention in economic policy, he argued, inevitably leads to intervention, and government intrusion into personal liberties, in a long list of other ways. Experience tells us that Hayek is right. But we also know that ultra-liberal economic policies can have the same effect. Where the international liberalization of markets, or the removal of state support for industry, has caused rapid deindustrialization, big government has tended to follow. Sometimes this has been in the form of public sector employment, but often it has been in the form of increased health, policing and welfare bills as unemployment and inactivity have given way to community decline and social problems. Perversely, ultra-liberal economic policies can lead to exactly the sort of government interventions, in social policy that many ultra-liberals, particularly market fundamentalists, despise.

Postmodernists and liberals

While market fundamentalists have followed thinkers like Hayek, concentrating mainly on economic policy, left-liberals have concentrated on social and cultural policies. And here, they have been influenced by a series of postmodern thinkers, starting with Michel Foucault.

The postmodernists were not liberals. They rejected the liberal conception of the individual, arguing that it projected white, Western and male experiences onto the whole of humanity. They rejected Marxist theory too, arguing that its emphasis on class structures was too simplistic. They were suspicious of science, reason and religion, arguing that knowledge and discourse exploit the weak and favour the strong. Instead, they argued, meta-narratives need to be replaced by much smaller and more personal mini-narratives.

Foucault concentrated on discourse: the language, customs and shared stories that amount to culture. And discourse, he argued, is oppressive. It controls people by controlling what can be known. And what is known is determined by the powerful. 'In any given culture and at any given moment', he wrote, 'there is always only one "episteme" that defines the conditions of possibility of all knowledge, whether expressed in theory or silently invested in a practice.'[76] Humans themselves are constructs of culture and therefore controlled by oppressive power structures. We are not autonomous agents, but pawns directed by discourses that reflect the interests of the powerful.

This analysis – and in particular the need to 'deconstruct' oppressive discourse – had significant influence on the American thinkers behind the rise of identity politics. The Combahee River Collective Statement, made in 1977 by a group of black feminist lesbians from Boston, is believed to be the first document to refer to identity politics. 'We believe that the most profound and potentially most radical politics come directly out of our own identity', the statement declared. 'Our situation as Black people necessitates that we have solidarity around the fact of race, which white women of course do not need to have with white men, unless it is their negative solidarity as racial oppressors. We struggle together with Black men against racism, while we also struggle with Black men about sexism.'[77]

A little more than a decade later, Kimberlé Crenshaw deconstructed feminist and anti-racist discourse to produce the concept of intersectionality. 'Black women are sometimes excluded from feminist theory and antiracist policy discourse because both are predicated on a discrete set of experiences that often does not accurately reflect the interaction of race and gender', she wrote. 'Because the intersectional experience is greater than the sum of racism and sexism, any analysis that does not take intersectionality into account cannot sufficiently address the particular manner in which Black women are subordinated.'[78]

Judith Butler, the American gender theorist, discusses 'the mundane way in which social agents constitute social reality through language, gesture, and all manner of symbolic social sign'. She therefore argues that 'gender is in no way a stable identity or locus of agency from which various acts proceed; rather, it is an identity tenuously constituted in time – an identity instituted through a *stylized repetition of acts*. Further, gender is instituted through the stylization of the body.' This, she says,

> moves the conception of gender off the ground of a substantial model of identity to one that requires a conception of a constituted *social temporality*. Significantly, if gender is instituted through acts which are internally discontinuous, then the *appearance of substance* is precisely that, a constructed identity, a performative accomplishment which the mundane social audience, including the actors themselves, come to believe and to perform in the mode of belief.[79]

There are many problems with this intellectual trend. If discourse is oppressive and dictated by the powerful, language and culture are the means by which an exploitative hierarchy is maintained. That means it is justified not simply to end the hierarchy, but to turn it on its head. If white men are oppressors, then whiteness and masculinity are not neutral identities, but negative identities that should be treated as such and penalized. If discourse reflects the interests of the powerful, and oppresses others, the essential liberal ideal of a society granting equal political rights to its citizens is an illusion.

If people are not even aware of the ways in which their social identities and roles are constructed for them, they cannot understand the meaning of their own words and actions. Thus a writer cannot know the true message or purpose of his words, and a speaker cannot know the true meaning of his remarks. The opinions of anybody who reads or listens should carry just as much weight. In fact, the opinions of those with oppressed identities should carry even greater weight. Consider the increasingly frequent use of the phrase, 'speaking as a woman', or as any number of other oppressed identities. The purpose of speaking in this way is to suggest that the person's identity gives them a superior moral perspective compared to others. The perceptions and experiences of those with oppressed identities become more important than reason and objective facts.

Institutions are suspect, too, because they play a crucial part in subjugating oppressed groups. Older and more traditional institutions are even worse, because they are tainted by association with colonialism, racism and sexism. They must therefore face boycotts, protests and calls to compensate for perceived misdemeanours from their pasts. The nation itself is a source of guilt and shame.

Language becomes increasingly controversial. If discourse is a means of oppression, words themselves are a form of violence. So violence itself is an acceptable response to language. Freedom of speech is anyway a dangerous deceit, postmodernists and their successors believe, because people are not truly in control of what they say. There is no case, therefore, to preserve our right to say what we like, and certainly no case for the right to offend. That would be a licence to commit 'microaggressions' against oppressed groups.

What is especially insidious about oppressive discourse, the postmodernists and their left-liberal successors believe, is its subtlety. White people who consider themselves to be anti-racist unwittingly entrench racial prejudice through their actions. Minorities themselves deepen their own disadvantage through the stories they believe and repeat. According to Alana Lentin, an Australian academic, 'the rejection of racism by proponents of positions that hinder the cause of racial justice is the ... next step in "post-racial" racism.' She concludes, '"not racism" is a form of racist violence.'[80]

And so complainants no longer need to prove that the accused has said or done something with racist intent. They do not even have to prove inadvertent racism. They can identify racist violence even when it is 'not racism'. They can allege that somebody has repeated a 'trope' used by racists in the past. And they can demand reparations from almost any Western institution old enough to have existed before decolonization.

It is also, incidentally, one factor behind the recent rise of anti-Semitism across the West. Jewish people are not seen as another minority group in need of protection. Because Western imperialism is driven by financial interests, and because financial interests are supposedly controlled by Jewish families, anti-Semites see Jews as part of the system of oppression. In this sick worldview, Jews are said to perpetuate social, economic and political disadvantage among members of minority groups, while reinforcing the wealth and power of privileged elites.

This is how militant identity politics endanger the principles of essential liberalism. Pluralism, equal political rights, freedom of speech, mediating institutions and even the rule of law come under attack. Essential liberalism is – like any other body of thought – simply another oppressive discourse that damages the interests of identity groups including women, homosexuals and ethnic minorities.

And yet many liberals have chosen not to resist the rise of militant identity politics, but welcome it. Ultra-liberals on the left, on the centre and sometimes even on the right have chosen to embrace militant identity politics. And not far behind them are the wealthy elites, universities and big business, who fall over themselves to prove their distance from white privilege and past colonialism, and demonstrate their adherence to the ever-changing rules of the identity game. After all, proving their 'woke' credentials is a lot simpler for these individuals and institutions than rediscovering the solidarity and sense of citizenship they abandoned a long time ago.

Identity politics in practice

Identity politics – understood as leading government and political debate with the welfare of specific groups in mind – should not necessarily be a problem. We have already seen how respecting, not ignoring, the continued significance of class can help to inform political decision-making. If we ignore group identity, we risk ignoring the human need for recognition from our fellow citizens. And without respecting the significance of group interests – which might, for example, include the welfare of a particular ethnic minority, discrimination against homosexuals, or the equal treatment of men and women – we would undoubtedly be a more unequal and less fair society.

Few today would question the achievements, or the legitimacy of the arguments, of the Suffragette and Suffragist movements, or Martin Luther King and his fellow civil rights leaders, for example. In their different ways, each of these important figures was a leading and successful practitioner of identity politics. Thanks in part to campaigners like them, there has been a great transformation in social attitudes in Britain over the course of the last twenty or thirty years. Huge majorities now reject homophobia, racism and sexism.[81] The difference between these campaigners and contemporary, identity-obsessed left-liberals, however, is that they were fighting for equal rights and an equal political status for men and women and for white and black people. Today's identitarians, in contrast, demand that we recognize and value difference.

And so identity politics is on the rise. And the identities that are becoming more politically prominent are based on sexuality, ethnicity, religion and gender. More traditional identities, based on community, class and nation, are becoming less prominent in political discourse than in the past. A more militant form of identity politics – in which all political issues must be judged through the prism of identity, minorities are expected to identify politically with their group, non-members are seen as incapable of representing minority group interests, and a special status is granted to minority groups – is now widespread.

The first problem with this militant identity politics is that it is dehumanizing and reductive. There is plenty more to a black woman than her black identity or her gender. She might be a mother or a sister or an aunt, a wife, a friend to many, a nurse or an engineer or soldier. She might be a conservative, she might be a socialist or liberal. She might believe in God. She might have hard-line views about the criminal justice system, or she might be a penal reformer. She might like football, or she might detest it. Her status as a black woman affects who she is, but it does not define her. Most members of identity groups want to be respected as individuals in their own right.

Yet the individuality of people from minority backgrounds counts for little with the practitioners of militant identity politics. When Boris Johnson appointed the most ethnically diverse Cabinet in Britain's history, the response from identity-obsessed left-liberals was not to welcome the news, but to condemn the black and Asian ministers he appointed. Clive Lewis, the Labour MP, tweeted: 'Genuine congratulations James [Cleverly]. I mean it. I'm just sorry you & the other black members of that cabinet had to sell your souls & self-respect to get there.'[82] A left-wing journalist – who happens to be white – said: 'Someone from a minority group who chooses to serve in a far right government is no longer a person of colour. They're a turncoat of colour. It's one thing to opt out of fighting oppression, quite another to legitimise it with your own skin.'[83]

Militant identity politics runs into the familiar and inevitable clash between human values and interests. In 2019, when a school in Birmingham taught pupils about homosexuality and sought to challenge homophobia, hundreds of Muslim parents protested outside the school gates and 600 children were withdrawn from lessons. At one protest, parents held signs that read, 'say no to promoting of homosexuality and LGBT ways of life to our children', 'stop exploiting children's innocence', and 'education not indoctrination'. The local Labour MPs Roger Godsiff and Shabana Mahmood defended the parents and their behaviour. Mahmood claimed 'it is all about the age appropriateness of conversations with young children in the context of religious backgrounds.' Minority rights must be protected, she insisted, but they must apply to people with strict religious beliefs too.[84]

We have already seen how liberalism can become illiberal, but here we see how liberal universalism can give way to relativism. Other examples abound. Thousands of cases of 'honour violence' are recorded every year, mainly against women. Forced marriage and polygamy are illegal, yet believed by the authorities to be widespread. An estimated 170,000 women in Britain live with the consequences of female genital mutilation.[85] The authorities, often reluctant to intervene in what they see as cultural matters, frequently let these crimes go unchecked. There has only ever been one prosecution in Britain for female genital mutilation.[86]

In a series of horrific court cases, child grooming gangs consisting mainly of Asian, Muslim men have been found to have systematically abused mainly troubled, white working-class girls in towns and cities including Bristol, Oxford, Rochdale, Rotherham and Telford. In Rotherham alone, gang members abused at least 1,400 girls over a period of around fifteen years.[87] The scale of these crimes – and the failure of the state to prevent them over long periods – is not only a gross injustice suffered by the victims, it is a festering social wound. Agitators and campaigners on the extreme right, like Tommy Robinson, have repeatedly cited Asian grooming gangs as they try to whip up hate.

While we know that child sex abusers are not disproportionately likely to be from any one racial or religious group, this is not the case when it comes to grooming gangs, which the statistics show are more likely to be perpetrated by Pakistani-heritage men targeting vulnerable, white working-class girls. An official study by the Child Exploitation and Online Protection agency shows that for gangs that targeted underage girls because of their vulnerability to exploitation, rather than because of sexual interest in children, 75 per cent of the perpetrators were Asian.[88] The independent inquiry into the Rotherham scandal concluded, 'in Rotherham, the majority of known perpetrators were Pakistani heritage' but the authorities had failed to take action because they had been 'inhibited by the fear of affecting community relations.'[89] A former social worker reported, 'if we mentioned Asian taxi drivers we were told we were racist and the young people were seen [by the authorities] as prostitutes.'[90]

The journey from universalism to moral relativism is not the only perverse consequence of identity-based left-liberalism. Members of the Labour Party are increasingly concerned that the use of all-women shortlists, designed to increase female representation in Parliament, is now undermining attempts to increase black and ethnic minority representation in the House of Commons.[91] According to the logic of militant identity politics, women are a disadvantaged group who need to be protected. Clearly men can make way for them, but what if those men are black and therefore members of another disadvantaged group? And what about that dramatically under-represented group, the working class?

As the debate about transgender rights has accelerated, and as feminists and gay rights campaigners have raised concerns that certain changes might end up detrimental to women and homosexuals, they have found themselves under attack. Figures including Julie Bindel, Germaine Greer and Peter Tatchell have found themselves 'no-platformed' at universities.[92] Martina Navratilova, the former tennis star and trailblazer for lesbians in the 1980s, was forced to resign from Athlete Ally, an organization established to support LGBT athletes, after she questioned whether transsexuals should be able to compete in women's competitions.[93]

These examples all demonstrate how identity-obsessed left-liberalism ends up causing tensions and rivalries between the groups it is supposed to be supporting. But this is nothing compared to what it does to attitudes towards the majority group. In order to retain their status as groups that deserve special support, militant identity politics requires continuous evidence that specific groups are disadvantaged, and to do this, they need to perpetuate a sense of victimhood. Left-liberals therefore need to castigate wider society and the majority group – in other words, white people – as oppressive. This is one reason why the definition of racism is constantly expanded and often goes beyond what a reasonable person would agree is racism.

It is also why we see campus campaigns to pull down statues of old imperialists, such as that of Cecil Rhodes at Oriel College, Oxford. It is why, in the United States, there is a growing campaign – backed by senior Democrats including Elizabeth Warren – for reparations to be paid to African Americans in recognition of the slave trade, which was abolished more than 150 years ago. It is easy to write off these examples as outliers, but the logic of militant identity politics can have damaging consequences.

In 2017, following the appalling fire in Grenfell Tower, David Lammy, a black Labour MP from a constituency in a different part of London, assumed the role of spokesman for the victims and their neighbours and families. When Sir Martin Moore-Bick, a respected retired judge, was appointed to lead the subsequent public inquiry, Lammy whipped up anger and outrage:

> He is a white upper middle class man who I suspect has never visited a tower block housing estate ... It's a shame that we couldn't find a woman to lead the inquiry, or indeed an ethnic minority. I think the victims will also say to themselves when push comes to shove there are some powerful people here – contractors, sub-contractors, local authorities, governments – and they look like this judge. Whose side will he be on?[94]

Separately, Lammy speculated, without any evidence, that the police had deliberately undercounted the number of people killed in the fire.[95]

To argue that a judge cannot be a judge because he does not look like the victims of the case into which he is inquiring is clearly perverse. But Lammy's intervention demonstrates the many destructive problems with identity-obsessed left-liberalism. It undermines trust in civic, legal and democratic institutions. It can be repressive for individuals, who are expected to conform by expressing their views only through the prism of their group identity. And it can undermine people's affiliation with other, vital identities, such as their attachment to their immediate locality, region and nation. As Jonathan Haidt has argued, militant identity politics ignores the pursuit of common humanity and instead promotes the politics of the common enemy.[96] Without broader, genuinely diverse and more inclusive identities, solidarity becomes difficult to realize.

Culture wars

Identity is at the heart of the culture wars that are increasingly fought out in Britain. Whereas the traditional political dividing line was socioeconomic, increasingly it now appears to be cultural. And this divide is not only evident in politics and government, but in the media, on university campuses, and in the arts and entertainment.

The change is brought home by the 'ClockFace' model, produced by the research and strategy company, Populus (see figures 2 and 3). Based on census data, figure 2 shows the profiles of people living in

Based on Census data analysis. Shows the information we reveal about ourselves can be reduced to two main axes: SECURITY (a measure of health, wealth and well-being) and DIVERSITY (Physical and demographic proximity to your neighbour).

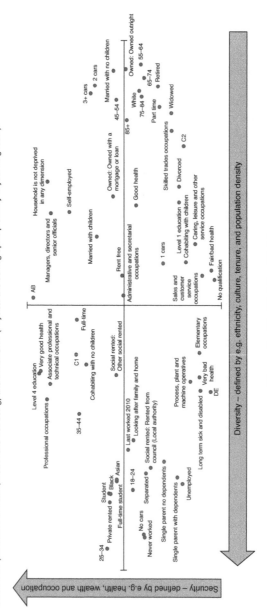

Figure 2 *The ClockFace Model*

© Populus, reproduced by kind permission of Rick Nye

communities mapped out against two axes: one showing increasing diversity and the other increasing security. Figure 3 shows how communities voted in different elections – in Britain and the US – on the same axes. Elections that are fought on socioeconomic matters show a dividing line that reaches from the bottom-left quadrant to the top-right quadrant. Elections that are fought on cultural matters – like US presidential elections and the Brexit referendum – show dividing lines that do the opposite: stretching from the top-left to the bottom-right. The question is whether, for normal British elections, the dividing line is moving in the direction of a permanent cultural divide. As figure 3 shows, the movement between 2015 and 2017 suggests this might indeed be what is happening.

We should be alarmed by the prospect of politics fought permanently about cultural matters. A socioeconomic divide allows the mainstream parties to argue about how to balance economic efficiency and economic equality. It ought, in theory at least, to allow the parties to accommodate one another's changes and recalibrate government policy in line with the wishes of the public. In contrast, a cultural divide is, by nature, much more zero-sum and, partly as a result, much more poisonous.

Consider the culture wars in the United States. They have their roots in the 1960s, and popular protests against the Vietnam War and the treatment of black Americans. When, to some people, those protests began to appear anti-American and anti-patriotic, they unleashed a backlash. Increasingly, US culture wars are fought over a growing number of symbolic issues, each becoming more extreme than the last. Debates over abortion rights, gun control and the provision of healthcare are not conducted with calmness and respect but in a frenzy and with hatred. Now gay rights and immigration control – 'build a wall' – are on the list of issues caught up in the culture wars; it is getting harder and harder to forge a national consensus on anything.

The same is true for Britain's Brexit referendum, when the dividing line was undoubtedly cultural. Countless studies have shown that the vote to leave the EU was not driven by poverty or by party affiliation. One third of Labour supporters, and two-thirds of Labour constituencies, voted to leave, as did a third of Liberal Democrats. Leave voters

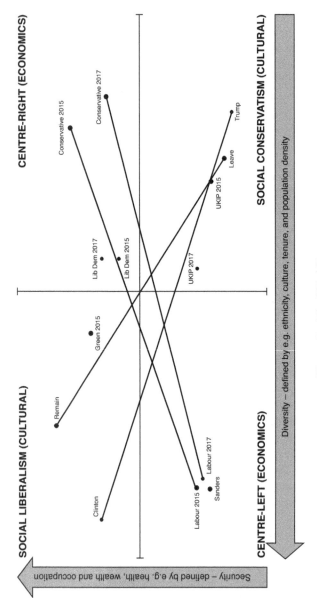

Figure 3 *The Global Picture*

© Populus, reproduced by kind permission of Rick Nye

tended to be older than Remain voters, and more likely to be working class. But the striking correlation was between education and voting behaviour. Seventy per cent of people whose highest qualifications were GCSEs voted to leave the EU, while 68 per cent of university graduates voted to remain.[97]

The pattern was clear. Those with 'ascribed' identities – based on home town, class and nationality – voted largely to leave the European Union. Those with 'achieved' identities mainly voted to remain. And since the referendum, this divide – between the Somewheres and Anywheres described by David Goodhart – has only grown wider. Remainers are often criticized for being aloof, snobbish and unpatriotic. Leavers are mocked for being racist, stupid and too old to have a stake in the future. And as the Populus research shows, this is beginning to have an effect on the party system: Somewheres are increasingly likely to vote Conservative, and Anywheres to vote Labour.

The culture war is not limited to electoral politics. Increasingly, radical campaign groups threaten direct action. Some try to disrupt the deportation of illegal immigrants. Others disrupt mass transport systems or strike against globalization or climate change. Some, like 'Stop Funding Hate', try to pressure private businesses into withdrawing offensive publications, such as the *Daily Mail*. Others try to force universities to 'decolonize' the curriculum. Left-liberal councils have even refused to enforce immigration laws. 'It is not the responsibility of Labour councils', they say, 'to inform on vulnerable migrants when they come to us seeking shelter and support.'[98]

Hypocrisy abounds as the culture wars go on. Elite liberals and left-liberals dislike support for the traditional family, but prefer to get married and stay married to bring up their children. Elite liberals justify their ideology by pointing to the supposed rational autonomy of individuals, but decry the irrationality of the electorate when they disagree with democratically made decisions. They want to tax sugar, ban smoking and regulate the price of alcohol, but favour legalizing the hard drugs they often use themselves. They say they hate discrimination – and are always keen to signal their virtue – but their belief in equality rarely stretches beyond the members of their own social classes. Their determination to eliminate carbon emissions kills jobs at home and transfers industrial emissions to countries that use dirtier sources of energy, but environmentalism feels good, and helps to wash away their white, Western privilege.

These are all reasons why culture wars are divisive and polarizing and difficult to escape. As the American liberal writer, Mark Lilla, has said, the identity politics that fuel culture wars are 'expressive not persuasive', and so lead people into angry and adversarial factions.[99]

White decline

One group that is increasingly angry and frustrated is the white working class. We have already seen how their fortunes have waned compared to richer white people, some other ethnic groups, and previous generations of working-class families. But instead of showing solidarity with them, and offering practical and policy support, ultra-liberals have offered only scorn.

For identity-obsessed left-liberals, white people – as the majority group and the descendants of colonizers and oppressors – are the problem. This is of course historically ignorant – almost all peoples have through time been conquerors, occupiers and slave owners – but it is the sad logic of militant identity politics. Minorities have to continuously prove their disadvantage – or have it proved for them by well-meaning liberals – to merit their status as special groups in need of support. To do this, they must maintain their status as victims, and by definition victims must be oppressed. White people – excluding of course the identity-obsessed left-liberals who police the system fiercely – are the oppressors. They carry with them the original sin: white privilege.

Nothing could feel more absurd to the white working classes than the idea that they are born privileged. Yet elite liberals and left-liberals routinely castigate them, in politics, the media and the arts and entertainment. Their patriotism is seen as racist, their Euroscepticism as xenophobic. Their concerns about job security and the decline of their communities is hopelessly parochial to ultra-liberals excited about globalization, disruptive technologies and militant identity politics. Language that would be considered unacceptable about any other group – 'white trash', 'chavs', and 'the underclass' – is often used laughingly and without guilt in elite liberal and left-liberal circles.

The white working classes feel not only this lost solidarity, but also their deprivation relative to others. According to Justin Gest, who has researched attitudes among the white working classes in Britain and America, the sense of injustice brought about by relative deprivation is driven not only by the loss of economic security and prosperity, but also by cultural, political and social loss too.[100]

Roger Eatwell and Matthew Goodwin say this anxiety is fundamental to the success of populist parties and politicians across the West in recent years. What motivated working-class voters to support populists, they suggest, 'was a sense that, relative to others, they and their group had lost out, whether to more affluent middle-class citizens or to immigrants. Not only had they been demoted from the centre of their nation's consciousness to its fringes, but affirmative action had given further advantages to minorities while anti-racism campaigns had silenced any criticism about these rapid and deeply unsettling social changes.'[101]

Eric Kaufmann, an academic who has studied white communities as they respond to cultural change, goes further. He argues, 'demography and culture, not economic and political developments, hold the key to understanding the populist moment. Immigration is central. Ethnic change – the size and nature of the immigrant inflow and its capacity to challenge ethnic boundaries – is the story.'[102]

Kaufmann points out that 'white exceptionalism' – the idea that unlike any other racial groups, white people have no attachment to their ethnic and cultural identity – is ridiculous. 'When Harlem is gentrified by whites and Asians, or Brixton by hipsters, this is experienced as a loss by blacks', he argues. 'So, too, when a historically ethnic-majority area with strong local traditions like Barking, England, becomes superdiverse, this is experienced [by some local people] as a tragedy.' This does not mean change must be stopped, he insists, but 'the desire to slow ethnic change is a legitimate expression of the ethnic majority's cultural interest.'[103]

The pace of demographic change experienced by the white majority in Britain, and in other Western countries, has been rapid. In the United States, white people made up 87 per cent of the population in 1950, a number that will fall to 47 per cent by 2050.[104] In Britain, projections suggest that the non-white population will reach up to

35 per cent by 2050.[105] A similar story, to varying degrees, is playing out across Western Europe.

In 2011, the census showed that 41 per cent of non-white British ethnic minorities were living in council wards where whites were in a minority. This was up from 25 per cent in the preceding census in 2001.[106] Quietly, these rapid changes are causing deep anxiety among white populations. Research shows that as particular communities become more racially diverse, white people move away. This is true not only in Britain, but also in the United States and across Europe, including in traditionally liberal countries such as the Netherlands and Sweden. Unlike the stereotype of ethnic ghettos, where minorities of one particular ethnic background congregate, unwilling to mix with others, it is white people who are 'sticking to their own'.[107]

Even in super-diverse London, where people are more likely to meet people from different ethnic backgrounds, Londoners' friendship groups are less likely to reflect the age, income and ethnic mix of the community they live in than anywhere else in the country.[108] Research shows that white people who live in diverse communities maintain largely white friendship groups. White people living in council wards that are 30 per cent white, for example, have friends who are on average 68 per cent white. As many as 65 per cent of whites in these wards interact with people of different ethnicities at work, but only 14.5 per cent did so in one another's homes.[109]

When it comes to education, school segregation is even more pronounced than the segregation of children in the broader population. Sixty per cent of ethnic minority children attend schools where minorities form the majority of pupils.[110] In 2015, there were 511 schools across 43 local authorities in which more than half the pupils were from Pakistani and Bangladeshi backgrounds.[111] According to Kaufmann's research, schools where white British children comprise more than 80 per cent of pupils attract yet more white British children. When the number falls below 70 per cent, schools start to lose white British children and gain more ethnic minority and foreign-born white pupils.[112]

These decisions made are not born of racism. Increasingly, Britain is a more open and tolerant society. One in eight households in England and Wales now includes more than one ethnic group. In London, the number rises to one in five. Twelve per cent of couples are inter-ethnic among those younger than fifty, compared to 6 per cent for couples older than fifty.[113] Kaufmann's explanation is that rather than 'escape', a more convincing motivation for this self-segregation is that white people are 'gravitating to whiter areas to find social cohesion or a sense of community', a theory bolstered by the fact that white liberals are just as likely to move towards whiter areas as conservatives.[114]

This is a difficult issue to understand and address, but the anxiety is real. White people are as attached to their ethnic and cultural identity as any other group and, faced with the reality of rapid demographic decline, many feel a sense of loss. And this loss is compounded by the economic and social crisis experienced by many white working-class families.

It is reasonable to argue that some minorities have it worse than white people, and in many ways that is true. Pakistani and Bangladeshi communities struggle in particular. Family breakdown and poor educational attainment can be as common among black people as among whites. Racism, less prevalent than it once was, undoubtedly persists. These are all injustices that need to be confronted. But we cannot ignore the crisis of the white working class. It is a far larger group than any minority. It is spread across the whole country and dominates many communities. Even if ultra-liberal politicians do not want to help solve the crisis for reasons of solidarity, they will eventually need to confront the reality of many millions of disaffected and frustrated voters.

The biggest broken promise

More than any other, the issue that has broken the bond of trust between ultra-liberals and the working classes is immigration.

We know from almost every poll published that most people think immigration is too high and ought to be reduced. Research shows that this view is shared across every age group and every part of the country, including liberal London and Scotland.[115] As the pollsters Ipsos MORI say, historical research shows 'there are always 60%+ who want immigration reduced'.[116] In every general election since 2010, and the Brexit referendum, the winning side was the one promising to reduce immigration.

Britain has experienced waves of immigration in the past. The migration of Commonwealth subjects after the Second World War, mainly from Africa, the Caribbean and the Indian subcontinent, saw hundreds of thousands of people come to live and work in Britain. While legislation introducing new immigration controls was passed in the 1960s and 1970s, this had only a limited effect on the numbers of people arriving, as so-called 'secondary immigration' occurred and families reunited in Britain.

Nonetheless, far from being a 'nation of immigrants', as campaigners often like to say, Britain's population has been remarkably stable through the centuries. If anything, we have been a 'nation of emigrants', as British subjects settled in colonies and other countries. Annual net migration, despite the rise in post-war Commonwealth immigration, never exceeded the tens of thousands until the late 1990s. Before then, it peaked in 1994, when net migration reached 77,000. Often net migration was negative, meaning more people left the country than came to live here.

But then, suddenly, in 1998, one year into Tony Blair's first term as Prime Minister, net migration leapt to 140,000. And since then, the annual inflow has only been higher. On average, net migration has run at more than 230,000 since 1998, and over that period net migration has increased the size of the UK population by five million people, the equivalent of five cities the size of Birmingham.[117]

No politician ever promised to oversee immigration on this scale. In 1997, Tony Blair's election manifesto promised 'firm control over immigration'.[118] In 2010, David Cameron promised to get annual net migration back to the 'tens of thousands a year'.[119] But by 2015, the numbers had reached more than three times the promised level – 332,000 – and a record high.[120] As a pollster once said to me, 'Britain never had a Pentagon Papers moment, a single event that destroyed trust in government, like America did. But the repeat failure to control immigration, and the broken promises to bring the numbers down, are the British equivalent. Immigration has obliterated trust in politics in this country.'[121]

Ultra-liberal supporters of mass immigration often say it is futile trying to control the numbers. In the modern world, they say, with relatively cheap international travel and easy communications, it is simply impossible to hold back the tide. But this is not true. Where levers exist to control immigration, and ministers have been prepared to pull them, the numbers come down. The number of student visas issued, for example, fell dramatically after bogus colleges were shut down and foreign students were expected to prove their eligibility for higher education. The number of family visas issued fell after the government toughened up the requirements. As a result of these changes, and a cap on the number of work permits issued, net migration to Britain fell by almost one third between 2010 and 2012.[122] The numbers have risen again since because governments have not taken action to keep them down.

So it is possible to control the numbers: it is just that ministers rarely try to do so. Tony Blair's government liberalized family, work and student visas and unsurprisingly the numbers went up. It introduced the Human Rights Act, which made it harder to enforce immigration law. When Poland and seven other countries joined the EU in 2004, it chose not to apply transitional immigration controls, as was allowed under European law. Instead of adding 13,000 per year to net migration, as the government predicted, more than 1.5 million people came.[123] These were all deliberate policy choices that contributed to the huge rise in immigration after 1998.

Ultra-liberals claim mass immigration makes us better off, but this is also untrue. Academic studies suggest it makes little economic difference overall. According to the OECD, 'the [fiscal] impact of the cumulative waves of migration that arrived over the past fifty years in OECD countries is on average close to zero.'[124] And while mass immigration increases the size of our economy, it only does so by increasing the size of the population. On a per capita basis, studies show the effect is broadly neutral. As Robert Rowthorn, an economist from Cambridge University, has said, depending on the profile of immigration, its effect on GDP per capita 'could be positive or negative, but either way it is unlikely to be very large'.[125]

For some workers, the effects of immigration are certainly negative. While there is no fixed number of jobs in the economy – an idea economists reject as the 'lump of labour' fallacy – there is evidence that mass immigration can force down wages for workers with lower skills and training, and squeeze some people out of work altogether.[126] Because it can provide a ready-made supply of trained workers, willing to live on low wages, mass immigration removes incentives for businesses to train local workers or for government to provide widely available decent technical education.

It can also put pressure on infrastructure and services. Official figures show that immigration is behind more than a third of the increased demand for housing in England.[127] Supporters of immigration are right to point out that the NHS depends on foreign workers, but surgeries and hospitals can struggle when the local population grows quickly. And so too can the school system: due to immigration and high birth rates among migrant mothers, England needs 418,000 new secondary school places – an increase of nearly 15 per cent – by 2027.[128]

These are economic reasons for immigration control. But one of the main reasons voters want to reduce and control immigration is to protect their cultural identity. Research by Eric Kaufmann suggests that while people are less hostile to skilled immigration than unskilled immigration, when they believe that even skilled immigration will bring faster ethnic change, they oppose it by a margin of around three to one. 'Skill mix matters', reports Kaufmann, 'but [it] is overridden by concerns about cultural change.'[129]

Asymmetrical multiculturalism

While identity-obsessed ultra-liberals strive to offer cultural protection for minority groups, they insist that the majority group – the white British – should simply accept cultural change even if it makes them uncomfortable. This is what Kaufmann calls 'asymmetrical multiculturalism', the idea that ultra-liberals should encourage minorities to maintain and protect their cultural identities, while whites should 'morph into cosmopolites'.[130]

Whether multiculturalism is asymmetric or not, however, it is almost undeniably a policy that has failed. As Trevor Phillips, the former head of the Commission for Racial Equality, has argued, 'we've emphasized what divides us over what unites us. We have allowed tolerance of diversity to harden into the effective isolation of communities, in which some people think special separate values ought to apply.'[131]

It is certainly true that Britain's different ethnic and cultural groups lead remarkably separate lives. We have already seen how, as communities become more diverse, white people tend to move away. And we have seen how English schools are more racially segregated than the already segregated communities they serve. But there is yet more evidence of the parallel lives led in modern Britain.

Half of all British black and minority ethnic citizens live in just three cities: London, Birmingham and Manchester.[132] In 2018, a government study reported that densely concentrated minority communities are growing in number. Whereas in 2001, 199 council wards were 'minority majority', by 2011, 429 wards were majority non-white.[133] According to other government reports, segregation is more prevalent among Muslims and people of Pakistani and Bangladeshi ethnicity. Birmingham, Blackburn, Bradford and Burnley all have wards with Muslim populations of between 70 and 85 per cent.[134]

Across England, 770,000 adults cannot speak English.[135] Around one in five adults from Pakistani (18.9 per cent) and Bangladeshi (21.9 per cent) backgrounds either speak English poorly or not at all.[136] And women are disproportionately affected: the number rises to 30 per cent for women with Bangladeshi backgrounds.[137]

While segregated communities consisting mainly of one ethnic or religious group can provide useful help and support for their members, this degree of geographical and linguistic isolation brings social, cultural and economic isolation from wider society. The more isolated your community, for example, the less likely you will be to have friends – or a spouse or partner – outside your ethnic group. And the less integrated you are, the less likely you are to work and earn a good wage. Some 57.2 per cent of Pakistani and Bangladeshi women are economically inactive. Of those with jobs, one in four Pakistani men work as taxi drivers, while two in five Bangladeshi men work in restaurants.[138]

We have been aware of these problems for many years. Following riots in northern English towns in 2001, the then Labour government commissioned Ted Cantle to review the circumstances of the communities where the riots occurred. He reported, 'separate educational arrangements, community and voluntary bodies, employment, places of worship, language, social and cultural networks, means that many communities operate on the basis of a series of parallel lives.'[139]

By the time Dame Louise Casey reviewed the integration of Britain's various communities and cultural groups, fifteen years later, her findings were no better than Cantle's. She identified 'discrimination and disadvantage feeding a sense of grievance and unfairness, isolating communities from modern British society'. But she also found 'high levels of social and economic isolation in some places and cultural and religious practices' that hold citizens back but also 'run contrary to British values and sometimes our laws'.[140]

The problem has been caused by a double failure of liberalism. The first is the failure of the identity-obsessed left-liberals, who value minority identities only and disparage majority culture. They see no problem with the parallel lives led by members of different communities: indeed, such differences are the very basis of their worldview.

The second is a failure of a more conventional liberalism to understand citizenship. Its own view of citizenship is transactional, not relational. Liberalism is ignorant about place, careless about relationships, hostile to tradition, forgetful of institutions, ambivalent about the nation, and – with the exception of identity-obsessed left-liberals – blind about culture. It sees citizenship as simply a contract, in which the state protects a list of certain rights. It imagines citizens as autonomous individuals who should throw off prejudice and superstition and lead fully rational lives. And it is impatiently universalistic: its contract between state and citizen should hold anywhere in the world and at any time in history.

Citizenship and identity

Citizenship requires much more than the transactional relationship envisaged by liberals. Unlike their minimalistic view of citizenship, fuller, richer, civic conceptions of citizenship recognize that we need strong institutions to shape our behaviour and help us to resolve conflicts of values and interests. They accept that we need to respect traditions to help us to identify with one another, and recognize the implicit promise of reciprocity made by citizenship: that if we do right by another, they will do right by us. And they understand, too, that citizenship is not a one-way relationship in which we can take without giving back. To paraphrase President Kennedy, this conception of citizenship asks citizens not to think of what their country can do for them, but what they can do for their country.

As the failures of multiculturalism have become more apparent, even some elite liberal politicians realized something needed to change. Driven mainly by concern about the rise of homegrown extremism and terrorism, political leaders including even Tony Blair began to question the principles of multiculturalism. Yet while their condemnation was clear, their policy response was hollow. Speeches and strategies that had British values at their heart ran aground because of the familiar problem that human values and interests often conflict. Policies to strengthen institutions or build entirely new ones never came. No political leader has yet managed to produce a coherent strategy or policy based on a truly civic conception of citizenship.

Neither has any political leader been prepared to ask the most difficult questions. What if understanding even this fuller, civic conception of citizenship is not enough? What if we also need to consider the importance of ethnic and cultural conception of identity too? This is normally considered a taboo subject, because for some it carries the connotation that foreign nationals who choose to build a life in Britain cannot become British, or that citizens with minority backgrounds are not British, even if they or their forebears were born in Britain. If this were the purpose of raising the issue of ethnic identity, it would be wrong, because citizenship in a multiracial society like Britain must be inclusive. In England and Wales, 7.5 million people, or 13 per cent of the population, were born outside the UK. At least one in five British nationals identifies as something other than white British.[141] These citizens – with black, Asian, European and many other backgrounds – are as British as anybody else, and the ethnic identity of white Britons must not be used to undermine them.

Nevertheless, it is hasty to ignore the significance of ethnic and cultural identity and its relationship with citizenship. As we discussed in the first chapter, identity depends to a certain extent on context. I might describe myself as a European in Asia, but British in Europe. In Britain I might call myself English or say I am from Birmingham. In just the same way, it would have been ridiculous for a white British person to refer to their white identity in the 1950s. But today, with one in five people identifying as something other than white British, the salience of white identity is growing. And as it does so, patience with asymmetrical multiculturalism and the liberal, minimalist view of citizenship is wearing thin.

Few people outside ultra-liberal circles want Britain to be reduced to a values-free platform upon which anybody in the world can live and work respecting only a minimalistic liberal social contract. The liberal conception of citizenship is failing because on one hand it asks too little of us, but on the other hand it asks the impossible of us. This is because it expects the values of citizens to align exactly with the values of the liberal order. As we have seen repeatedly, such an alignment in values is impossible.

Instead, we need to find a way of making a reality of civic citizenship, based on institutions, traditions and social norms, and a solidarity and patriotism that means we will act for one another and for the greater good. And as we do so, we need to think about how ethnic and cultural identities relate to citizenship. It is undeniable that our most important institutions and traditions come from deep in our history, and many of the examples of solidarity and patriotism we can learn from also come from our past.

There is nothing inherently dangerous, therefore, in allowing the majority group to express and enjoy their ethnic and cultural identities in a peaceful and positive manner. Indeed, doing so is vital in telling the national stories that maintain the bonds of citizenship and faith in our institutions and respect for our traditions. Disparaging Britain's history, as many ultra-liberals do, or ignoring it because it is dominated by privileged, white men, is therefore counter-productive and damaging.

We do, however, need to think about what this means for citizens who have different ethnic and cultural identities to the majority group. For white British people, it is easy to identify with Britain's long history and the many stories that come from it. That means their attachment to institutions, traditions and norms is often implicit, simple and almost automatic. For minorities with ancestries in countries connected to Britain through history, culture and sizeable diasporas already in the country – in the Commonwealth, for example – there is also a common story.

But for some minorities, their attachment to Britain can feel less straightforward. They might feel little connection with Elizabeth I or William Shakespeare. They might view some figures from British history, such as Oliver Cromwell, or Winston Churchill, with suspicion because of their actions in countries like Ireland and India. They might look at some institutions – Parliament perhaps, or the Conservative Party – with suspicion, or some traditions – connected with Christianity, maybe – with ambivalence. How we go about building a strong sense of citizenship, therefore, needs to respect and understand differences in ethnic and cultural identities. It needs to respect the fact that there are many different ways of feeling an attachment to national identity, and many different reasons for doing so. But ultimately it also needs to respect and understand the ethnic and cultural identities of white Britons, and the long story, spanning hundreds of generations, of our national life.

The rejection of nation

National identity and patriotism are embarrassing topics of conversation for most ultra-liberals. They are often associated in public debate with racism or chauvinism. But national identity is what makes meaningful citizenship – and the obligations and sacrifices we are willing to accept as citizens – possible.

It is no coincidence that the development of Britain's welfare state, the provision of extensive public services, and the increase in progressive taxation and public spending occurred immediately after the Second World War and at a time when the nation state was strong. Support for policies that make a reality of solidarity can only be strong when identification with the nation state – and the spirit of citizenship it engenders – is also strong.

Yet since the Second World War, the nation has come under relentless pressure. On the one hand, globalization and, in particular, the power of international financial markets has undermined the ability of national governments to determine policies. On the other, international and even supranational organizations have been created to consciously limit what governments can do.

In many respects, these have been changes for the better. Despite the pain caused by the latest wave of globalization described in chapter 1, nobody can deny that the world is a more prosperous place as a result of the increases in trade since the Second World War. Likewise, any student of how the world stumbled into the First World War appreciates that a world without international governance is chaotic and dangerous. Today, as the balance of power between the East and West changes, the failure to modernize global institutions such as the International Monetary Fund, the United Nations and the World Bank is contributing towards the instability we are witnessing across the world.

There is undoubtedly an important role for international governance. As a result of organizations like the World Trade Organization and the United Nations, trade has become smoother and international relations more predictable. Some international organizations, however, have caused political decisions to be made further away from ordinary people, and with less democratic accountability, than ever before.

The European Convention on Human Rights (ECHR), backed by the European Court in Strasbourg, constrains national governments in matters from the deportation of foreign terrorists to the conduct of their soldiers on the battlefield. While the Convention makes it harder for countries like Britain to keep their civilians safe, it does nothing – despite the claims of its supporters – to prevent the abuse of the judicial system in countries like Romania, or the murder of President Putin's political opponents and journalists in Russia. The Human Rights Act – which incorporates the Convention into British law – compels judges to follow Strasbourg's case law and judge whether laws passed by Parliament are compatible with the Convention. Thanks to the Human Rights Act, the ECHR has, with very little debate, become Britain's de facto written constitution.

Then there is the European Union. Britain joined the EU – or what was then called the European Economic Community – in 1973. As the EU's single market developed, trade between European countries became more fluid, with hidden trade restrictions such as differential product standards and professional licences eliminated. But over the same time period, more and more control was ceded to the EU and its institutions. Member states gave up their veto in the Council of Ministers. The Council surrendered more control to the European Parliament. The European Court of Justice extended the application of European laws on everything from taxation to immigration control. And the British courts confirmed the supremacy of European law over

British law, ruling that any domestic legislation deemed incompatible with EU laws must be struck down automatically.

In many ways the European Union is the quintessential ultra-liberal project, in that the right and left have for their different reasons driven the country relentlessly in an ultra-liberal direction. Market fundamentalists on the right see a free market in goods and services, and approve, while left-liberals see open borders and a supranational governance model, and also approve.

But the effect of European integration has been to undermine sovereignty and democratic government. As we have already seen, there have been consistent majorities in favour of reducing immigration to Britain for years. Yet EU free movement rules made it impossible to restrict migration from Europe. Certain taxes, such as VAT on energy bills, could never be reduced because of European laws. EU laws have constrained national choices on everything from public procurement rules to the investigation of terrorists. Voters have become used to politicians promising to fix problems, only to say they could not do so because of the European Union.

This weakening of the nation state might not mean much for many of David Goodhart's Anywheres. They can enjoy easy international travel, and the chance to study and work in different countries. Back in Britain, they can benefit from cheaper services provided by nannies, plumbers and waiters from foreign countries. And undoubtedly, the convinced ultra-liberals among them will enjoy the feel-good factor of rising above parochial ideas like national identity.

But for the Somewheres, the reality is less happy. They lack the opportunity, and often the desire, to travel, study and work abroad. They face competition, for jobs and wages, from cheaper migrant workers, and are more likely to use schools and other services struggling to cope with increasing numbers of users. They have not shed their national identity in favour of internationalism, and they expect the solidarity that comes with a shared national identity to continue.

The impact assessments produced by the Whitehall utilitarians might have shown that EU membership – and the uncontrolled immigration it brings – makes Britain, in net economic terms, marginally better off. But for the Somewheres, the majority of whom voted to leave the EU, this was an answer – which they probably judged inaccurate anyway – to the wrong question. Instead, they wanted to know why a country like Britain could not govern itself. They wanted to know why politicians seemed so keen to turn their backs on the nation state. They wanted the nation state – and the obligations of citizenship, the solidarity and the democratic accountability it brings – back in their lives.

The decline of community

The ultra-liberal rejection of the nation has occurred simultaneously with the decline of community. And this phenomenon, too, has its roots at least partially in philosophical thinking.

Community is a vital component of a functioning society. As we discovered in chapter 1, we are relational beings. We do not want to discard the bonds of relationships and communities; we want to retain them. We do not want to escape; we want to belong. Yet liberalism perceives us to be autonomous and individualistic, constantly striving to escape the influences of others. As Robert Nisbet, the influential American sociologist, argued, this is not true. 'Genuine freedom is not based upon the negative psychology of release', he wrote, 'its roots are in positive acts of dedication to ends and values. Freedom presupposes the autonomous existence of values that men wish to be free to follow and live up to. Such values are social in the precise sense that they arise out of, and are nurtured by, voluntary associations which men form.'[142]

These voluntary associations are what we mean when we discuss community, and they mediate our relationship as individuals with wider society. The most obvious form of association is the family, but the many other varied examples include faith groups, trades unions, charities, sports teams, and local residents' organizations. The difference between these relationships and market transactions is that we are prepared to suppress our individual interests if we believe it benefits the wider group. As we noted earlier, psychologists like Jonathan Haidt have established that humans are capable of great acts of altruism, but we tend to be altruistic only to fellow members of our own groups.

So it is that parents forego personal luxuries to provide opportunities for their children, trades unionists go out on strike to defend the rights of their fellow workers, and volunteers give up their time to do something good for their neighbours. This is how we achieve our status – or recognition from others – in the community. It is how we learn to cooperate with one another and reciprocate favours and good behaviour. And it is how we learn to differentiate between good and bad, and right and wrong. Closely connected to community are the institutions that police behaviour and norms and traditions that build and engender trust.

A society with a strong sense of community, therefore, will have more trust between its citizens, better cooperation and less crime and anti-social behaviour. It will be more willing to pay taxes for a welfare state and healthcare for all. But a society with little sense of community will suffer the opposite. When economic opportunity is limited and trust is low, economic activity is more likely to be seen as a zero-sum exercise. Consider payday lenders with their exorbitant interest rates, bookmakers with fixed-odds betting terminals, and energy companies that rip off customers who do not switch providers. Think, too, of the absence of ethical standards in banking before the financial crash. Strong communities can stand up to crony capitalism and challenge political corruption. For these reasons, they are vital to the health of capitalism and democracy. 'Where there is widespread conviction that community has been lost', Nisbet warned, 'there will be a conscious quest for community in the form of association that seems to promise greatest moral refuge.'[143] This is what can lead to popular support for extremists and populists.

Community in modern Britain has come under a twin attack. On one front, elite liberals' and market fundamentalists' relentless individualism and emphasis on market forces has eroded our neighbourliness and commitment to community. The uniformity and scale of capitalist mass manufacture and marketing have undermined culture and tradition and exposed us all to a more atomized way of life. Many places have suffered rapid deindustrialization, economic hardship, the loss of important institutions, brain drains and declining social capital. The bonds of solidarity are breaking.

On another front, confronted by these consequences of ultra-liberalism, elite liberals and left-liberals have relied on the centralized, utilitarian state to issue remedies. But no true sense of community can develop when decision-making is distant and ignorant of local circumstances. Community needs associations and institutions that are born of real needs and play a meaningful, significant role in meeting those needs. Institutions that no longer serve a real purpose wither and die. This is why centralized government solutions, such as tax credits to subsidize low-skilled, low-paid work, public sector jobs to make up for declining private sector employment, and infrastructure and investment decisions taken many miles away, end up undermining, not enhancing, community. They leave little or no space for local initiative.

The evidence for the decline of community in Britain is all around us. For people with lower educational qualifications and in lower-paid work, trust is lower than among the better educated and better paid.[144] In places where family breakdown is common, young people often seek recognition and status through gang membership, which increases crime and anti-social behaviour. In places with poor education and training records, neither the market nor the state is providing solutions. And neither is local government, which remains enfeebled, nor our depleted community institutions.

The family, in particular, is under pressure. As we have already seen, family breakdown is far more prevalent among white working class and black families than among Asians and more prosperous white families. And the nature and shape of the family is changing. Couples get married and have children later in life than their parents and grandparents. Some couples do not marry. Many children live with a lone parent – more often than not, their mother – and many grow up with step-parents and half-siblings. The state should support commitment and ease the pressures of family life, but it will need to do so recognizing the great diversity of modern families.

It also needs to respect the diversity of what parents want. According to Catherine Hakim, the sociologist, women's attitudes to the balance between home and work can be divided into three broad categories. Around 20 per cent are 'home-centred', preferring to stay at home to care for their children; around 20 per cent are 'work-centred', prioritizing their careers; and around 60 per cent are 'adaptive'. These women want to work but also play a significant role at home caring for their children. Unsurprisingly, Hakim finds that more female graduates – the Anywheres – are likely to be work-centred, and more of those with lower qualifications – the Somewheres – are more likely to be home-centred.[145] Yet policy-makers, with their exclusively elite equality agendas, design policies that push mothers back into the workplace as soon as possible. Policies that support families and ease the pressure on parents, especially in the early years of a child's life, ought to reflect the diversity of parents' views and present their choices in a more neutral way. This way, parents, not ultra-liberal policy-makers, can decide what is best for their families.

Governments of left and right have made efforts to address the decline of community, but none has made much progress. Devolution to elected mayors who represent large, metropolitan areas has been a step in the right direction. But these mayoralties are relatively weak institutions, with limited resources and legal powers. Central government remains reluctant to cede control. And the nature of devolution – both to Scotland and Wales and to the city regions – has so far been messy and incoherent, with powers granted in an ad hoc, almost random manner.

David Cameron's 'Big Society' was a well-intended attempt to rebuild community, but it missed the point that community has lost many of its functions to the market and the state because the market and the state can do them better. The community might once have played a part in childbirth, for example, or the provision of palliative care, in days before universal health services. It might have played a greater part in the alleviation of poverty before the welfare state. But nobody wants important services to be provided by untrained generalists and amateurs today. And nobody expects inexpert citizens to play major roles in the governance of public services. The solution to the weakness of community is not to try to take things back to 'the way things were', to impose romantic amateurism on public services, or place burdens on people leading already complex lives.

The complexity of modern life, however, is why we need a revival of community. Without it, we will have too little trust and social capital, too few checks on government and big business, and not enough help and support for one another. But the key to the revival of community will be an understanding of our relational nature, and an appreciation that associations and institutions must have both purpose and empowerment to meet the challenges and complexity of today. To do that, we will need to overcome the assumptions and biases of ultra-liberalism, which has led us to our isolated and atomized modern condition.

The decline of trust

For all the reasons we have discussed so far, Britain is experiencing a crisis of trust. And this crisis is a real danger, because free and open societies require trust and reciprocity to prosper. This virtuous behaviour is reinforced by strong institutions, a healthy civil society, the rule of law, and customs and traditions that encourage us to do right by one another.

According to the *British Social Attitudes* survey, 54 per cent of us say that, generally speaking, people can be trusted.[146] This is apparently a better number than the survey has found in previous years. But scratch beneath the surface and we should be concerned. As we have just seen, trust is lower among people with lower educational qualifications and those with lower-paid jobs. People with degrees (64 per cent) and in professional occupations (63 per cent) are more likely than those with few or no qualifications (42 per cent) or in routine jobs (41 per cent) to believe that other people can be trusted. People who are more engaged in social activities – in leisure, cultural or sports groups, for example – are also more likely to trust others.[147]

According to the Edelman Trust Barometer, only 43 per cent of us have trust in Britain's institutions, a number lower than countries including the United States and the Netherlands, and below the global average. Trust in government and the political parties has plummeted. More than half of us think the way businesses operate is not in the public interest. And divisions caused by Brexit are deep and widespread. Sixty-nine per cent believe people have become angrier about politics and society since the referendum. One in six of us has fallen out with friends or family over Britain's departure from the European Union.[148]

The trust crisis is not tainting every British institution. Trust in the National Health Service, for example, has risen by two-thirds since the early 1990s. Support for the monarchy has increased over the same period. But trust in the police, the media and specific industries such as banking has fallen.[149]

The causes can be traced back to many of the issues we have already considered. We are experiencing the effects of entrenched inequality, the great stagnation, the abuse of unaccountable power, the decline of social mobility, the corrosion of institutions, a weakening sense of shared identity, and a loss of solidarity.

These are all consequences of the ultra-liberal policies Britain has pursued for decades. And the removal of real political choices by ultra-liberal politicians from our democracy has made matters worse. Successive governments of different parties – and combinations of parties – have ignored the majority view on subjects as diverse as tuition fees, the privatization of public services, immigration and Britain's membership of the European Union. This has been reinforced by the rise of the liberal technocrats, who have, as we discovered in chapter 1, promoted a programme that purports to be non-ideological but in truth reflects choices based on values and denies the validity of policies that challenge ultra-liberalism.

Politicians and activists have used other methods to shut down debate and get their way. Some perfectly legitimate views – on subjects like white British cultural identity – are portrayed as unacceptable. Some policy choices have been removed because politicians used unaccountable processes and mechanisms – such as supranational government, international law, quangos, independent central banks, and the courts – rather than win an argument in an open, democratic forum.

And there is another great change fuelling the trust crisis. As technology changes, and the traditional media declines, our ability to hold politicians, businesses and the powerful to account also declines. The proportion of us who get news from television has declined from 79 per cent to 66 per cent since 2013. Fifty-nine per cent of us relied on the print press in 2013, but now only 36 per cent of us do so. In contrast, 74 per cent of us check the news online, and 39 per cent use social media to find out what is going on.[150]

As newspapers themselves go online, some provide news and comment for free while others publish their content behind paywalls. Regardless of their business models, however, all newspapers face a severe financial challenge. Sales revenues are down, print advertising revenues have collapsed, and online advertising income will not fill the gap. Many people read news reports and opinion pieces on Facebook, rather than the original news organization's app or website, which means the advertising revenues never make it to the original source. According to Alan Rusbridger, the former editor of the *Guardian*,

Facebook took £20 million from his newspaper's projected advertising revenues in one year alone.[151]

The scale is extraordinary. Facebook has 2.3 billion monthly active users.[152] Between them, Facebook and Google account for 65.8 per cent of the UK digital advertising market, a percentage forecast to rise to 71.6 per cent in 2020.[153] As these giant web companies increasingly filter the news for us, we get the news they believe we want, leaving us in enormous echo chambers that confirm our biases and prejudices. Worse still, whistleblowers claim these companies sometimes abuse their power by selecting the news we see to suit their own interests and ideological, ultra-liberal beliefs.[154] By accident and design, what the public learns about how they are governed is becoming more skewed.

The changing nature of news and communication is revolutionizing political communication. Internet technologies, the sophisticated use of data and micro-targeting potential voters means political discourse is increasingly taking place in private and unobserved, away from sensible scrutiny.

When communication with voters is reduced to millions of different personalized micro-messages for individual people, for example, there can be little or no meaningful national conversation, and this will cause social and cultural divisions to grow even wider. It is harder to scrutinize what politicians are saying, and harder to hold them to account. And there is less persuasion. Instead, campaigners try to anger and inflame voters to encourage them to turn out and vote. If we could invent a model of political communication to favour populists and demagogues, this would be it. Without change, the trust crisis, and our wider cultural crisis, will only get worse.

This need not be inevitable, however. Understanding that diversity of values and interests is an inevitable fact of life, we need to learn to accept and tolerate our differences. But we should also be straining to create unity out of our diversity: a cohesive community. The problem is that ultra-liberal ideology is destroying the very things that bring us together. Instead of *e pluribus unum* – 'out of many, one' – we risk *e pluribus nihil*. Out of many, nothing.

4

REFLECTIONS ON
TWO REVOLUTIONS

As the economic and cultural crises rage, ultra-liberals have responded by burying their heads in the sand. On some issues, such as the decline of community, they appear not to have noticed at all. On others, like the crisis of the white working class, they seem to have noticed, but not responded. With some problems, like the regional economic disparities we face, their answers are to do more of the same: more market and more utilitarian sticking plasters, but no long-term solutions that challenge ultra-liberal logic.

In fact, regardless of the evidence of the crises around us, the ultra-liberal response has been to pursue more of the policies that caused the crises in the first place: more unchecked individualism, more market forces, more technocratic government, more supranationalism, more globalization, more immigration, more asymmetrical multiculturalism and more militant identity politics.

As public dissatisfaction with the status quo has become more apparent, some critics have begun to speak out. Writers like Edward Luce have blamed mainly economic factors for what he calls the retreat of Western liberalism. Robert Reich, the academic and former US Labor Secretary, believes capitalism needs to be saved from the imbalance between capital and labour. David Goodhart, Matthew Goodwin and Eric Kaufmann have all emphasized the cultural crisis to explain the changes we are witnessing in Western politics.

The truth is that the public's disaffection is driven by both economic and cultural changes, which relate to one another and reinforce one another in complicated ways. If public anger related only to economic deprivation, why have voters not turned leftward, demanding simply to tax the rich and spend more on redistributive policies? Why have they demanded, through the Brexit vote, a return to national self-government and, through opinion polls and election results, to reduce immigration? Why has there been a voter backlash in Britain, Europe and the United States, but not in Japan, a culturally homogeneous country that experienced austerity and stagnation long before we did?

Equally, however, it cannot be the case that the public is angry only about cultural change. If it was, why did anger increase following the financial crash and its aftermath? Why, given demographic change has been happening gradually over decades, did anger not increase before, or after an earlier recession? Why has the voter backlash included many black and minority ethnic voters, in Britain and elsewhere?

We cannot pretend that public anger with the way we are governed, or with the way our lives are changing, is caused only by either economic or cultural shifts. It is the combination of the two issues that causes the sense of 'relative deprivation' we discussed in chapter 3. As Roger Eatwell and Matthew Goodwin observe, relative deprivation

is intimately bound up with people's worries about the broader economic and social position of their wider group and how this compares to others in society. But it is also linked closely to people's specific concern that rapid demographic change is threatening their group, not only economically but also socially and culturally. These feelings of loss and worries about ethnic change fuel an animosity towards established politicians, who either failed to prevent this from happening or sometimes actively encouraged it.[1]

Further academic research backs up these conclusions. An international study published in 2019, for example, found that popular opposition to mass immigration is based on cultural concerns, not economic worries, but economic anxiety strongly influences perceptions of social decline.[2] Justin Gest, who researched opinions among the white working classes in Britain and America, agrees that a popular sense of injustice is driven by both economic insecurity and cultural loss.[3]

This presents us with an obvious problem. Fixing one crisis is hard enough, but fixing two is more than twice as difficult. This is because the obvious policy responses to one crisis might make the other crisis worse. The ultra-liberal response to declining economic growth, for example, would be to seek an even more flexible economic model. In practice, this would mean fewer workplace rights and protections, more workers exposed to global competition, and more immigration. It would not address the vast economic disparities and inequalities that exist in modern Britain, and it would compound, not cure, the cultural crisis we are experiencing. New solutions are therefore necessary, and if they are not forthcoming, voters will seek them in extreme and unscrupulous leaders.

Remember the warning we heard from Isaiah Berlin in chapter 1. 'I may not be seeking for a rational plan of social life, the self-perfection of a dispassionate sage', he said. 'What I may seek to avoid is simply being ignored, or patronized or despised, or being taken too much for granted – in short, not being treated as an individual, having my uniqueness insufficiently recognized, being classed as a member of some featureless amalgam, a statistical unit without identifiable, specifically human features and purposes of my own.'[4]

And remember, too, Robert Nisbet's warning. 'In an age of real or supposed disintegration', he wrote, 'men will abandon all truths and values that do not contain the promise of communal belonging and secure moral status. Where there is widespread conviction that community has been lost, there will be a conscious quest for community in the form of association that seems to promise the greatest moral refuge.'[5] Step forward extremists and populists.

The dangerous deceit of illiberal democracy

Ultra-liberals are quick to label their opponents as populists. But it is not always clear what they, or anybody else, mean by populism. Often it seems nothing more than a term of abuse, deployed when rivals have adopted policies that are popular, but with which ultra-liberals disagree. In turn, the insult is often worn as a badge of pride by those who claim to speak for the people.

Before we discuss what populism is, however, we first need to be clear about what it is not. Populism is often said to be fascist in character, but this is inaccurate and unhelpful. Fascism is an ideology based on nationalism, usually racist in nature, and offers an authoritarian third way between capitalism and socialism. Populism is more about how politics are conducted rather than the substance of what the populist promises. Fascists tend to be populists, but most populists are not fascists. And this is crucial: if we confuse populism for fascism, we will be unable to identify populists even when they stare us in the face.

In fact, populism can be found on both the left and right. And there is great diversity in the politics of the populists we see around the West. Italy's Lega and Five Star coalition government prioritized welfare payments for the poor; Donald Trump has cut taxes for the rich. Spain's left-wing Podemos wants more support for migrants and refugees; Austria's government wants to stop them reaching Europe in the first place. Geert Wilders says he opposes Islamic migration to protect Dutch liberal values; the increasingly authoritarian Viktor Orbán promises a new age of 'illiberal democracy'.

What these politicians and parties have in common is their style of politics. As Jan-Werner Müller notes, populists are always anti-elitist, but what differentiates them from mainstream politicians is that they are also anti-pluralist. They argue that diversity is division, and division is bad for the country. They claim that they – and only they – can truly represent the people. 'The core claim of populism is thus a moralized form of antipluralism', says Müller.[6]

The policy solutions they propose are always simple. And because the solutions are obvious, the reason governments have not implemented them already is that they must be corrupt, or serving other interests, such as minority groups or foreign powers. And these interests are powerful: if populists in government fail, the failure is normally blamed on dark forces – at home or abroad – that are working to undermine the interests of the people. This is one reason why conspiracy theories circulate so frequently among populists and their supporters.

All we need, populists tend to argue, is an honest and strong leader, untainted by the traditional party system and willing to speak for the people, who can remove institutional roadblocks to get things done. And this is where the gravest danger of populism lies. The logic of populism means the checks and balances required by liberal democracy – independent courts, a free media, parliamentary scrutiny, a strong civil society, rights and protections for minorities – come under attack.

In opposition, the attack is limited to rhetoric, but in government, populists use the power of the state to undermine these vital checks and balances. The media is brought under control. The judiciary is undermined. Party loyalists are given jobs that are normally reserved for apolitical bureaucrats. The government engages in what Müller calls 'mass clientelism', in which party supporters are openly rewarded with government funds.[7] Contracts are awarded to specific companies, grants made to favoured organizations, subsidies given to certain regions, and payments made to members of loyal social groups. And civil society is marginalized and suppressed. A rival network of more compliant organizations, often supported or funded by the government, is established to take its place.

Populism is therefore dangerous to liberal democracy. But that does not mean it is straightforwardly anti-democratic. In fact, populists often stand for a very pure form of democracy. They want to appeal directly to the people, and often favour the regular use of referenda. It is not democracy itself the populists are trying to attack but the liberal elements of liberal democracy.

We have already noted the paradox of liberal democracy: democracy needs to be limited and constrained if it is to survive. The paradox of populism is the mirror image: the populists' belief in unmediated democracy risks killing the institutions and rights that make democracy meaningful.

'Illiberal democracy' is not, therefore, a contradiction in terms, but it is a deceit, and a dangerous one. If civil society and its different groups are not free to scrutinize their governments, if the media cannot freely report the news, and if the courts cannot prevent abuses of power, we might as well give up electing our governments altogether.

Illiberal democracy and the radical left

The reinvention of Labour in recent years as a radical left-wing party has been an unambiguously populist story. As we have seen, populism can be found on the left as well as the right, and most of Labour's recent methods have been populist in nature.

Labour's politics turned decisively anti-pluralist. Within the party, the hard left captured the most important positions and institutions. Misogynistic bullying and anti-Semitism became rife as hard left activists intimidated their mainstream opponents. Moderate MPs were marginalized, isolated, and exposed to 'mandatory reselection', a phony exercise in local party democracy designed to impose hard left candidates on the wider electorate.

To their enemies outside the Labour Party, the hard left was even more brutal. Rival candidates reported intimidation and threats of violence unknown in modern British elections. Journalists who did not join the sycophantic praise of Labour's leadership found themselves excluded from events, booed and jeered by activists, and threatened with acts of violence. Jews were attacked as Zionist 'oppressors' of the Palestinians, international financiers who exploit the working classes, and supporters of Israel who cannot therefore be truly British.

Political violence was not only defended but promoted and put into practice. Jeremy Corbyn spent years associating with violent revolutionaries, including not only Hamas and Hezbollah in the Middle East, but the IRA in the United Kingdom. John McDonnell, Corbyn's shadow chancellor and de facto deputy, praised the 'bombs and the bullets' of the IRA, urged supporters to 'lynch' a female Conservative MP, who instead of naming he called 'the bitch', and praised rioters for 'kicking the shit' out of Conservative Campaign Headquarters during violent protests. The attack on CCHQ was, McDonnell said, 'the best of our movement'.[8]

There are other ways in which the radicalized Labour Party showed its disregard for the law. When one Labour MP told a party meeting, 'we should … bring an end to [the May] government with a general strike', she won a standing ovation from her audience.[9] Dawn Butler, a shadow minister, praised the hard left council that ran Liverpool in the 1980s for setting illegal budgets and saying it was 'better to break the law than break the poor'.[10]

This is all drawn from the populist playbook. All the country needs is a strong and honest leader, untainted by traditional party politics, who can break through the paralysed and corrupt system. Labour's simple solutions – based on the renationalization of industry, huge redistribution of wealth and massive public spending – had not been implemented before, their supporters said, because other politicians were in the pay of the City and Jewish speculators. Conspiracy theories – from the idea that the 'deep state' will keep Labour out of power, to the claim that Jewish families like the Rothschilds control mainstream politicians – still abound among Labour activists and advisers.

This all points to the main danger of populism: in opposition, populists attack the institutions of liberal democracy with rhetoric, but in government they use the levers of the state to expand their own power and destroy the checks and balances that get in their way. Opposition parties that are willing to intimidate critics and opponents, defend political violence as a legitimate tactic, and advocate illegal behaviour cannot be expected to respect the rules of liberal democracy when in power. For this reason, Labour's left-wing radicals are as dangerous to liberal democracy as any populist party, of right or left, anywhere else in the West.

Towards a communitarian correction

The change we need is not a wholesale rejection of the essential liberalism described in chapter 1. We must not undermine the values, norms and institutions that have made Britain – and the rest of the democratic world – successful, prosperous and free. It is the tenets of essential liberalism that made possible great discoveries, social progress and fairly distributed economic growth.

The change we need is a communitarian correction, a shift in policy to address the problems ultra-liberalism has caused, compounded or ignored altogether. This correction needs to return the 'people' and 'place' of policy to our politics. The decline of community and the decay of important institutions must be addressed. A cohesive society, based on an inclusive but still distinctly British culture and identity, must be built. And we must do these things as we work out how to achieve sustainable economic growth – and share its proceeds fairly – as technology and the global economy change at an increasing speed.

The answers do not lie with the populists of extreme left and right. A communitarian correction is not only feasible; it is entirely consistent with the philosophical traditions of both conservatives and social democrats.

The radical left, as we have seen, are illiberal democrats. They risk our democratic rights, and they risk impoverishing us with their economic policies. They reject the vital tenets of essential liberalism, and none more so than free markets. Their belief in commanding and controlling a complex economy – which is no more possible in an age of artificial intelligence than it was during the eras of Stalin or Chavez – risks disinvestment, a flight of capital, shortages, poverty and political corruption. It therefore risks depriving us of our ability to make simple decisions for ourselves and our families.

Yet while the radical left reject essential liberalism, they remain firm adherents to cultural ultra-liberalism. They might oppose the economic aspects of globalization, but they welcome the diversity caused by mass immigration. They might not support some of the economic policies of the European Union, but they support supranationalism as superior to national sovereignty and parliamentary democracy. They enthusiastically believe in militant identity politics, and practise asymmetrical multiculturalism without a second thought. In doing so, they undermine the very objectives the Labour Party was founded to deliver: solidarity and equality between the classes. For this reason, they would do nothing to resolve our cultural crisis. Indeed, they would make it far worse.

This does not mean the left is incapable of finding solutions to our crises. Not for nothing did Harold Wilson say Labour 'owes more to Methodism than Marxism': the party has had many philosophical influences since its formation in 1900. From the beginning, it was a coalition of working-class trades unionists and middle-class Fabians, socialists, social democrats and defecting radical liberals. What brought Labour's different interests together was their belief in collectivism, as opposed to the individualism of the Liberals and – sometimes but not always – the Conservatives.

As Marc Stears, a professor of political theory and former Labour adviser, says, what unites Labour's different intellectual strands is the belief that 'our personal relationships improve as our common life improves.'[11] This emphasis on the importance of the community should not mean the suppression of individual difference or opinion, and should not inevitably mean a levelling downwards. Instead, it should mean that the life of the individual is made better by improving the community he lives in.

This is the principle behind Labour's traditional support for progressive taxation, public services and the welfare state. But it also explains why previous generations of Labour politicians were unabashed in advocating apparently culturally conservative policies that protect local communities, like controlled immigration, and the nation itself, like the maintenance of strong defences. They understood that putting the community before the individual requires a willingness to define and defend the community. Of course a community requires inclusivity, but by definition it also demands exclusivity, because the rights and obligations that are conferred on community members cannot be granted to non-members. This is a lesson that, slowly but surely, some on the centre-left are beginning to learn. In Denmark, for example, the Social Democrats were elected in 2019 on a platform that included a promise to reduce immigration and ban the burqa and niqab in public places.

If Labour learned from its own history, and the tradition of Clement Attlee and Ernest Bevin, it would know, as the Blue Labour thinker Maurice Glasman puts it, that 'Labour is not the liberal party.' Instead, it needs to understand that ultra-liberalism undermines the sense of community that makes Labour's mission possible. The party must therefore concentrate, as Glasman says, on 'renewing relationships, institutions, [and] the practices of reciprocity, mutuality and solidarity' that have been undermined by decades of ultra-liberalism.[12]

So the left is capable of delivering the communitarian correction we need. But so too are conservatives. And this is a vitally important point. We must not leave it to populists and extremists to challenge ultra-liberalism for its failures. Nor should we want only the left or only the right to appreciate the need for a correction. As we have already discussed, an electoral dividing line that is cultural rather than socioeconomic will lead quickly to divisiveness, bitterness and a culture war from which we cannot escape. Instead, we should want both conservatives and social democrats to forge a new settlement, in which both sides respect the vital tenets of essential liberalism, but recognize too the need to move policy in a more communitarian direction.

Conservatism and liberalism

For those who are used to hearing that conservatism is about individualism, this might come as a surprise. But true conservatism – as opposed to the liberalism and libertarianism supported by many Conservative politicians – is not about how we can escape one another, but about how we relate to one another. It is not a theory that purports to have discovered a single truth about the world. It is a guide that relies on instincts, traditions and institutions. It respects reason, but is sceptical about the unlimited faith many liberal thinkers accord to reason. It is not about blind support for the market, but about community and good government. It is not about believing in the inevitability of progress, but neither is it about trying to hold back change. It is an approach to change that respects experience, and the customs, traditions and laws of a country.

The philosophical essence of conservatism is of course related to the conservative disposition. As Michael Oakeshott once described, conservatives tend to 'prefer the familiar to the unknown, the tried to the untried, fact to mystery, the actual to the possible, the limited to the unbounded, the near to the distant, the sufficient to the superabundant, the convenient to the perfect, [and] present laughter to utopian bliss'.[13]

But conservatism is not only a disposition: it is a philosophy. And as a philosophy it is about much more than resistance to change, as its critics often allege. Of course, it is cautious, sceptical and averse to grand theories, but as Edmund Burke articulated, it still embraces progress. 'A state without the means of some change', he argued, 'is without the means of its own conservation.'[14]

But what kind of change do conservatives believe in? Do they just believe in directionless change, a diluted form of whatever their more ideological opponents propose? In *The Constitution of Liberty*, Hayek complained that conservatism 'may succeed by its resistance to current tendencies in slowing down undesirable developments, but, since it does not indicate another direction, it cannot prevent their continuance'.[15] In *Phineas Finn*, Mr Monk, the fictional Radical MP, describes how, 'when we split among ourselves, as we always do, [the conservatives] come in and finish our job for us. It must be unpleasant for them to be always doing that which they always say should never be done at all.'[16]

Consider the varied actions of conservatives in government, and this criticism might seem fair. After all, how can the same philosophical tradition spawn the near-socialism of Harold Macmillan and the free market beliefs of Margaret Thatcher? To the uninitiated, conservatism might appear to be a mix of contradictions. Support for the market can undermine the community. Support for the community can restrict individual freedom. A fixation with freedom can mean hostility to government. Without government, there can be no order. And without order, there can be no market, no community and no freedom.

To unpick these contradictions, we need to understand the origins of modern conservative philosophy. Conservative thinkers like Burke agreed with liberal theorists about the importance of individual freedom, and they also believed that the proper authority for political power is popular sovereignty. They argued, however, that liberty is the happy consequence of a well-ordered society, in which citizens have obligations as well as rights. Inherited traditions and institutions protect us from an over-mighty state and encourage us to be good and trustworthy citizens. The law is written with experience and wisdom in mind, not abstract theory, and it evolves gradually through time.

Liberals, in their adherence to abstract theory, were guilty of divorcing social and political organization from its historical, cultural and institutional context. It was preposterous to theorize on the basis of a state of nature that never existed and indeed could never have existed. Every member of every generation is born into families, societies and nations, as members of institutions and keepers of traditions. It is the responsibility of every generation to maintain these institutions and traditions in good health. We are all born with obligations as well as rights, and those obligations are to past and future generations as well as our contemporaries.

This was more than a mere conceptual argument. Burke's best articulation of conservative philosophy was written just as liberal principles were being applied ruthlessly and violently during the French Revolution. Government should be grounded not in abstract ideas, he argued, but in experience. Traditions and institutions should be defended, as they encourage trust, reciprocity and good behaviour. Community life, and local civic organizations – the 'little platoons' – help us to help one another. There is an important role for the

state, but a strong society protects the individual from arbitrary government. Rights are not universal: citizens acquire them through gradual
legal change.

This is, of course, no wholesale rejection of the essential liberalism we
discussed in chapter 1. Roger Scruton, the contemporary conservative
thinker, says: 'conservatism began life more as a hesitation within liberalism than as a doctrine and a philosophy in its own right'. Explaining
its paradox, Scruton says, 'conservatism is about freedom, yes. But it
is also about the institutions and attitudes that shape the responsible
citizen, and ensure that freedom is a benefit to us all. Conservatism is
therefore also about the limits to freedom.'[17]

If this characterization of conservatism seems difficult to reconcile
with the beliefs of some modern Conservatives, that is because it is.
Those who believe conservatism is only about the aggressive pursuit of
greater individual freedom do not understand the conservative's commitment to others. Those who believe that markets provide perfectly
when left pure and untouched forget Adam Smith's lesson that, while
market economies generate wealth, they must be policed to protect us
from those who would game or abuse the system.

Conservatism is not liberalism, and it is about far more than the pursuit of individual freedom. But of course this remains an unsatisfactory
explanation of what it means to be a conservative. We need to consider
not only what conservatism is not, but what it is.

A human enterprise

Unlike some of its more ideological rivals, conservatism has no mas-
terplan or blueprint from which we can learn how to order society.
Instead, we have to explore a series of books and essays by conservative
thinkers, study the speeches of conservative statesmen, and examine
the application of conservative principles by governments if we want to
understand its real meaning.

Above all, to be a conservative is to reject abstract theory and ideology. It is to be sceptical about the inevitability of progress, and to be
mindful of the risks of losing what we already enjoy. It is to know that we
are not solitary individuals, but social animals who belong to families,
communities and nations. It is to believe we must cooperate as much

as compete with one another. It is to respect individuality and personal freedom, but also accept constraints on freedom and our obligations towards others. It is to understand that the culture and institutions we inherit represent knowledge and wisdom that we must preserve for future generations. It is to appreciate that we understand the world not from grand theory but from the experience of life as it is lived.

This rejection of ideology makes conservatism a uniquely human enterprise. Ideologists are engaged in a rebellion against human nature. They want to make the world something it is not, and something it can never be. They want to force people to conform to the expectations of their theories. And they hate the people – and the communities, traditions and institutions they hold dear – when they fail to conform. The ideologist, as Burke said of Rousseau, is 'a lover of his kind, but a hater of his kindred'.[18] Their utopias – socialist, fascist or liberal – are inevitably oppressive, because anybody who challenges their actions and principles must be irrational or nefarious. Ironically, given the ideologist's complaint that it is the conservative who opposes change, it is the ideologist who refuses to tolerate change, because his system, he believes, is built on perfect principles.

Respect for people as they really are, and respect for the significance of place in all of our lives, is therefore at the heart of conservatism. And because the conservative learns from life as it is lived, he understands that human values and interests are diverse and conflict. He understands that we are born into communities, but when communities decline or die, we seek out new identities and groups – not all of them constructive or positive – from which we can meet our need to connect and relate to others. The conservative understands that institutions are necessary to manage and reconcile conflicts of values and interests. And he recognizes that communities that are capable of uniting people – such as the nation – are necessary if we are to avoid smaller, exclusive communities based on more uniform identities and interests that pit us against one another.

Conservatism does not place one value above all others. Individual freedom alone does not trump our obligations to others, for example, when it comes to security or solidarity. Correspondingly, conservatism does not err too far in the opposite direction. It should not stifle or intrude upon our personal freedom. The whole is important, but so too is the individual, which is why conservatives have a respect for individuality and a tolerance for quirkiness and eccentricity. It is also why no true conservative is a puritan who tries to limit people's enjoyment of life.

This leads the conservative to a strong support for the essential liberalism described in chapter 1. He supports not only democracy but liberal democracy, complete with its checks and balances and rights to protect minorities. He supports a market economy, which allows for a fair and efficient allocation of finite resources, and lets citizens make decisions for themselves and their families. He supports a pluralistic society, in which common customs and institutions bind us together and help us to resolve conflicts of values and interests.

Of course, tensions can emerge between the conservative's commitment to a pluralistic society and his desire to maintain common customs and institutions. For example, the decline of Christianity and the growth of minority communities practising other faiths means the Church of England is no longer the unifying institution it once was. Although they might mourn the decline of a once-important institution, and look for other ways to bring the country together, this is a trend conservatives can accept as organic and inevitable. But sometimes the clash between pluralism and our common life can be problematic. A commitment to pluralism cannot mean the tolerance of behaviour and cultural practices that undermine our sense of shared identity. This is why conservatives abhor the moral relativism and asymmetric multiculturalism promoted by identity-obsessed left-liberals.

Conservatives worry when the boundaries of either negative or positive liberty are drawn too broadly. If negative liberty is drawn too broadly – if the core of personal freedoms that can never be touched is too large – then the strong and powerful can undermine the freedom and wellbeing of others. Think, for example, of the business left to freely abuse the rights of its workers. This is why conservatives understand that libertarianism is a danger.

But conservatives also know that if positive liberty is drawn too broadly – and government becomes too intrusive in trying to cure the social ills that it believes restricts the liberty of its citizens – it can undermine the core freedoms of us all. This could be in the form of excessive taxation, nannying public health policies, or the over-regulation of business. Too broadly defined, positive liberty can even, in extreme cases, undermine self-government and democracy itself. If a political movement, or state, asks people to think of themselves as simply part of a broader identity – such as a racial group, tribe or totalitarian party – the rights of the individual can quickly become subordinated to whatever is deemed to be the interests of the group.

The conservative recognition that human values and interests are many and conflicting is at the heart of its pragmatism. Accept this fact, and the desire to impose uniformity on the world appears to be ridiculous. Accept the role of customs and institutions in reconciling difference, and the universalism of ideologists becomes just as absurd. Accept our relational nature, and our innate desire to belong, and the rights-based individualism of ultra-liberalism looks completely wrongheaded.

Accepting that values are multitudinous raises further questions, however. The conservative cannot accept that every human value is as important as another. Nor can he accept that the balance between one value and another will remain the same throughout time and regardless of context. Individual freedom might be threatened most by an oppressive state in some contexts, but by anarchy in others. With the internet and modern technologies, privacy means something different in this century compared to the last, and that has repercussions for freedom, security and our sense of ownership.

The empiricism at the heart of conservatism inevitably throws up tensions, paradoxes and contradictions. And this can often lead to misunderstandings about conservatism and the intentions of conservatives. Sometimes, these misunderstandings are even made by people who call themselves conservatives. But the paradoxes of conservatism simply reflect the paradoxes and complexity of human society. Freedom is only possible when freedom itself is constrained. Our individualism is most endangered when the customs, institutions and obligations of community life are eroded. Capitalism is made possible by the bonds of family and community that capitalism itself can destroy.

Freedom and belonging

We have already seen that conservatives reject the concept of the state of nature and the individualistic theories that grow from it.

But this does not mean that conservatism is stiflingly communitarian or collectivist.

Conservatives revere individual freedom and understand that it needs to be guarded against many threats. If the state is too big, for example, it can become too intrusive. And this is not only the case with totalitarian regimes, but democracies too. Just think of how excessive taxation or regulation can restrict business activity, block new competitors from challenging incumbents, and affect employment and savings. But the state is not the only threat to freedom. Anarchy, or at least the dangers posed by the loss of order, can be just as big a worry. Think of how cybercrime is limiting the ability of the state to protect us from threats ranging from child abuse to terrorism.

Other individuals can endanger our personal freedom, through acts of criminality and anti-social behaviour, or by exploiting us as workers or consumers. Those who practise the most militant forms of identity politics want people to subordinate their own personalities and beliefs to their identities as ethnic minorities, for example, or homosexuals or women. Sometimes religious practices or cultural norms can infringe personal liberty. Think about the scale of so-called honour violence and female genital mutilation.

Personal freedom is precious because it gives us the dignity of being able to take decisions for ourselves and for our families. It grants us the control we desire to spend our time and money on our own priorities. It is closely bound up with our desire for recognition – the recognition we crave from others – because it means we are able to stand on our own two feet and provide for those we care most about. Without freedom we lose purpose, recognition and self-respect.

But freedom is only meaningful if we have the means to live our lives freely. If deep and entrenched inequality renders it difficult for even a small number of citizens to lead dignified and fulfilled lives, their liberty is illusory. If extreme inequality has similar effects for much larger groups, it can jeopardize the order upon which our freedom depends. If the freedom of the rich and the powerful needs to be constrained in some ways, for example through progressive taxation or by obligations placed on business, in order to reduce extreme inequality and make freedom meaningful for everybody, the conservative should agree to do so readily.

But not all constraints on freedom need to be imposed on us. We do not seek to escape social ties: we seek to belong. We form families, seek friendships and join clubs. We come together to solve collective problems: we create guilds, trades unions and charities. We forge traditions, follow customs and embrace our regional and national identities. We care for our relatives and help out our neighbours. We vote in elections and run for office. We participate in jury service.

We do not do these things because, back in the state of nature or at some later point, we chose, coldly and rationally, to do so. We do these things, in many cases, because we inherit our identities, customs and membership of groups. We are born into families and nations and faiths and churches, for example. But we also choose to join new groups: friendships, unions, charities, and so on. In the case of immigrants, they choose to join a country and, implicitly or explicitly, accept its ways of life. And we teach our children to do what we have done and generations before us have done: to maintain the traditions and institutions we inherit, and to join and form other groups too.

In different ways, we are encouraged, through membership of these groups and traditions, to curb our personal freedom. We make sacrifices for our children. We care for our parents. We give to charities. We pay taxes. We avoid behaviour that hurts or undermines the interests of others. We respect contracts, even when they no longer suit us. We observe laws, even when we disagree with them. At times of crisis, we are prepared to fight and maybe even die for one another.

We would not do these things if we were solitary beings. We do them because we are inherently social. We do not rationalize collective action, compromise or self-sacrifice. We do not, with each generation, learn to do them afresh. Often, as with our family commitments, we are simply born to do them. But often, we continue to do them through customs, rituals and traditions. We do them because we are encouraged, persuaded or even mandated to do so by institutions or laws. With wisdom and leadership, we add to our obligations and responsibilities, modify them, create new ones and discard those that no longer serve a purpose.

As Edmund Burke said, the limits on freedom must come from within us as well as without. The more we restrain ourselves, he argued, the less the state needs to restrain us. Our self-restraint, he wrote, comes from 'moral chains' we place on ourselves.[19] Liberty is not, he said, 'solitary, unconnected, individual, selfish liberty, as if every man was to regulate the whole of his conduct by his own will. The liberty I mean is *social* freedom. It is that state of things in which liberty is secured by the equality of restraint.'[20]

To ultra-liberals, many of these constraints are unnecessary encumbrances. They represent prejudice and irrationality. They are just old-fashioned ways of doing things. They stand in the way of progress. They stand in the way of individual freedom. They are hindrances that need to be removed, they believe, so we can all be set free.

But to conservatives, they are vital aspects of communal life. They teach us to respect one another, trust one another and care for one another. They help to build our confidence in fairness and reciprocity: they reassure us that if we do right by somebody else, they will do right by us.

The conservative knows that, paradoxically, without these limitations on freedom, freedom itself is in danger. Without the institutions and relationships that comprise community, there is nothing that lies between the individual and the state. There is nothing to protect us from overmighty government or oppressive rule. Big government becomes inevitable because where community withers, prosperity declines and social problems grow. Worse still, in the absence of a real community, people turn to populists, who promise to restore community in the name of nationalism, socialism and religious extremism.

Capitalism and community

Conservatism, then, is about a balance of freedom and belonging. And the struggle to find this balance is most often manifested in another tension within conservatism: the tension between capitalism and community.

Conservatives believe in free markets. Yes, capitalism can sometimes seem vulgar, with its mass manufactured goods, its relentless focus on growth and profit, and its obvious reliance on the self-interest of investors, makers, service providers and workers and customers. But like it or not, conservatives understand that our self-interest is one of the things that make the world go round. 'It is not from the benevolence of the butcher, the brewer or the baker that we expect our dinner', said Adam Smith, 'but from their regard to their self-interest.'[21] Winston Churchill agreed: 'The idea that all service is valueless unless disinterested is a fallacy', he argued. 'Mutually advantageous exchange of goods and services between communities is the foundation alike of the prosperity and peace of the world.'[22]

This is not an argument for ethics and morality to be removed from commercial exchange. True markets do not exist without governments and laws. Private property needs to be protected. Contracts need to be honoured. And the market itself must work fairly. Consumers are protected from fraud and faulty or dangerous products. Workers are protected from exploitation and poor working conditions. Smaller businesses and entrepreneurs are protected from incumbent firms rigging markets. 'A "free" market is not completely untrammelled', says the conservative writer and politician David Willetts, 'any more than a "free" man is outside all law and discipline.'[23]

Nonetheless, the free market is fundamental to a fair, peaceful and prosperous society. Adam Smith was the first to make this case from philosophical principles. We are all born, he argued, with an innate desire to better ourselves. 'An augmentation of fortune is the means by which the greater part of men propose and wish to better their condition.' This, he said, drives society as a whole to become more prosperous, because it is 'powerful enough to maintain the natural progress of things towards improvement, in spite both of the extravagance of government and of the greatest errors of administration'.[24]

Just as important was Smith's rejection of mercantilism, the idea that trade is a zero-sum game in which one side wins and the other loses. Instead, he argued, trade makes us all better off, because it allows us to specialize. As we become more specialized in our particular fields, our expertise, efficiency and productivity grow, and that is how we all become more prosperous. Because mercantilism sees wealth as an unchanging stock, it encourages the powerful to guard their own wealth jealously, while exploiting others. It can therefore lead to civil disorder at home, and confrontation between states and even war overseas. Because free trade encourages transactions across borders, and makes people more prosperous in different countries, it makes international cooperation more likely, and war less likely.

The genius of free markets does not end there. Instead of protecting producers, whose interests are concentrated and easy to represent to government, truly free markets protect the interests of all of us, as consumers. Instead of luxury goods and high-quality services remaining the preserve of the privileged few, free markets make things more widely available and more affordable for everybody. Instead of trying to set prices through a command-and-control economy, which as we have already noted is impossible, free markets allow pricing to determine the fair allocation of finite resources.

But free markets are about much more than efficiency. There is a strong moral case for them too. The free market is the means by which we all earn a wage, or businesses make a profit, and is therefore the means by which we care for our families, save for our pensions, buy our own homes and acquire our own possessions. In other words, it is about how we play a part, and earn a stake in, wider society.

And free markets go hand-in-hand with democracy. If prices were set by government and not the market, imagine what power that would put into the hands of the state. In a free market, wealth is peacefully and equitably transferred from citizen to citizen in a series of free choices based on individual wants and tastes and the quality of goods and services on offer. A command-and-control economy, as experience repeatedly shows us, can lead quickly to arbitrary government and oppressive rule. Private enterprise and private property, therefore, form the foundations of a strong civil society.

This does not mean that capitalism always works perfectly, or that conservatives believe in the infallibility of markets. Conservatives know that markets can fail, because traders do not have the information they need to agree the right price for a product. Businesses might cause damage or harm for wider society – to the environment, perhaps, or the labour market – that is not reflected in their own costs. The market might not accurately reflect distortions caused by subsidies and other forms of support given to some businesses by their governments. Conservatives know, then, that governments need to be prepared to intervene to correct market failures, regulate business activity, and ensure – through education and training, infrastructure policies, tax and regulation – that Britain's economy remains internationally competitive.

And as we saw in chapter 2, fundamental changes in the way the economy works are challenging our views about the free market. Globalization, and the changing nature of production networks, is making international economic competition more individual. The result is that the world's super-rich are getting richer, the world's poorest are climbing out of poverty, but the West's working classes are being squeezed. The idea that increasing specialization is making all of us richer is ringing increasingly hollow with many Western workers who find themselves earning less than they did a decade ago. Similarly, new technologies are changing the entire shape of our economies, and as artificial intelligence develops, the pace of change will only grow faster. Meanwhile, China's mass industrial espionage and America's protectionism and trade wars indicate a worrying new trend of neo-mercantilism.

Conservatives also understand that capitalism relies upon non-market relationships and institutions – families, public services, wider society – to survive. And, as we have already seen, unchecked capitalism can undermine and even destroy these vital public goods. Some of Britain's greatest economic and social challenges lie in communities that have suffered rapid deindustrialization, the decline and death of major civic institutions and their replacement with big government. Knowing that, once lost, institutions and traditions are difficult to revive or replace, a conservative should always guard against the most destructive tendencies of capitalism. He should also strive, not to rebuild exactly what has been lost, but to restore human and social capital, and infrastructure and institutions, in the forgotten places that have lost them.

Conservatism demands a balance between capitalism and community. It recognizes that we need to cooperate as well as compete. It knows there is more to life than Amazon and eBay, Primark and Lidl, or Facebook and Twitter; there is a need for family, community and culture. It knows too that there is more to life than disruption and destruction, there is a need for continuity and conservation. And it knows that capitalism always has within it the power to destroy the social foundations upon which it, and everything else, rests.

Equality and solidarity

Few politicians and thinkers believe, in legal terms, that a country's citizens should be anything other than equal. We are equal before the law, we have equal voting rights, and we all entitled to run for elected office. We are not equal, however, when it comes to income or wealth.

The proposition that government should ensure economic equality is an enticing one. It sounds so fair and so simple. But it is wrought with practical and moral problems.

First, it destroys incentives to work. If the parents of one family both go out to work, earn decent salaries and save hard, they might have more money than the family next door. That family might choose not to work, and live off benefits, or they might choose to work but squander their earnings through spending that leaves them with nothing saved up for a rainy day. At what point does the egalitarian say that the two families' incomes or savings should be equalized? And what would that do to the incentives for families across the country who want to work hard and build up their savings?

Any attempt to equalize incomes would destroy the ability of markets to price according to the value created by the entrepreneur or worker. If one worker earns more than another it is because his employer has calculated that he will add more value to the company's product or service. Attempts to artificially increase earnings risk distorting the market by increasing costs or making it harder to recruit talented workers, thereby making companies less productive and less competitive. Attempts to equalize incomes through punitive taxation will, as experience teaches us, lead to brain drains and flights of capital to other countries.

It is not only incomes egalitarians are interested in equalizing, however, for they are also keen to equalize wealth. Here, the same moral and practical questions apply. Why should the prudence of one family be punished, and the extravagance of another be rewarded? How could equalizing wealth be achieved without scaring successful businesses and investors to other countries? These problems are difficult enough, but any attempts to equalize wealth come up against the reality of human life. For obvious reasons, younger people have less accumulated wealth than older people, but, historically, pensioners have tended to have lower incomes than working-age people. Students tend to have lower incomes than anybody else, but they are studying for degrees that they hope will give them the chance to earn higher salaries in future. How does the egalitarian determine what is a fair and equal income for them?

The pursuit of economic equality, as we know from history, can end up destroying civil society, democracy and freedom. Any state that tries to bring about equality of income or wealth places enormous powers in its own hands. It usurps the market and sets prices. It removes control from people's day-to-day lives. Because it undermines economic growth, it prioritizes the redistribution of existing wealth rather than helping it to grow. And inevitably, it brings the state into conflict with two of the most important institutions in a free society: private property and the family.

The private ownership of property is fundamental to a strong civil society. It gives us security against dangers like ill health and redundancy, and it gives us a stake in our community. Widely spread, the private ownership of property provides stability and continuity, and protects us against the dangers of arbitrary and oppressive government. But private property inevitably means differences in the wealth enjoyed by different individuals and families. There can be no equalization of wealth, therefore, as long as the private ownership of property is permitted.

Similarly, the pursuit of economic equality creates a conflict with the family. This is because, while we are all born into families, we are not born with equally talented or equally wealthy parents. Over the course of their lives, parents earn and accumulate different levels of wealth. And of course they have different levels of diligence, education and intelligence. This brings advantages to some children that are not available to others. This is why egalitarians are often at best ambivalent about the family, if not hostile. Some of the most extreme governments the world has known have tended to undermine families for this very reason.

The conservative understands, then, that the pursuit of exact equality is a fool's errand. It goes against the grain of human instinct, and it is both economically and socially ruinous. It is a good example of how, when the definition of positive liberty is drawn too broadly, it can undermine the core individual freedoms granted by essential liberalism. And inequality itself is not simply an injustice to be tolerated: in fact, it can be a force for good. Capitalism needs some inequality to function. Not everybody deserves the same income and wealth: how much we earn and accrue should depend on our talent and hard work. It is our determination to compete with others and provide more for our families that drives us to work, invest and innovate.

But conservatism demands cooperation between citizens, not just competition, and the conservative cannot be relaxed about inequality regardless of its extent. If conservatives believe that private property is so important to the individual, the family and society at large, then they should want it to be within reach for more people. As we have already seen, entrenched inequality can make a mockery of the idea of individual freedom and undermine the order upon which a successful society is based.

Yet as we saw in chapter 3, as a result of huge structural changes in the world economy, and problems that are particular to the British economy, working- and middle-class people are being squeezed hard. There is deep income inequality, and an asset divide that will only grow wider. The unspoken promise of Western liberal democracy – that there will be consistent economic growth and its returns will be shared fairly – is breaking down.

And history teaches us, when economic growth fails or when societies become too divided, politics can become ugly very quickly. Right-wing populists pick on minorities and left-wing populists turn to class warfare. A breakdown of order – the thing the conservative fears most – does not necessarily mean coups, riots or revolutions. It can come gradually, imperceptibly, through legal, political and social changes made in full public view.

So the conservative may be comfortable with the existence of limited inequality, but he must not be tolerant of inequality when it is extreme, entrenched or widespread. Conservatives should therefore be as interested in solidarity with their fellow citizens as they are in simply respecting their freedom. This was the lesson taught us by Benjamin Disraeli, when he warned conservatives not to accept Britain's slide into 'two nations' of rich and poor. Disraeli was prepared to take on the interests of the rich and powerful – and restrict their freedom as investors, employers and landlords – in the name of protecting workers in factories and improving working-class housing. Conservatives today must understand that while equality itself is no desirable goal, solidarity with our fellow citizens is, and to act in this manner will require us to challenge and limit the freedom of the rich and powerful.

Inclusion and exclusion

Solidarity, however, requires community. And community requires a common identity. For conservatives understand that community is not based on the brotherhood of man, the unrealistic universalism of ultra-liberals and other ideologists, but on human relationships.

Those relationships are forged in the day-to-day reality of life. They are made in families, friendships and in local communities. They grow in institutions like trades unions and churches and charities. They deepen through traditions like Bonfire Night, Hogmanay and Remembrance Sunday. They stem from collective memories of tragedy, like the Hillsborough disaster, and great pride, like Britain's role in defeating fascism in the Second World War. They are helped along by shared moments from royal wedding street parties to discussing the football and BBC dramas in the office. They contribute towards the tacit commitments we make to one another, and build an expectation of duty, trust and reciprocity.

These relationships comprise millions of individual, family, professional and social interactions. They are based on culture, history and identity. And they add up, in their totality, to our national identity. A man might identify as a proud son of Leeds, a Yorkshireman, an Englishman, as British, a Hindu, somebody with Indian ancestry, who supports England at football and India at cricket. He might also identify himself through his job, his family, and his hobbies and interests. We all have multi-layered identities, but at the apex of them all is our national identity. No political unit in the history of mankind has been so successful in building the solidarity required for its citizens to support redistribution, welfare spending and free-to-use public services, nor to support the peaceful transfer of power from one side to another after elections.

Attempts to define 'Britishness' have always failed because they have made claims to values that are supposed to be uniquely British, yet completely inclusive. But as we have seen repeatedly, values conflict all the time, so there can be no such thing as definitively British values. Of course, there are values we as a society admire, and there are values we can agree have no place in Britain. Cultural norms that subjugate women, or disrespect people because of their sexuality or ethnicity, should be rejected because they offend our sense of equality and justice. Those who seek social, economic or political power through intimidation and violence should be confronted and punished, because they disrespect the dignity of others. Just because we accept that values are multitudinous and conflicting does not mean we have to accept that all values are equally valid. We should defend – in muscular fashion – the values our society has chosen to prize.

Nonetheless, a nation cannot be reduced to concepts as vague as a 'sense of fair play' and a belief in democracy. Nor can it be defined by a commitment to its most popular institutions, such as the BBC and the NHS. Institutions matter, but our national identity is based on a long and messy story that takes in our history, our shared stories and our collective experiences, as well as the institutions that bind us together.

Britishness is therefore about countless things. It is about the cup final at Wembley and the cricket at Lord's. Wimbledon and the Six Nations. Bonfire Night and Hogmanay. The Last Night of the Proms and the Royal Opera House. Coronation Street and Eastenders. The Trooping of the Colour, the Edinburgh Tattoo and royal weddings, babies and jubilees. Yes, it is the BBC and the NHS. But it is also the Oxford-Cambridge Boat Race. Remembrance Sunday. The abolition of slavery. The London Marathon and the local fun run. The 2012 Olympics. Monty Python. The Queen and the Commonwealth. Isambard Kingdom Brunel and Sir Tim Berners-Lee. It is haggis, neeps and tatties and steak and kidney pie. The balti and chicken tikka masala. A pint of bitter and a G and T. The local pub and Saturday night TV. 1066 and all that. 1966 and little since. Magna Carta and the Glorious Revolution. The Act of Union. The mother of parliaments and rowdy PMQs. Milton and Shakespeare. Elgar and Holst. Henry VIII. The King James Bible. The Beatles and the Stones. Sir Mo Farah. Mo Salah. The white cliffs of Dover, the Scottish Highlands, and the Brecon Beacons. St Paul's Cathedral. The village church. A pork pie and Cheddar cheese. A Devonshire cream tea. Nelson and the Royal Navy. Roundheads and Cavaliers. Mackams and Geordies, the Wars of the Roses, and local rivalries that go on and on. The honest bobby. The rule of law. Rorke's Drift. The Somme. Dunkirk. The Battle of Britain and El Alamein. Standing alone. Blood, sweat and tears.

Of course, it is possible to dispute some of the contents of this list. It is far from exhaustive and readers will no doubt have many other examples to add. And yes, it presents a rose-tinted view of Britain's national story. Britain did not quite stand alone in 1940: the Empire stood with us. Along with other nations, we participated in the slave trade before its abolition. And there are other moments of shame in our history, such as the Gordon Riots of 1780 and the Amritsar Massacre of 1919. But that is not what matters. All nations have good and bad in their histories. These stories make us who we are.

We might tell ourselves different variations of these stories, and some of us might choose to emphasize some elements of Britishness over others. Some people love village life; others enjoy urban culture. Some want the freedom to be left alone; others want to join clubs and volunteer. Some enjoy high culture; others enjoy life's simpler pleasures. A refugee might love Britain for its tranquillity. An immigrant might appreciate the opportunity to educate his children and build a future for his family. Many of us simply take these things for granted. There are many ways to take pride in Britain and feel British, but what matters is that our national identity is derived from stories, traditions and institutions – and a reverence of particular places – that are uniquely ours.

Inevitably, this makes our national identity – like others – exclusive. Because society is based on our shared identity, society is also exclusive. Societies grant rights, privileges and protections to their members, and refuse them to non-members. This ought to be axiomatic: if a society granted rights, privileges and protections to anybody, those benefits end up a reality for nobody. The society would cease to function.

Remember what we discussed in chapter 1. As Jonathan Haidt, the moral psychologist, says, humans are both 'selfish and groupish'. We are 'profoundly altruistic', he argues, 'but that altruism is mostly aimed at members of our own groups'.[25] Multiple academic studies confirm that as societies become more diverse, trust, solidarity and support for redistributive policies all fall.[26] And remember what we discussed in chapter 3. Liberalism has a warped view of citizenship, which is transactional, not relational. Its worldview is individualistic and universalistic: it fails to understand the significance of our relationships, traditions, institutions, cultures and treasured places. In particular, it is hopelessly blind about the importance of nation.

The conservative understands that this is wrong. For a society to function it must, to some degree, be exclusive. Not everybody should be allowed to join, and it should be up to the society itself who is allowed to join. But that does not mean a society should not also be inclusive. Every member should be a full member, with equal rights. Discrimination against anybody on the basis of a disability or illness, or their gender, race, sexuality or social class should be prohibited. Everybody should have the ability to go as far as their talents and hard work will take them. And newcomers should be welcomed and helped to play a full and constructive role in their new chosen home.

This is why conservatives understand that immigration must be controlled, and immigrants should be expected to integrate and accept the laws and ways of life in their new country. They need to get to know and understand the country's long story, and the institutions and customs that have grown out of it. They need to know and accept the law of the land. They must also respect the fact that many of Britain's customs and institutions have grown out of its Christian and European heritage. But conservatives also need to respect the fact that once a society has decided to accept migrants, there is an important responsibility to be inclusive. Newcomers should be welcomed and respected. They should be protected from discrimination. And they should be given help and support to settle down and integrate. If conservatives believe community and nation are fundamental to a good life and a strong society, they must ensure every citizen is included in both.

Challenges for conservatives

Conservatism, then, is about managing and maintaining a balance between competing values and interests. We need to find the right balance between freedom and belonging. We have to understand the relationship between capitalism and community. We can accept some inequality, but need to prevent it becoming entrenched. We must accept that society by definition must exclude outsiders, but it must also be inclusive for all its members. The precise nature of the balance we strive to find, and the means by which we maintain it, changes constantly as the world around us also changes.

This recognition that values and interests clash, and this adamant rejection of ideology, means conservatives take an unashamedly empirical view of the world. This can sometimes prompt accusations that conservatism means nothing at all. To the ideologist, who sees the need for progress to a fixed end-point, who believes in unchanging universal principles, and who carries with him prescriptive ideas of how to govern, conservatism can seem empty. But as we have seen, ideologies are inherently flawed and dangerous. They try to force people to conform with their theories of human nature, and they become oppressive when people do not do so. Fascism, communism and socialism have all committed this sin, and so, increasingly, does ultra-liberalism.

But just because conservatism lacks a grand plan, and makes no singular timeless and universal claim about the world, it is not true to say it lacks a coherent body of thought. Nor does it mean conservatism makes no moral demands of us. Because community is fundamental to a strong society, conservatism insists we accept our obligations towards others. Because customs and traditions help to build a shared identity and trust, we have to accept our responsibility to nurture them and hand them on to future generations. Because we depend on one another, we have to accept curbs on our individual freedom. Conservatives understand that through our many different identities – in families, in the workplace, in groups, communities and the nation – we have many different roles. Fundamental to all of these roles is our duty towards others.

In several important instances, however, the conservative's empiricism needs to be applied more thoroughly. This is because conservatism itself can sometimes veer towards the ideological. To avoid that, we have to challenge several core assumptions often made by conservatives.

Chief among these challenges is the conservative's attitude towards personal freedom. We have already considered the reasons why conservatives revere individual liberty. But we have seen, too, how freedom is only one value that needs to be balanced against others. When freedom becomes the pre-eminent single value for somebody who considers himself a conservative, he has lost sight of the meaning of conservatism. When conservatives forget about solidarity, they promote policies – from the marketization of certain services, to an obsession with reducing taxes – that grant greater freedom for the fortunate at the expense of the less fortunate. When they forget about community, they sometimes permit capitalism to destroy the public goods upon which we all rely. When they forget about customs and institutions, they lose the glue that binds us together.

Conservatives can be complacent about the power of the 'invisible hand' of the market and of society. It is of course true that neither the market nor society can be planned or directed by the state. We live in a 'spontaneous order' brought about by the billions of decisions made by millions of citizens, most of whom will never meet one another, or their political leaders. Our civilization is the happy outcome of countless human acts, errors, tragedies and triumphs. But this does not mean that either the market or wider society should be a free-for-all. The conservative recognizes that laws are needed to govern both. Markets can only work where the rule of law guarantees contracts, and society can only function where the rule of law guarantees our rights and freedoms.

The conservative ought to understand, too, that there are communities in crisis where the invisible hand has not come to the rescue. As we have seen already, the communities that struggle the most are those where businesses and investors have fled. In these forgotten places, economic and social decline have gone hand-in-hand. There is, in these communities, still a sense of solidarity with one another, and a hope that things can get better. But the conservative cannot simply wait for the invisible hand to work its magic. He must establish how the social capital, human capital, infrastructure, institutions and investment – in other words, the public goods that make communities and economies strong – can be restored.

Conservatives also need to reassess their thinking about community. Too often they debate the correct balance between the individual and the state. But this way of thinking inevitably leads us towards a hopelessly atomized society, consisting of isolated, insecure and untrusting individuals, governed by a state that grows and grows as it responds to social and economic crises caused by the decline of community. As we have seen, in this atomized condition, people are likely to seek out new forms of belonging and community through extremism and populism.

Strong communities, on the other hand, help us to help one another, and protect us from the dangers of an overmighty state. Yet it is undeniable that our sense of community has been undermined. Some of the community's roles have been taken by the state, and some by the market. Economic and social changes have made us more remote and untrusting. And some of the customs and institutions that are vital to strong communities have not just been neglected but attacked by those in positions of power. Sometimes those attacks have come from conservatives, who have seen certain customs and institutions either as barriers to freedom and progress, or as vested interests that need to be confronted.

Too often, when conservatives have shown an interest in reviving community, they have sought to use community organizations as a cheap alternative to services provided by the state. But this is the wrong way to look at things. A strong community will reduce demand for services provided by the state, because a strong community enjoys a stronger economy and fewer social problems. The 'little platoons' revered by Burke, the family, the church, the groups we join, all add up to a strong society, but they are not an alternative to the state. They complement the state, and they protect us from the state. But customs and institutions can only survive if they continue to serve a purpose. If the state or the market performs a function better than the little platoons, the little platoons will wither. The conservative needs to seek balance between community, market and the state, and needs also to revive community not by trying to restore what once was, nor by encouraging a romantic amateurism that cannot compete with the scale and efficiencies of market and state, but by forming and reforming customs and institutions with purpose and relevance to life now and in the future.

Foremost among the institutions respected by conservatives is the family, our most basic and important natural social unit. The family has existed, in different shapes and forms, throughout history, and in every different kind of society. It is where we are nurtured, at our most vulnerable, and where we are taught how to behave in wider society. It is where we learn language, and discover essential social skills like manners and respect, and cultural knowledge, such as traditions and norms. We are born into families and emerge from them capable of participation in community life and forming families of our own.

It is undeniable that the nature of family life is changing. Some conservatives regret this fact, and seek to do more to protect what they call the 'traditional' family. They point to research suggesting that children brought up by both of their biological parents in the same household fare better than those who do not. But there is no research that proves it is better for children to be brought up in unhappy, angry and even violent families. In fact, international studies show that children exposed to these unfortunate relationships suffer behavioural problems and replicate the actions of their parents in later life.[27] It is no good trying to force people against their wishes to remain in unhappy and troubled relationships. Conservatives should support the family, and the commitments we make to one another, but if they want to support the family, conservatives need to support it in all its shapes and sizes.

Ever present in all these dilemmas and challenges is the conservative's attitude towards the state. Many modern conservatives express a distaste and even hostility towards government action. Their goal is to reduce the size of the state, and reduce public spending further and further. Yet while conservatism is wary of the big state, and the dangers it presents to individual freedom and community life, conservatives believe there is an important role for government to play.

Edmund Burke argued that government is 'a contrivance of human wisdom to provide for human wants. Men have a right that these wants be provided for by their wisdom.'[28] Clearly this should include the legal frameworks needed to maintain order in society and trust in markets, and the power to enforce both. But if conservatives accept that community has been undermined by capitalism and big state interventions, acknowledge that deep inequality, particularly wealth inequality, disadvantages too many people, and the invisible hand is failing to address these problems, there must be a role for government in providing the remedies we need. This does not mean that the conservative ought to believe that individuals, families, businesses and communities should become permanently dependent on state subsidies. But it is naïve to believe that the solution to many entrenched social and economic problems is simply for government to withdraw. Where human and social capital are as depleted as they are in many communities, the state has a crucial role to play in recovery. Ultra-liberal ideologists may refute this, but conservatives do not.

Conservatism and change

Because conservatism is not an ideology, it can sometimes overlap with other bodies of thought. In accepting the tenets of the essential liberalism described in chapter 1, conservatives can find themselves on the side of liberals as they defend our core freedoms and the institutions that protect them. In accepting that there needs to be a balance between negative and positive liberty, conservatives sometimes find themselves in agreement with social democrats.

This does not mean conservatives go 'all in' with the fashionable ideas of the time. Conservatives accept that political life must have balance, which is why 'trimming' has been an important tradition for them for centuries. Trimming is sometimes interpreted to mean compromise and accepting prevailing wisdom, but in fact it is the opposite. The conservative tradition of trimming, first articulated before Burke in the seventeenth century by Lord Halifax, meant seeking balance by weakening the stronger side, rather than joining it. As Ian Gilmour wrote, 'in the past, Conservatives "trimmed" in favour of the state and against laissez faire. Today, they "trim" against the state and in favour of the individual. And both today and in the past, the purpose of their "trimming" was … to achieve balance.'[29]

But this does not mean the old familiar charge – that conservatism is simply resistance to change – is true. Of course, conservatives respect what has endured. This is down to their respect for real-world experience and wisdom, and their rejection of abstract theory. The knowledge conservatives revere is transferred through customs and institutions, many of which are centuries old. Conservatives respect what has endured because it has stood the test of time. But conservatism accepts change as inevitable, and necessary.

Also unfair is the related accusation that conservatism is simply relativism: a disposition to defend any existing order. Consider Burke's different reactions to the American and French revolutions. The latter, he contended, was the result of abstract political thought and a rejection of the political and social context in which the revolutionaries wanted to govern. It overturned institutions, and the rights it promised could not be upheld or enforced. It was therefore doomed to failure and risked upheaval, violence and the loss of the rights already enjoyed in France. The earlier American Revolution, he argued, was different. The US Constitution and Bill of Rights represented the protection of rights and privileges once guaranteed but then abandoned by the British when they taxed Americans without allowing political representation. The American Revolution was built on the common law, not abstract principles, and was the latest step in the long evolution of legal rights from Magna Carta onward. It was therefore the sort of change a conservative should support.

So conservatism is not about resisting change, nor even reacting or acquiescing to change dictated by others. But what kind of change do conservatives believe in? Without an ideology, without a fixed end-point that conservatives can try to reach, it can sometimes feel uncertain. Conservatism can sometimes feel as though it is without direction, and this is why its practitioners are accused of cynicism, or seeking power for its own sake.

In fact, conservatives do have guiding principles when it comes to change. Disraeli, echoing Burke, made the distinction between change 'carried out in deference to the manners, the customs, the laws, and the traditions of a people', and change carried out 'in deference to abstract principles, and arbitrary and general doctrines'.[30] The former was acceptable to him; the latter was not.

Michael Oakeshott criticized the 'rationalist' and his attitude to change.

> To the rationalist, nothing is of value merely because it exists (and certainly not because it has existed for many generations), familiarity has no worth, and nothing is to be left standing for want of scrutiny. And his disposition makes both destruction and creation easier for him to understand and in engage in, than acceptance or reform ... He does not recognise change unless it is a self-consciously induced change, and consequently he falls easily into the error of identifying the customary and traditional with the changeless.

The rationalist, who sounds very much like many an ultra-liberal, claims the character of the engineer. But 'the assimilation of politics to engineering is ... the myth of rationalist politics.'[31] In other words, society must change, but it must take care to preserve its customs and

institutions as it does so. Change can be gradual, organic and sometimes even incidental, but it must not be destructive. Yet destruction is
what ideological change often brings.

Not all customs and institutions deserve to survive, however. They
need to continue to serve a purpose to wider society, and if they do not,
then naturally they wither. Any customs and institutions that require
coercion of some form to continue – so-called 'closed shop' trade union
agreements, for example, or religious or cultural honour codes that are
policed violently – clearly lack legitimacy. But some customs and institutions need support and encouragement, both to get off the ground in
the first place and to survive thereafter. Conservatives tend to accept
this about older social institutions like the family, but they need to
accept it too about the need for new institutions that can rebuild communities where economic and social capital have been lost.

This is an important point, because conservatives accept that the
things that matter to a community – knowledge, trust, customs, institutions, commerce and so on – can be lost. Progress is not inevitable, and
neither are continuity and stability. If chaos and anarchy have existed in
the past, then they can exist in the future. If it was institutions and social
and economic capital that brought order and prosperity to a place, then
the loss of those same things might cause the loss, once again, of order
and prosperity.

Once we accept that progress is not inevitable, and what we already
enjoy cannot be taken for granted, then we become more sceptical
about change. And it becomes more understandable, and more acceptable, to resist it. Working out what change to resist, what to manage,
and what to deliberately bring about is therefore a complicated task.

When conservatives get this judgement wrong, they live to regret it.
Their failure, at the turn of the twentieth century, to introduce a basic
state pension in line with conservative values did not stop the pension's
introduction. It just meant Lloyd George introduced it a few years later,
and he decided the pension should be non-contributory. Partly thanks
to that foundation stone, Britain's modern welfare state remains non-
contributory, which is a source of regret to many conservative welfare
reformers. The same can be said about the failure of conservatives to
overturn early trades union court rulings, which led to a radicalization
of the unions and poor industrial relations.

Conversely, when conservatives have judged that change is right, inevitable or both, and embraced it, they have rarely regretted doing so. By embracing change, they have been able to shape it, and preserve the things that matter most. From the emancipation of the Catholics in the nineteenth century, and the extension of the electoral franchise, the Factory Acts and the universal provision of free education, until modern changes such as council house sales and the introduction of equal marriage, conservatives have been behind changes that have benefited minority groups and society as a whole.

The conservative mission is to improve the world, without trying to perfect it. This is why conservatives support change that preserves what is good and does not try to change or confront human nature. Ideologists try to force people to conform with their theories. Conservatives accept people as they are and work with them accordingly.

One Nation

This difference is vital. The determination of the ideologist to make the world something it is not makes him divisive. To the ideologist, you are either with him or against him. Stand in the way of progress towards his objectives, or question or challenge his methods, and you become his enemy. In contrast, because conservatism is not ideological, one of its main advantages is that it can avoid division.

This desire to avoid division is where the conservative tradition of 'One Nation' originates. Contrary to popular assumption, the 'One Nation' name did not quite originate with Disraeli, although its spirit did. In his novel, *Sybil*, he describes 'two nations', of rich and poor, 'between whom there is no intercourse and no sympathy; who are as ignorant of each other's habits, thoughts and feelings, as if they were dwellers in different zones, or inhabitants of different planets; who are formed by a different breeding, are fed by a different food, are ordered by different manners, and are not governed by the same laws.'[32]

It was Stanley Baldwin who later picked up this theme. 'We stand for the union of those two nations of which Disraeli spoke two generations ago', he said, 'to make one nation of our own people which, if secured, nothing else matters in the world.'[33] A generation later than Baldwin, a group of Conservative MPs including Edward Heath, Iain Macleod and Enoch Powell wrote a famous pamphlet under the 'One Nation' banner.[34] The tradition was not about the left or right of conservatism but the application of conservative principles to solidarity and the need to lift the condition of the people.

Even here, however, conservatives need to address important criticisms. The first is whether all of this is really true. 'One Nation' is a handy label that implies moderation, and it conjures romantic feelings for many conservatives, but is it not true that conservatives themselves have often divided the country? Look back to the 1980s, and this criticism feels valid. But the Conservative Party has tended to be most divisive when it is most ideological, and not conservative at all. However vital many of the 1980s reforms were, the Thatcher governments were radical and, from an economic perspective, mostly ultra-liberal. Conservatism understood in its true sense – always seeking a balance between competing values and interests – does not make this mistake.

And what about Brexit? Nobody can deny that Britain's decision to leave the European Union divided the country. But what the referendum showed – with more people voting for Brexit than had voted for anything else in British history – was that Britain's membership of the European Union had been divisive for many years. There is no unifying way of delivering Brexit, because in the end the decision was, and remains, binary. Britain is either a member of the European Union or it is not. The best thing a conservative can do, therefore, is to accept Britain's independence from the EU, and to strive to reunite the country and balance its competing values and interests in other ways.

The second criticism of One Nation is that because conservatism accepts the inevitability of inequality, it cannot be a unifying force. But as we have seen, it is the ideological pursuit of absolute economic equality that can become divisive and oppressive. Inequality is not only an inevitable fact of life; it is welcome, because it rewards hard work and responsible behaviour, and encourages enterprise and innovation.

Any society that is built on institutions like the family, which transfers knowledge and genetic advantages unevenly, and free association, which allows people to make use of their differing talents and aptitudes, will experience inequality. Even systems of government that reject capitalism and pursue economic equality – the Soviet Union, for example,

or the Chavez government in Venezuela – end up with social strati-
fication and unevenly shared economic goods. But in acknowledging
the inevitability of inequality, conservatives avoid this hypocrisy. The
crucial One Nation insight, however, is that we must not succumb to
sectional interests, but maintain a unity across the regions, and between
men and women, the social classes, and different ethnic and cultural
identities. This demands a strong commitment to solidarity, and a
respect for our responsibilities and obligations to our fellow citizens. It
demands, in other words, a strong sense of community.

But what if the conservative love of community becomes stifling and
illiberal? This is the third criticism of the One Nation tradition. But
which form of community do the critics say this about?

Despite its common modern misuse, community does not mean
membership of one particular identity group or another. When a conservative talks about community, he does not mean 'the gay community'
or 'the Muslim community'. He means the small and local associations
we join and which form a great chain of other associations, ultimately
comprising the nation, our largest form of community. As Burke said,
'to be attached to this subdivision, to love the little platoon we belong
to in society, is the first principle (the germ as it were) of public affec-
tions. It is the first link in the series by which we proceed towards a love
to our country and to mankind.'[35]

In other words, there are different levels of community. The first
is local, and immediate: the little platoons we form to support one
another, from the family to the village pub to the charity that supports
the local hospice. The second may be larger, representing perhaps a
city, or a county, or a trade union or a military regiment. These days,
they might also include networks and communities made possible by
internet-based communications. Third, there is the nation, a community of communities that reflects great diversity and many different
interests and values, but the unit that makes democratic government,
collective security and different forms of solidarity possible.

Given the conservative's belief in individual freedom, this love of
community cannot become stultifying. Social norms imposed and
policed by community can be a force for good, as they encourage us to
limit our freedom voluntarily in the name of responsibility to others.
This is why we say please and thank you to strangers and avoid dropping

litter. But norms that demean others must not be tolerated. Ostracizing people on the basis of their race, religion or sexuality should be unacceptable to conservatives.

Likewise, the conservative's patriotism should not become jingoism or xenophobia. A conservative might be suspicious of supranational government and utopian calls for world government, but he understands the need for international cooperation and global institutions. And he believes, in Burke's words, in 'commonwealths of culture'. In international relations, Burke reflected, 'we lay too much weight upon the formality of treaties and compacts ... Nothing is so strong a tie of amity between nation and nation as correspondence in laws, customs, manners and habits of life. They have more than the force of treaties in themselves. They are obligations written in the heart.'[36]

Nor should the conservative's love of country be mistaken for state worship, in which citizens are expected to subordinate their own thoughts and beliefs to others in the name of a broader identity. Conservatives understand that community and the state are different things. Just as much as the anarchy the state protects us from, a bossy and intrusive state puts community at risk.

The One Nation tradition avoids these pitfalls because of its recognition that values and interests inevitably and ceaselessly conflict. These clashes need to be resolved through institutions, laws and norms that accommodate our differences. And patriotism and the desire for national unity need to be expressed in ways that allow for the great diversity of a country the size of Britain. Yes, a country is a community, but conservatives recognize that a country also consists of many different communities with different interests.

All this is possible because conservatism accepts the need for balance between negative and positive liberty. Negative liberty protects our core freedoms that defend us 'from' despotism. Positive liberty allows for self-government and helps us to become free 'to' lead fulfilled lives. But conservatism also understands that both negative and positive liberty need strict boundaries to be drawn around them. This is why conservatism is unabashed in its support for balance and moderation and unashamed of its outright rejection of ideology.

5

REMAKING ONE NATION

How does the conservative make a reality of these beliefs? How can they be turned into meaningful policy and action? What is the conservative answer to the twin crises we examined earlier in the book?

The answers lie in a conservatism radically different from the kinds we have experienced in recent decades. This chapter will set out some proposals for a radical agenda that makes a reality of this new conservatism, but first we need to explain how conservatism can reassess its relationship with liberalism.

Conservatism is comfortable with the essential liberalism that we explored in chapter 1. It favours market economics and the rule of law. It supports pluralism as the way in which we can manage our differences. It prizes institutions because they help to mediate clashes of values and interests, and help us to build a common identity. It understands the need to compromise, exercise restraint in power, and accept the result of democratic elections and referenda. But conservatism needs to reject the ultra-liberalism that is driving our economic and cultural crises.

This does not mean conservatives cannot support new policies with a liberal flavour. There is a strong case, for example, for divorce law to be reformed to make it less adversarial and less damaging to divorcing parents and their children. Conservatives want to support the family, of course, but they must also recognize that the nature of the family is changing, and forcing couples to stay together against their better judgement, and making the process of divorce unnecessarily adversarial and rancorous, does nothing to help children. In fact, children are better off when divorcing parents maintain a civil and respectful relationship, which is something simpler and faster divorce laws would help.

There is a case, too, for the legalization of cannabis, a drug that has been effectively decriminalized while its supply and distribution remain in the hands of criminal gangs. There are undoubted physical and social harms caused by smoking cannabis, but legalization would allow regulation, with stronger forms of the drug still prohibited. It would free the police to pursue other crimes and take a tougher approach to harder drugs. Tax revenues raised by the legitimate trade in cannabis could be used in part to fund police resources and treatments for drug addicts.

And there is a case for the legalization of assisted dying for people suffering terminal illnesses. This is already the case in countries like Canada, the Netherlands and Switzerland, and in several US states including California, Colorado and New Jersey. These examples prove it is possible to construct a legal framework that prevents abuse and carefully safeguards the interests of patients with terminal illnesses. And there is growing support for legalization in Britain, with one study finding that 84 per cent of the public support a change in the law.[1]

But ultra-liberalism – in all its forms – needs to be resisted and reversed by conservatives.

This does not just mean that conservatives should simply oppose change or react to the calls for change made by others. And nor should conservatism be reduced to managerialism. There is an urgent need for a new conservative agenda that can address our crises and make Britain one nation once more.

Remaking one nation will require an acceptance of the world as it is today, and what it will become in the years ahead. It will require vision. And it will require adept and nimble leadership. But most of all it will require a new partnership of three: between government, market and community. It will therefore require conservatives to think more positively about the state, and more creatively about community.

Too often our political debate is about the balance only between the state and the market. And too often it has been a zero-sum argument, as though one must always be in conflict with the other. Of course conflicts occur – an overmighty state can undermine the market, and both the state and the market can undermine community – but in a successful society, market, state and community can all reinforce the other. A strong community lays the platform for a strong market economy. A market economy provides the resources to fund the state. The state regulates the market, and builds social and human capital in the community. The market can make communities strong, by giving individuals and families the dignity of freedom and responsibility. A strong community reduces the burdens on the state by reducing the bills of social failure.

A new conservative approach – which we might call 'enterprise conservatism' – would therefore incorporate not only private enterprise but state enterprise and social enterprise too. It understands that private enterprise is what creates jobs and prosperity, but it knows too that no business succeeds alone. Its goods are transported by road, its workers are educated in schools and colleges, and its customers are a part of sophisticated networks that include the private sector, public sector and charities. Often its knowledge and research originated in public institutions. Private enterprise needs freedom for creators and innovators, but it also needs a strong society, good government and moral virtues, including honesty, integrity and prudence. These virtues must be expected of everybody, and business leaders must remember their obligations and responsibilities to society.

Social enterprise is what makes our communities and institutions strong, but it can only exist where people have the skills, confidence, money, networks and time – the social capital – to make things happen. Social enterprise therefore needs the fruits of private enterprise to succeed. And where there are barriers that prevent it, and where there is insufficient social capital for it to occur, social enterprise also needs the state to pass enabling legislation and build capacity in communities where there is too little.

The state, all conservatives agree, is what provides the order that makes liberty possible. But that cannot be government's only function. Of course, the state must not be allowed to become overmighty, risking individual liberty, civic life and economic growth, but state enterprise is necessary to facilitate private enterprise, through providing infrastructure, skills and the right business climate, and to restore our society to good health, by investing in human and social capital through, for example, family and education policies.

Alongside this new approach must come an understanding that a diverse society needs to accept pluralism as not only necessary but attractive and desirable. But pluralism cannot, as we have discussed, give rise to militant identity politics or a moral or even legal relativism in minority communities. Instead, we need a new principle of ordered pluralism, which embraces the freedom of individuals to live their lives as they choose, and for cultural and ethnic groups to celebrate their identities, yet still builds a stronger civic identity. This identity must be inclusive and pluralistic, and it will need to recognize that there are different ways of feeling part of a whole, and different reasons for doing so. But the identity must also be distinctly British. Ordered pluralism would confer rights and obligations on citizens that would be unavailable to outsiders, and in so doing, restore the popular commitment to solidarity. Voting rights could be limited to British citizens, for example. Identity cards – or perhaps less controversially a public services access card – would prove somebody was in the country legally and entitled to use schools and health services and rely on the welfare system.

Ordered pluralism will therefore require cultural conservatism. Distinct from social conservatism, which is often associated with opposition to noble causes such as racial justice, gender equality and gay rights, cultural conservatism would defend those socially liberal causes as vital components of modern British life. Cultural conservatism would recognize that there are many different ways of ordering a successful society, and no such thing as universal rights interpreted uniformly and applied the world over. It would not therefore seek to impose on other parts of the world Western values, based on Western philosophical assumptions and our own cultural heritage, but it would defend Western culture robustly here at home.

Responding to a changing world

The facts of the world have changed, and yet our politics have not. Western hegemony is no more, and countries like China, India, Indonesia, Brazil and Mexico will become richer and more powerful.

The world needs a new multilateralism, in which the rise of these powers is reflected at the United Nations, and new institutions are created to ensure peaceful economic competition between East and West. The West needs to create a new forum in which democratic governments can work together to regulate cyberspace. But to maintain democratic legitimacy and public support, multilateral organizations need to remain intergovernmental and not supranational.

Britain will remain a strong international player. As an existing permanent member of the United Nations Security Council, with significant military and security capabilities, and nuclear weapons, Britain's voice will matter. According to projections, while fast-growing and populous developing countries will overtake many Western economies in size, by 2050, the UK will remain in the world's top ten economies.[2]

We need the strength to defend our interests in a more complex and dangerous world, but we also need to end the unsuccessful, wasteful and debilitating wars fought in the name of liberal interventionism. While we should make every effort to avoid involving ourselves in the sectarian war being fought across the Islamic world, we need to protect ourselves from its fallout, including the risk of extremism and terrorism and mass migration. We need to be realistic about the imperial nature of Chinese policy in Asia, Africa and elsewhere, and become more strategic about our own foreign policy. We need to recognize that China is the principal strategic rival of our most important ally, the United States, and so we cannot go 'all in' as China rises. We must also recognize that China's *modus operandi* – setting debt traps for countries to gain leverage over them and engaging in industrial-scale industrial espionage – is a danger to Britain's interests. We need to develop a special relationship with India and find a way of normalizing our relations with Russia. We need the means to protect our interests from threats around the world. Overall, we need a more hard-headed attitude to foreign policy, defence, aid and trade. This means that while Brexit must see Britain remain genuinely independent of the European

Union, it will need to negotiate a close future relationship, incorporating not only trade but cooperation on security too.

At home, we need a radically different economic model that addresses the challenges posed by globalization, changing technology and our ageing society. We will need to think differently about free markets, the role of the state in the economy, the level of public spending, the ways we raise taxes, the balance between labour and capital, and international trade.

In particular, we need to think again about the way globalization is working. As we saw in chapter 2, as production networks have become multinational, international economic competition has become less between nations and more between individuals. We therefore have to question whether our assumptions about the benefits of comparative advantage are still true. Does increased specialization, to the degree we are experiencing today, still make us inexorably richer? Or does it consign ever more Western workers to lower skilled and lower paid jobs? Traditional methods of measuring economic strength – the size of GDP or GDP per capita – might no longer be appropriate. We might need to start thinking about economic strength in ways that show how prosperity is shared across society as a whole. More and more unrestricted free trade might no longer be the inevitable route to prosperity many conservatives believe it is. International trade agreements will need to be negotiated to reflect this growing realization – giving Western workers much-needed respite – but it will be important to avoid throwing the baby out with the bath water. The world does not need a neo-mercantilist descent into trade wars and industrial espionage.

Despite its difficulties, globalization – and growing international competition – is here to stay. So we will still need to think differently about our international competitiveness. Policy-makers have always understood that competitiveness comes from lower production costs and investment in physical and human capital. But in these latest stages of globalization, some investments are smarter than others. It is an easy mistake for governments to pursue policies where the home country pays the bill, but the benefits end up elsewhere. Corporation tax cuts, for example, might reduce the taxes paid by companies on their profits, but they will do little to encourage firms to manufacture goods in

Britain. Instead, policy-makers should focus their efforts on factors that are less internationally mobile and have greater local spillover effects.

This means we need to invest far more in people and places. We need to make the most of our world-class universities. But we also need to provide better technical and vocational education, both during school and college years and at more advanced stages. That means better funding, new teaching institutions that work closely with employers, and high-quality, respected qualifications. Given the pace of change caused by new technologies, we also need the resources and structures to provide adult education and training, skilling and reskilling people through their working lives. We should introduce individual lifetime learning budgets.

Educating people better is not enough, however. In the modern, knowledge economy, spatial clustering is just as important. Access to knowledge and talent are what matters, so high-skilled workers and high-growth companies specializing in similar fields increasingly tend to cluster in the same places. London shows how the power of agglomeration can work. The banks and other financial services companies are not located in the City because of a tax break here or there, but because of the talent London has to offer, and the presence of related companies and services: lawyers, insurers and others. Policy-makers have compounded these advantages by making sure the tax regime and regulatory environment is competitive, and infrastructure – the Underground's Jubilee Line, the Docklands Light Railway, and Crossrail, for example – is provided. Add in the quality of life in London for well-paid City workers, and it is clear how the capital has benefited from clustering.

Cities that have little for companies, investors and talented workers to cluster around, however, find themselves struggling. Communities that once depended on a single industry – steel in Sheffield, for example – have struggled to recover when the old employers have closed down or moved on. These places often lack the skilled workers, the infrastructure and the cultural capital to attract new businesses. And businesses do not want to bear the risk of being first movers: once a cluster has emerged, the costs and benefits of joining it are clear, but moving to a city in the hope that a cluster might form is an unnecessary risk. This does not mean, however, that policy-makers should simply wait for the invisible hand of the market to work its magic. If we want our cities to succeed – and cities are the engines of growth in the modern, knowledge economy – we need to help them to establish new clusters and benefit from the resulting agglomeration.

We need massive new investment to improve connectivity between Britain's cities, and with cities across the world. That means better road and rail connections, but it also means significantly more airport capacity, even after Heathrow's third runway is built. We need far better connectivity within Britain's metropolitan areas as well. So we need better local trains and light railway services to make commuter journeys affordable, reliable and fast. And we need much better investment in buses, which remain the most common form of public transport, especially outside London, and especially for people on lower incomes. We should pilot, in British towns and cities, versions of the Dunkerque bus system. There, buses have been made free to use, and routes simplified into five core routes, each with a guaranteed service every ten minutes. Within a year of the system's launch, the number of bus passengers increased by 65 per cent during the week and 125 per cent at weekends.[3]

We need the right tax and regulatory regimes for the industries we want to encourage and the clusters we want to create. But we also need to make all our cities – and not just London – more appealing to the talented and mobile workers they need to succeed. So attractive and affordable housing matters, and so does clean air and green spaces. The urban design of city centres – clean and easy to get around for pedestrians and cyclists – is vital. Local universities will play a crucial role in attracting and retaining talented workers and conducting research and development alongside business. And the cultural offer – the museums, galleries, shops, restaurants and venues for live events – is also crucial. By charging foreign visitors for access to museums and galleries, for example, we could fund new regional satellites of the country's great cultural attractions and create wholly new regional cultural institutions.

This kind of plan will require government to give more powers – and bigger budgets – to the mayors who run the metropolitan areas like Greater Manchester and the West Midlands. But there is more, still, for government to do. It could, for example, address the 'first mover' problem by moving first itself. If ministers grouped together various government agencies – the economic regulators, for example, or research and data bodies – and invited mayors to bid to host them, they could lay the foundations of new clusters in the regional cities. The winning bids would have to include a spatial plan, a skills plan, the right infrastructure, university expertise, and a strategy to encourage private sector spillovers.

The supply side reforms needed for the modern economy are different to those in the past. Yes, unnecessary regulations need to be swept away, and bad regulations need to be reformed. Brexit might allow Britain to create free ports, scrap the EU's burdensome procurement rules, and escape its restrictive precautionary principle. The planning system needs to be completely overhauled. Industrial energy costs need to be kept down. And taxes need to be kept competitive. More generous capital allowances – encouraging firms to invest in plant and machinery – and allowances designed to get companies investing in human capital should be the priority. Tax changes like these will create more local spillover effects and win a greater return on investment than further reductions in corporation tax.

But modern supply-side reforms also require government action and spending. They require the devolution of budgets and powers to mayors, investment in infrastructure and human capital, and an industrial strategy to improve the performance of the economy outside the South East of England. This will require conservatives to accept a different attitude to the role of government and to public spending. Fiscal policy will need to be more generous, and the Treasury's fiscal rules will need to permit more government borrowing to fund infrastructure projects. Traditional quantitative easing is unlikely to be desirable or effective in the future. Instead, ministers should view direct investment in digital and physical infrastructure as a better-targeted alternative. New investment rules will need to be established to ensure funding reaches the regions that need it most, and not just London and the South East of England.

Extra investment need not come only from the taxpayer. Capitalism is supposed to provide capital for innovators and business leaders to turn their ideas into reality, creating jobs and growing the economy. But because our tax and regulatory systems favour debt over equity finance, we are potentially starving the economy of billions of pounds of investments. Equity finance is taxed four times – at purchase, dividend, sale and corporation tax – while debt finance is tax-deductible:

the taxpayer spends billions every year subsidizing the debts of big business. This works very well for the corporate giants, many of which are sclerotic, as they can manage and refinance their obligations. But how does it incentivize the start-ups and small to medium-sized companies that are most likely to drive growth and create jobs? A switch in policy that treated debt and equity finance equally would unleash huge new investments for our economy and increase the resilience of British companies. It would need to be implemented gradually, to give time for over-leveraged firms to adjust, but this change would make start-ups faster growing and more dynamic, improve productivity and bring to an end the perverse incentives that cause firms to build up ever-growing debts. If government wanted to improve regional investment, it might also recapitalize one of Britain's banks – which only survived the financial crash thanks to the taxpayer – to create a regional banking system.

Government will need to play a part, too, in making sure Britain can succeed with new technologies. Britain is the leading European nation when it comes to so-called 'unicorns': private tech companies worth more than $1 billion. In the last two decades, UK-based entrepreneurs have created 72 tech unicorns, compared to 29 in Germany, Europe's second most successful tech nation. Thirty-five per cent of the tech unicorns set up in Europe and Israel are based in Britain.[4]

But the world is in the midst of a tech arms race, and Europe is far behind the leaders. The United States has created 703 unicorn companies, and China 206.[5] China plans to become the world leader in artificial intelligence by 2030. It has established a $2 billion artificial technology park in Beijing, and to enhance its machine learning research it is investing $143 billion in its semiconductor industry alone.[6] In the US, more investment comes from private sector companies such as Amazon and Google, but the White House has published its own artificial intelligence strategy, and government agencies are rebalancing their budgets to promote research and development.

Other nations are working hard to compete. Germany's industrial strategy plans to make huge volumes of data available to researchers and developers, and will lighten regulations to encourage the development and application of artificial intelligence. The German government will spend €3 billion to implement its artificial intelligence strategy alone.[7] Canada has created the Vector Institute in Toronto, which aims to produce more postgraduates expert in deep learning and machine learning than any other institution in the world.

This is technology like none before it, and it is vital that Britain produces – and maintains – homegrown companies specializing in artificial intelligence. Britain needs an ambitious artificial intelligence strategy, backed by billions of pounds of public and private investment. But financing alone is not enough, of course. The state has the capacity to make Britain one of the most attractive places in the world for tech investment. It should aim to set a world-leading regulatory framework for digital technologies and make as much data as possible freely available. In particular, the National Health Service should be fully digitized and its anonymized data made available for researchers. New institutions should be created: an artificial intelligence institute, for example, and a new world-class research university, similar to the Massachusetts Institute of Technology.

The state will also need to protect British assets in artificial intelligence. DeepMind, the British company discussed in chapter 2, was sold to Google for £400 million in 2014 without even a golden share for government. It is now priceless, almost certainly not for sale at any price. If Britain wants to develop its own artificial intelligence capabilities, build new clusters of artificial intelligence businesses, and have a place at the table when the world works out how to govern and regulate this revolutionary technology, it will need to keep its artificial intelligence assets independent, and capable of growing into world-leading companies, rather than being eaten up by the likes of Amazon and Alibaba.

In the long run, if we reach a stage when future knowledge and discovery is generated by machines and not humans, we will need to decide who should own the assets and the profits derived from these discoveries. We will need to debate whether these assets and profits rightly belong to the inventors and investors behind the machines, and their heirs and successors who had nothing to do with them, or whether instead we should treat them as a public good. This might be anathema to market fundamentalists, but if artificial intelligence proves to be as transformative as many experts predict, there will be a strong case for settling upon the latter.

Reviving civic capitalism

Changing technology is one reason why the balance between labour and capital has grown out of kilter. Another reason, as we discussed in chapter 2, is the decline of 'countervailing power', the fact that the laws and regulations that govern markets have been slowly and quietly changed to suit big business, investors and the executive classes, and to work against the interests of ordinary people. As a result, jobs are more precarious and pay and conditions are less generous than they have been for decades.

A fashionable solution to this problem is that we should introduce a form of Universal Basic Income (UBI). With technology likely to cause unemployment and lower pay, the logic goes, we should scrap all traditional means-tested benefits and replace them with a single, unconditional flat-rate payment to all citizens. The payment would be made whether or not the recipient was in work, and because it would be universal and flat, campaigners say there would be little need for complex bureaucracy. But this is a deeply flawed idea. First, and as we have already seen, technology is not likely to destroy jobs, but change them. Second, Universal Basic Income would destroy incentives for people to innovate and work hard for their families. And third, as a report from the University of Bath concluded, 'it is impossible to design a UBI scheme which is fiscally feasible, has no adverse distributional consequences, and is sufficiently generous to eliminate the need for means-testing.'[8] In other words, a Universal Basic Income is either prohibitively expensive or less efficient than existing policies at reducing inequality and poverty. It is a dangerous idea, and conservatives should reject it.

Neither can conservatives propose the full-on re-regulation of the labour market, nor the liberalization of trades union legislation. Britain's unions are too often ideological, adversarial and aggressive. Instead, the conservative solution should be to create institutions and frameworks that address job insecurity and low pay without second-guessing businesses and over-regulating the economy.

Corporate governance needs to be reformed. Executive pay, including bonuses and long-term incentive plans, should be made subject to annual binding votes by shareholders. Institutional investors should be required to publish their voting decisions and inform their fundholders – whose money they are investing – of their positions. Listed companies should be required to publish, without exemption, the full pay packages of their executives. And workers and consumers should be directly represented on company boards. They could even take a seat on company remuneration committees.

But, alone, even these changes are insufficient. Other measures to restore the balance between labour and capital are necessary. The National Living Wage should be increased so it goes beyond 66 per cent of median earnings, formally ending low pay in Britain. For workers in the middle of the pay scales – who are also facing downward pressure on their incomes – occupational licensing can help. New professional or sectoral organizations, a little like the guilds of the past, could provide training, qualifications, licensing and pay representation for their members. Trades unions could be awarded the status of these organizations, but this – and the receipt of any public funds – should be made strictly conditional on constructive labour relations.

We should learn from other countries, including Australia, where wage boards set minimum pay levels by sector and occupation. Studies show they have helped to limit income inequality without having a detrimental effect on employment.[9] Sectoral pay bargaining through wage boards would address Britain's decline in countervailing power and – particularly in sectors dominated by smaller employers – help workers in more dispersed industries.

Immigration needs to be controlled, so the country can meet skills shortages and attract top talent, but so mass immigration no longer displaces lower-skilled workers from the labour market nor puts downward pressure on wages. Work permits should be required for anybody who wants to take a job in Britain, and those permits should only be granted to those who have the skills the country needs. Student visas for university students should continue to be generous, but they should no longer provide the guarantee of the right to live and work in Britain after graduation. Instead, graduates – not all of whom are the brightest and the best in the world – should be allowed to work in Britain after study only if they meet the criteria for work permits. Family visas should be reformed, with higher income thresholds required of sponsors, and there should be an outright ban on marriages to first cousins to reduce the number of so-called 'fetching marriages'. Asylum claims should be processed in offshore centres to remove the incentive to claim asylum in the hope of remaining and working illegally in Britain. There should be sustained work to reduce the demand for immigration – by addressing skills shortages through better technical education, investing in automation to replace menial labour, and increasing pay in sectors like hospitality – and there must be a clear objective to cut immigration overall.

We need to learn the lessons of past deindustrialization. In particular, as the economy inevitably changes, we need to make sure communities do not lose the social capital they need to renew and prosper. We need to invest heavily in the regions – in human and social capital, not just infrastructure – and not just in the South East of England. In addition to individual lifetime learning budgets, we urgently need an ambitious national programme to retrain and reskill workers at risk of unemployment due to changing technologies. If such a programme is as ambitious as it needs to be, it will be expensive to run, but the costs will be nothing compared to the bills we will face later if we do not act.

We should change the rules governing mergers and acquisitions, so when companies are bought, the plans that are put to investors by bidders are legally binding. Defending companies should be given more time to audit the cost savings set out by hostile bidders. And the process should be changed to reflect the fact that when a company is sold, it is not only shareholders with a stake in its future, but also workers, local communities and, often, the whole nation. There should be a tough new 'strategic interest test', which would allow ministers to intervene and prevent takeovers that are likely to undermine strategically-important sectors of the economy or erode the country's skills base.

We need a new economic partnership, in which workers are given new rights and protections that reflect the reality of the modern economy. Employees of listed companies should be legally entitled to shares in the company as part of their remuneration. There should be comprehensive legislation that gives contract workers and people working in the gig economy new protections. A new round of enabling legislation could allow municipal leaders to establish their own schemes to protect local workers and consumers. There should be new rights to protect people suffering from mental health conditions, which are often intermittent and therefore beyond the scope of existing protections. And there should be more support for people returning to work after lengthy career breaks, like those who have cared for elderly parents or take time out to raise children.

The labour market is only one market that needs to be reformed: other markets need to face change too. The systematic over-reward for investors in regulated industries, described in chapter 2, needs to stop, cutting bills for energy and water customers and fares for airline and railway passengers. Where specific markets have become dysfunctional, there needs to be industry-by-industry reform.

Banking would be made more competitive, diverse and responsive to local needs if government created a regional banking system, as proposed above. A common utility platform – which in effect would put all bank accounts and their numbers onto a single system – would mean customers could switch banks instantaneously, while missed payments and other inconveniences could be reduced.

The railways should not be renationalized – consider for a moment the likely reduction in investment if they were run by the state – but the entire structure of the industry needs to change. In practice, the privatization of the railways replaced a single, state monopoly with several smaller monopolies, each enjoyed by a single franchise holder. There is little competition and little room – given the growing interventions made by the Department for Transport – for companies to innovate. This needs to change. Within the big conurbations, train services can be run by operators reporting to a commissioning authority, like Transport for London. But for longer distance routes, access to the lines need to be opened up to allow different companies to provide different kinds of services. There should be better integration between track, run by Network Rail, and train, run by the operating companies. Railway workers should be given the opportunity to create mutuals and run their own services, or be given a greater commercial stake in their firms. And the Byzantine fare system should be torn up to reduce the number of fares – which total 55 million in different bundles – and make it easier for customers to understand the cheapest way of travelling.[10] Fares should be unbundled and a single journey should become the basic pricing unit.

And we should not stop there. University tuition fees need to change, so fewer students are funnelled into unsuitable degrees with no return on investment. Telecoms and internet services need to be reformed to stop consumers getting ripped off, and to make sure the whole country has reliable high-speed internet access. The energy price cap should be retained, but the retail energy market, which systematically overcharges its most loyal customers, needs to be overhauled, with the number of tariffs offered by different providers reduced to make choice understandable and meaningful. And the overall price of energy needs to be kept down, for businesses and households alike. This will mean more than retail market reform, however, and a change in Britain's crazily unilateralist approach to climate change policy.

New markets created by new technologies need regulation too. The digital economy is bringing extraordinary new benefits to consumers – providing products that simply did not exist until recently; offering cheap, and sometimes free, services; creating systems that reduce the barriers to starting up new businesses – but they are fundamentally different to non-digital markets. Very often, the winner takes all, and the market is entirely concentrated. And the top firms are hoovering up potential rivals all the time: in the last ten years, the biggest five tech firms have made more than 400 international acquisitions. Not one has been blocked.[11]

There needs to be greater data mobility for users, and systems with open standards to allow for competition and consumer choice. There needs to be more intervention by the competition authorities to protect innovation and consumer rights. There needs to be better oversight of the use of artificial intelligence and machine learning algorithms to prevent market abuse. Much of this work can be done by national governments and regulators, but clearly some action will need to be taken at an international level. Democratic governments will need to create new institutions and agree new treaties that allow them to set expectations and standards for these powerful new companies.

One market more than any other that needs to be put right is housing. Britain's dysfunctional housing market is a factor behind almost every one of the country's social and economic problems. Supply has not kept up with increasing demand. Global interest rates have fallen and remain abnormally low. And prices have risen accordingly. Expensive housing restricts labour mobility, encumbers agglomeration in big cities, and reduces savings and investment. Instead of helping, government policies – such as quantitative easing and Help to Buy – have increased housing costs further. And as housing gets more expensive, wealth inequality will deepen. Capitalism, policy-makers are starting to realize, loses support when ordinary people cannot accrue capital of their own.

Increasing the number of houses we build is vital. This will inevitably mean changes to planning laws, but it need not mean sacrificing the green belt nor standards in our built environment. Strategically located new towns will need to be built, especially in the South East of England. There and elsewhere, new towns can be constructed around new rail lines, with revenues from the new housing contributing towards the costs of new infrastructure. In city centres, we need to build upwards, with higher-density housing developments. Outside city centres, we need clean, green and attractive street-based housing that families with children would love to own.

We need market reform in the over-consolidated construction sector. Between the 1960s and 1980s, smaller construction companies made significant contributions to the numbers. But since the 1980s, a steep decline in the number of smaller construction firms has occurred. In 1988, there were around 12,200 small companies building almost four in ten new homes. By 2014, the number had fallen to around 2,400 building just 12 per cent of new homes.[12] The dominant players now make huge profits, pay their executives record-breaking bonuses, and build too few houses. We need to change the planning system to allow smaller firms to compete with the dominant companies, sell public land for house building in ways that help smaller companies, and legislate to stop the big firms land-banking. We need to work with industry to increase the use of 3D printing and modular construction to reduce housebuilding costs. And we need to reform banking rules so smaller and newer construction companies can get the financing they need to get building.

Even still, we will need the state to make a greater contribution towards housebuilding. Britain has not built enough houses since local authorities built significant numbers, often totalling more than 100,000 per year, themselves.[13] We need to provide local authorities and housing associations with the funding and flexibility to build more homes.

We need to reform compulsory purchase powers – which overvalue land and make it prohibitively expensive for councils to acquire building sites – and help councils to capture the increase in land value when they build.

To encourage home ownership, councils might be mandated to sell the homes they build after a minimum period of, say, fifteen years. Council tenants in expensive rented homes could be allowed to use their Right to Buy discount to purchase cheaper homes elsewhere, and allow the local authority to raise new revenues from the sale of valuable housing assets. Mortgage regulations that cap the sums a family can borrow, based on multiples of their annual income, rest on assumptions about a return to higher interest rates that seems unlikely for the foreseeable future. These regulations should be relaxed to allow more families of modest means to afford a home of their own.

Bringing Britain together

Restoring civic capitalism is just one way in which we can bring Britain back together. But as we have seen, the crisis facing our country is not only about economic injustice – as deep as that is – but also cultural anxiety. We need to do far more to heal our fractured nation and make it one.

A good starting point would be to make fiscal policy fairer. We have already examined why the economy needs more investment, not less. We have seen, in chapter 2, how our ageing population will put pressure on the public finances. And we know that after a decade of austerity, there is little room for further spending cuts. Regardless of the size and speed of economic growth, if there is room for tax cuts in the foreseeable future, they will be funded by borrowing or tax increases elsewhere.

So the question is how taxes are raised fairly. Online firms like Amazon that avoid paying taxes in Britain should be made to pay a digital services tax – bigger than anything proposed by government to date – which could allow a reduction or even the abolition of business rates for small businesses on the high street. Some of Britain's highest earners are able to avoid income tax and National Insurance contributions by paying capital gains tax on their income, which has been earned by managing the investments of others, and should therefore be taxed as income. Closing this loophole would mean they would pay a fairer share of tax on their very high incomes.

If taxes on working families can be reduced, it is likely they will have to be offset by other sources of revenue. We could address the redistribution to the rich, caused deliberately by government policy, by asking the prosperous to take more of the strain and supporting workers on modest wages. Tax relief on pensions – which has disproportionately benefited the wealthy and costs the Treasury £38.6 billion per year – has recently been limited for higher earners, but it should do more for savers on lower wages.[14] Higher-rate taxpayers might also be asked to contribute more in National Insurance contributions, which unlike income tax is not structured progressively. In 2019–20, contracted workers paid National Insurance contributions of 12 per cent up to an income of £50,000 but only 2 per cent thereafter.[15] A more ambitious reform might be to scrap National Insurance altogether and roll it into income tax.

We will also need to reconsider the balance of taxation between income and wealth. Our ageing society and rising health costs mean we will need an extra £24 billion per year by 2030 and £63 billion per year by 2040 just to meet the additional costs of health, social care, pensions and pensioner benefits.[16] The choice appears to be to either cut back the welfare state, or to ask younger generations to shoulder the burden in the form of higher taxes or extra borrowing. But there is a third way, and that is to ask those who have accumulated wealth to contribute more. Wealth taxes are controversial in a country that has grown unused to them, but historically and internationally they are not unusual.

We could reform council tax to make sure that people who own high-value properties pay more. We could ask wealthy pensioners to contribute more to the cost of their social care. We could abolish stamp duty on new homes, and make all home sales subject to capital gains tax. We could reduce the thresholds for inheritance tax so they reflect the value of an average family home.

Some or all of these measures would allow us to raise more revenue to pay the rising costs of welfare and public services, and reduce the burden on younger, working families. At a time when income inequality remains stubbornly wide and wealth inequality is likely to grow, rebalancing the burden of taxation between income and wealth would make Britain a fairer country, in which opportunity is spread more evenly.

But taxing wealth more and income less can only be one part of a plan to create real equality of opportunity. We also need to do more to create wealth, and make sure it is shared widely. The pursuit of economic growth is not something to cause embarrassment: it is how we lift people out of poverty and ignorance and into prosperity and knowledge. We therefore need policies – like those listed above – that focus unapologetically on growth. And we need to make sure that the assets in which people invest and grow their wealth – housing, pensions and, in some cases, shareholding – are available to everybody.

International studies show that poor social mobility is connected to unequal access to education, labour markets and finance.[17] English school reform – overseen by different governments and over a period of years – has been a great success story. But it needs to go on. More organizations with the social capital to make free schools and academies work – private schools, universities, faith groups and selective schools – should play a greater role in opening good new schools in struggling communities. The legal ban on creating new selective schools should be lifted, and replaced with a policy that allows such schools to open, subject to conditions about admissions for working-class children, support for neighbouring schools, and to avoid a detrimental effect on other local schools, an upper limit on the percentage of selective school places in a particular community.

There needs to be far better technical and vocational education for students at school age and beyond. The funding model for tertiary education needs to be reformed, so fewer students are pushed into academic degrees of dubious value, and every eighteen-year-old gets a meaningful choice of further and higher education, including good technical and vocational study. To help avoid brain drains, tuition fees could be reduced and the terms of student loans made more generous for young people who choose to study good courses at local universities.

Many of the policies described above, such as immigration control and labour market reforms, would help improve access to work. So would adult retraining and lifetime learning budgets. And so would improved workplace rights and support for people who want to stay in, or return to, employment despite injury, illness – including mental illness – and caring responsibilities. Finance needs to become much more inclusive, with lending regulations made more generous for families with modest incomes, and share ownership made a compulsory part of remuneration packages.

All of these measures should help to improve social mobility. But that is not enough, because we cannot simply leave behind those who do not prosper. We need to show far greater social solidarity with every citizen. Good jobs need to be available for people across the spectrum of skills and abilities. And those jobs need to come with good pay and fair rights and protections. The welfare system needs to do nothing to discourage work – its guiding aim must always be to help people to help themselves – but it must be a reliable safety net. Industrial strategy and regional policy must work to bring growth to the regions and ensure investment and spending is shared fairly across the country.

The same goes for public services. If services are to be run in a way that makes them responsive to their users, they cannot be centralized and run from Whitehall. And that means variations in standards – the so-called 'postcode lottery' – are inevitable. Those varying standards should, in a system that works well, encourage innovation and improvement as all service providers learn from the best. But it is not acceptable for poorer families, and poorer parts of the country, to experience consistently worse public services than those who are better off.

Public services need to be organized and run in line with the experience of what works, but the values we prioritize too. The criminal justice system, for example, needs to be tougher and more transparent in its decision-making. Prisoners should no longer be automatically released halfway through their sentences. For violent criminals and terrorists, there should be more indeterminate sentences, where release can only come at the end of a minimum period and if a court is satisfied that the prisoner no longer poses a danger to the public. The public expect those who do the right thing to be rewarded, and those who behave irresponsibly to be punished. So for problems that might seem petty from Whitehall – like anti-social behaviour, fly-tipping and illegal traveller camps – mayors and local governments should have greater powers, and expect greater accountability, for putting things right.

The National Health Service is built on our commitment to solidarity, our belief that one citizen should not jump the queue for healthcare because of their ability to pay more. This is why attempts to implement market-based reforms to the NHS are always controversial, and why any attempts to privatize healthcare, and replace the NHS with a model of social insurance, are doomed to fail. Instead of trying to create quasi-markets within the Health Service, which cause unnecessary bureaucracy and waste, we should take advantage of the scale of the NHS and run it as efficiently as possible. And with modern medicine transformed by genomics, digital medicine and artificial intelligence, the massive scale of the NHS and its access to huge troves of data will be an important advantage.

This does not mean, however, that every service needs to be run in this way. School reform has been successful, for example, because it has granted more autonomy for school leaders and allowed greater parental choice where existing provision is poor. There is no reason for the state to own and run the railways or the utility companies. These markets should be better regulated and customers should be better protected, but there is no reason to believe – based on experience in Britain or elsewhere – that the state would do a good job running water companies and energy firms.

Conservatives cannot make Britain one nation once more without a strong focus on racial justice. As we saw in chapter 3, while Britain has been largely successful in its transition to a multiracial society, racial injustice persists. We need to be restless in seeking out these injustices and relentless in eliminating them. There should, for example, be far more transparency in sentencing policy, and action to prevent people from minority backgrounds receiving harsher punishments than white people. Black people suffering from mental health problems are more likely to find themselves in police custody than members of other ethnic groups, and deaths in custody often arise when police officers use inappropriate restraint techniques. Often, this disadvantage and injustice is not caused by any kind of bias or racial discrimination, but circumstances and cultural context. But that does not make it any the less pernicious. To help more people from Pakistani and Bangladeshi backgrounds into the workplace, for example, there should be a multiagency programme to work with younger people, especially women and girls, to help them to get the right qualifications, apply for jobs and travel back and forth to work.

One neglected group that as much as anybody needs support is the white, working class. If the crisis in white, working-class communities had been taking place among any other group, ultra-liberals would have been in uproar. Instead, the crisis has been allowed to continue and grow for many years. There should be programmes to target white working-class children in schools to make sure they are not – as now – being left behind. There should be interventions to help struggling families with life skills that most of us take for granted: how to pay the bills, cook healthy meals for children, and find work and learn new skills. There should be measures to encourage employers – and especially the public sector – to identify social class discrimination just as there are for race and sex discrimination. There should be special assistance for the white working-class towns, districts and suburbs that are struggling most.

There must also be immigration control. As we discussed in chapter 3, almost every opinion poll published shows clear majorities of people think immigration must be reduced. The public's reasoning might in part be economic – because of labour market effects, for example, or the pressure on infrastructure and services – but many voters are worried about cultural change. So when conservatives devise policies to control immigration, those policies should reflect not only skills shortages but also the likely ability of an immigrant to integrate well. English-language skills are already a requirement for some visas, but the immigration rules should give weight to people from countries with strong cultural connections to Britain. These might be based on bonds of language, geography or history. They might be based on the extent of integration – or the lack of it – by existing diasporas in Britain. But Britain's immigration rules should reflect the quite understandable desire of the majority group to slow the pace of change and protect and preserve their cultural identity.

Britain's integration policies must also become more effective at bringing the country together. These policies cannot be based on woolly thinking about abstract shared values, as they have in the past. Of course, there are some values that we as a society can broadly admire, and there are values that we can agree have no place in Britain.

We should stand up for the former and be uncompromising in our opposition to the latter. We can accept that values are multitudinous and conflicting but that does not mean we have to accept that all values are equally valid. But we must work to bring Britain together by building our policies on customs that build familiarity and trust, and institutions that mediate disputes and forge a common identity despite our differences. These policies need to be based on our duty – on the need for obligations and reciprocity – as citizens. And they need to be respectful of our long national story.

We need to ask more of newcomers from communities that do not integrate well. Foreign cultural norms – like forced marriage, honour crimes and female genital mutilation – have no place in Britain. Neither are hostile and repressive attitudes towards people of other faiths, homosexuals and women acceptable. The state must stop dealing with self-appointed 'community leaders' and organizations connected to extremist groups. It must enforce the law equally, regardless of the race or religion of the alleged perpetrators of crimes and their victims. The politicization of schools by religious radicals – protesting against things like the content of the curriculum, sex education and school uniforms – must be resisted. The manipulation of women and girls, and the deliberate construction of walls between communities, must end. The burqa and niqab should be banned in public places, as they are in several European countries including France. The calls for legally binding definitions of 'Islamophobia' should be confronted and explained for what they are: an attempt to create a modern blasphemy law for one religion and put extremists above scrutiny.

Equalities legislation and the policies it produces, in all sectors of the economy, should be reviewed to ensure it is effective, properly targeted and proportionate. We should aim to establish what might be called a 'natural' representation of social groups in certain professions and industries, based on empirical studies of the pipelines of qualified applicants. This work should be conducted with scientific rigour and an open mind about the causes of disparities. And there should be intensive efforts to address the deeper and more complex causes of disparities, such as educational attainment, access to employment and family breakdown.

There should continue to be a legal duty not to discriminate on the basis of race, gender and sexuality, but this duty should also protect white people, men and others whose characteristics are not protected by existing laws. To prevent cultural – and often ultra-liberal – groupthink, we need to do much more to ensure a true diversity of beliefs and perspectives in business, government and the private sector. We should presume people to be innocent until proven guilty beyond reasonable doubt when it comes to accusations of racism, sexism and other forms of bigotry. And those in positions of authority should stay steadfast in response to witch-hunts and trial-by-social media.

But we must also do much more to boost the social capital of newcomers and people living in isolated communities. People cannot integrate if they do not know the country's culture, laws and ways of life. Instead of waiting for migrants to apply for citizenship before we ask them to study life in Britain, we should ask more of people from the moment they start living and working here. All new immigrants – even those on visas lasting a year or so – should be required to attend courses about life in Britain, and compliance should be a condition of the migrant's visa. Similarly, a place-based, multi-agency programme designed to support specific communities – as suggested above – would help people living in isolation, particularly women and girls, to break out of their ghettos and get to know their fellow citizens. A fully comprehensive, and mandatory, form of National Citizen Service for every teenager would see young people from every racial, religious, regional and class background work together on projects for the common good.

Repairing democracy

There is no denying the deep sense of crisis in our political system. Trust in politicians has reached a new low. The two parties are under increasing strain. Brexit – and the reaction of many ultra-liberals to the vote to leave the European Union – has brought our constitution almost to breaking point. Meanwhile, the frustrations that many people have had with our political system – its remoteness, its inability to listen to what the public want, its domination by ultra-liberals, and its failure to simply get things done – continue unchecked.

We need more democratic accountability, less technocratic government, and institutions that better reflect the identity and needs of the British people. We need our institutions to manage clashes of values and interests, but we also need them to make decisions and deliver.

Perversely, our system both ignores the wishes of the public while also failing to get agreed and done the big things the country needs – infrastructure projects, for example, and serious economic reforms. To put this right, we need fewer and lighter bureaucratic and legal checks, and far more responsive democratic structures.

The rise of the liberal technocrats must be reversed. The Human Rights Act should be scrapped. The process of judicial review – used to challenge government decisions over and again and at great cost – should be reformed and restricted. The Treasury should be more attentive to monetary policy – the consequences of which can be far greater than fiscal policy – and more accountable to Parliament for the monetary policy decisions it makes. The civil service – unreformed since the nineteenth century – should be made more professional, more specialist, and open to people and ideas from beyond its own ranks. The special adviser system should be abolished, and replaced by a new model that allows Cabinet ministers to appoint advisers to specific, named positions subject to a proper recruitment process. More senior civil servants should be appointed by their secretaries of state and made more directly accountable to Parliament. Quangos should be more accountable to ministers, mayors and MPs. And the people appointed to run them must be more representative in every sense of the term: not only when it comes to race and gender but to personal beliefs and perspectives. Left-liberals have dominated these positions for long enough.

Supranational government must be resisted. Of course, there is a need for international institutions to maintain peace, ensure trade and mediate disputes. But supranational government destroys democratic accountability and makes decision-making more distant. In the European Union, national governments are represented in the Council of Ministers, where they can be outvoted. The technocratic yet powerful Commission is unelected. The Court of Justice acts as a motor of integration, constantly widening the application of European law. And while the European Parliament is elected, its members are elected from many different countries whose peoples do not see themselves as one.

Democratic accountability relies on the nation state – the only tried and tested, consistently successful unit of democratic organization – and strong local government. Membership of supranational organizations, like the European Union, is incompatible with national sovereignty and democratic government. For this reason, Britain should withdraw from the European Convention on Human Rights as well as the European Union, codifying individual rights in domestic law instead.

Parliament – and its role in our constitution – should also face change. Since 1999, Scotland and Wales have enjoyed devolved government, while England has not. Devolution has brought the government of Scotland and Wales closer to the people, but it has failed to stymie separatism: the Scottish Nationalists in particular continue to perform strongly, while in the 2014 referendum, Scottish independence was only narrowly averted. And it has led to a constitutional imbalance. While English MPs have no say over policies including health and education in Scotland and Wales, Scottish and Welsh MPs continue to vote on those policies as they apply to England.

Devolution is a lopsided solution that creates constitutional injustices and friction between the Union's constituent nations. It should be scrapped and the United Kingdom should move to a fully federal structure. Responsibility for foreign policy, international trade, aid, defence, security, immigration, monetary policy, the maintenance of the British single market, and the distribution of regional development funds would remain reserved for the UK government. Everything else would be devolved to the four nations of the United Kingdom.

The main argument against this move is that England is too big, compared to Scotland, Wales and Northern Ireland, to fit into a federal structure. But by that logic, the Union itself would be unsustainable. And right now the constitutional imbalance caused by devolution to Scotland and Wales makes it harder, for example, for an MP from Scotland to become Prime Minister of the United Kingdom than an MP representing an English constituency. Because it would grant control over almost every domestic political issue to each of the four nations, a fully federal UK would make the case for independence harder to advocate and bring government closer to all the peoples of the United Kingdom. It could also mean that the English government and parliament would sit in a regional city, rather than London, which would be a significant opportunity in the battle to rebalance the British economy.

The House of Lords can finally make way for an elected upper house. It is true, the Lords is home to some experts, but it is far from being the 'expert revising chamber' its supporters frequently claim it to be. Many peers were experts in their fields decades ago, and often represent vested interests from their former fields, not the public interest. Many are simply the beneficiaries of political patronage: former MPs, political advisers and party donors who have helped long-departed prime ministers and other party leaders. A maximum of ninety-two of them are hereditary peers, ninety of whom are elected from the ranks of the aristocracy in an absurd pantomime by peers already sitting in the House. And the Lords has shown itself willing to be more than simply a revising chamber. It has ignored convention and voted against legislation promised by the governing party's manifesto. It did everything it could to frustrate Britain's departure from the European Union. It should be replaced by an elected chamber with a clearly defined role, scrutinizing and amending legislation without challenging the primacy of the Commons.

These changes would require new constitutional laws. These laws would set out the relationship between the national governments and parliaments and the federal, United Kingdom parliament. And they would set out the roles of the reformed Lords and Commons and the relationship between them. But that is all these constitutional laws should do. After years of constitutional abuse and chicanery – consider the European Communities Act which subordinated British laws to European laws, the Human Rights Act which instructs British judges to follow case law established by the European Court of Human Rights, the Fixed Term Parliaments Act, and the behaviour of the Speaker of the Commons in arbitrarily changing Parliament's rules – it might feel very tempting to support the introduction of a codified constitution. But as the experience of the United States shows us, such a constitution can hinder the development of modern laws – on gun control, for example – because of principles set out in a different time. Whatever the intentions of those who support a codified constitution, it is highly likely that it would set in stone ultra-liberal beliefs and prejudices, which we will never be able to change again.

There are other ways in which our democracy can be reformed. The Human Rights Act should be scrapped and replaced with a Bill of Rights that would put Parliament in charge of deciding the balance between competing rights, and British judges in charge of individual cases. The Fixed Term Parliaments Act has caused chaos over Brexit, as the Commons blocked government policies but kept refusing to allow an election. The legislation – which was only invented to secure the Conservative/Lib Dem coalition government – should be abolished, and the power to call fresh elections should be returned to the Crown.

The mayors who run the city-regions can be given more powers with fewer needless hindrances. A new 'jury stage' could see citizens scrutinize legislation as it goes through Parliament. Select committees might be given greater legal powers to call witnesses and ensure they give evidence under oath. MPs who defect to other parties should be made to face automatic by-elections, and the public should be given stronger powers to recall MPs who break their promises. Voting might be made compulsory, as it is in Australia. The public funding of political parties would end the unhealthy influence of wealthy donors and ideological trades unions over party policies.

These are all important reforms. Undoubtedly, some will say conservatives should not countenance such significant change. Others will say constitutional reform is a distraction we can do without. But as we have seen with Brexit, how we make big decisions affects what those decisions are. Technocratic policies – like English votes on English laws, or bit-by-bit devolution – are not working. Where power lies matters. We have an opportunity to bring about the kind of change conservatives respect: by reforming in order to preserve what matters most, we can address very real contemporary problems while providing solutions that are consistent with British laws and traditions.

That is not all. Our democracy needs reform to help governments get things done. Successive governments have ducked decisions on energy infrastructure, airports, roads, railways and housing for decades. Whitehall should be reformed. The Cabinet Office should become a Prime Minister's Department capable of driving change across Whitehall. The Treasury's 'Green Book' – which sets out its spending rules – needs to be changed so investment decisions are no longer skewed in favour of London and the South East. The Treasury might also be stripped of its oversight of departmental spending, with the responsibility handed over to the new Prime Minister's Department. And politicians themselves need more space to deliver: the electoral timetable should be changed to elect governments every six years to encourage longer-term decision-making.

Our democracy also needs to catch up with the digital age. We need new electoral laws that reflect the nature of modern, online campaigning, with strict limits about what parties can do with personal data. Paid political advertising online should be prohibited, just as it is on television. Social media companies like Facebook and Twitter need to be treated like other media companies and made legally liable for the material they publish. Social media users should be required to prove their identity and use their real names to set up accounts and comment online.

The free press needs to be supported through the disruptive change it is experiencing. Just as government created the BBC at the dawn of the broadcasting era – precisely to maintain high standards and address concerns about media manipulation – government can do something similar for the internet era. A tax on internet service providers (ISPs) could fund a news platform – separate to the BBC and similar to a service like Netflix – through which users could read or watch news from established media outlets. An ISP tax could also fund training for investigative reporters. And the BBC – which risks being squeezed as the media bifurcates between live events like news and sport on one hand and expensive productions on the other – needs to be reformed to maintain its relevance in an age when companies like Amazon can spend up to $1 billion on a single series.

Restoring community

All of these plans rely on the ingenuity of the market and the strength of the state. But they rely just as much on the restoration of community.

As we noted earlier, community has declined because the ultra-liberal emphasis on individualism and market forces has eroded our sense of obligation to one another. So too has the rise of the centralized, distant, utilitarian state. But this does not mean the restoration of community has to mean the restoration of everything communities once did. We cannot turn back the clock. The market and the state have superseded community because in many ways they carry out functions that matter to us better. If we want to restore community, we need associations and institutions that can meet real and important modern needs better than government or private companies.

Of these associations and institutions, the most important by far is the family, humanity's natural social unit. Without strong families, society cannot function. It is within the family that babies are nurtured and children are taught how to interact with the wider world. The family teaches us language, social skills and cultural knowledge. It prepares us for life as adults, when we are capable of living and working independently, participating in and contributing towards the wider community, and forming families of our own. Experience tells us that where families are in crisis, society is in crisis.

We need to do far more to support families, especially those who need the most help. Many of the policies we have already discussed – reducing taxes on working families, increasing the National Living Wage, making finance more inclusive, extending home ownership, supporting people with caring responsibilities, and helping families in crisis – will make families stronger. But more still must be done. Families need to be better supported at the stages in life when they need help most. Statutory maternity pay should be extended and increased. Child benefit should be frontloaded so parents get more help in the early years of their children's life. A neutral 'family fund' to subsidize professional childcare, give parents transferable tax allowances, or recognize in other ways parents and grandparents who stay at home to bring up children, would reduce childcare costs without forcing parents into the workplace or out of it. We could establish a national childcare crèche network, based on the *école maternelle* in France. Families who want to care for elderly relatives should be recognized through transferable tax allowances or council tax rebates, and by making the costs of home renovations for caring purposes tax-deductible.

We need to build up associations and institutions in local neighbourhoods too. Community is eroded when power lies with distant decision-makers, ignorant of local needs and wants. It becomes stronger when responsibility for decisions lies with those who know the ground and who experience the consequences of their actions. There are limits to localism – there is an important role for national institutions and national government in aggregating interests and mediating clashes of values – but Britain desperately needs a renaissance of local institutions and local leadership. Doing so would bring government closer to local communities, make decision-makers more accountable, and not just tolerate but welcome difference.

More powers and bigger budgets for the metro mayors, as discussed above, would help. Local councils should be reformed so there are fewer layers of governance and less duplication, but the single tier of remaining local authorities should be given more autonomy. Councils should be encouraged to coordinate public procurement policies across cities, counties and regions to back local businesses and create local jobs. Local place-based solutions, operating across different agencies and government departments, should be used more to tackle ingrained problems such as isolated minority communities and families in crisis. Local communities should be given greater rights to acquire and control community assets. Parks, public spaces and even high streets could be run by committees of residents, and local sports clubs could take control of playing fields and pitches. Swathes of public sector land should be turned into community land trusts, allowing local residents to develop and run housing developments. When community assets – such as post offices, pubs and village shops – close, residents should have greater powers and financial support to take ownership and run them on a co-operative basis.

There is a host of other ways we can form new associations and institutions to boost community. By making National Citizen Service mandatory, we could ask young people to volunteer in support of public services, as hospital visitors, for example, or care home workers, and to help charities, at home or overseas. By creating modern forms of guilds – professional and sectoral organizations that provide training, occupational licensing, and so on – we could create new means of cooperation and collaboration on the basis of shared interests and challenges. By paying the country's great cultural assets – theatres, galleries and museums – to set up regional branches, we can improve the quality of life in more of our cities beyond London.

We could do more to make use of the social capital of older people, by encouraging them to mentor younger people as they study and work, or by taking up teaching roles. We could – just as we do with jury service – draw citizens' names and ask them to participate in particular community services, working with vulnerable families for example, for fixed periods. We could do far more to help families and voluntary organizations to sponsor refugees, helping them with their housing and integration into the community. We could do more to help people to spin out of the public sector and create mutuals and co-operatives that provide services locally and nationally.

Through an advanced industrial strategy, we can create powerful new institutions that represent neither the market nor the state. Chambers of commerce could be put on a statutory footing, for example, as they are in Germany, and charged with providing training, legal advice and trade support. Catapult centres, which boost research and development by bringing together scientists, researchers and industry, are still small in number and funded modestly. They should be expanded and their budgets should be increased. New networks should be created to encourage the exchange and transfer of knowledge between academia and industry. A new world-class research university, proposed above, could be consciously located outside the South East of England, in the Midlands or the North.

New regional banks would be market institutions, but market institutions grounded in their localities. Likewise, new investment vehicles – taking advantage of a policy shift towards a better balance between debt and equity corporate financing – could be established along regional lines. University investment funds, designed to attract equity funding for start-ups spinning out of academia, would be based on location. Other place-based investment funds might be set up, emphasizing to both entrepreneurs and investors their connections to particular locations.

We need a revival of associations and institutions at a national level too. Brexit, and a move away from supranational government, ought to be an opportunity to revitalize parliamentary democracy and our governing institutions. So, too, should a move towards a more federal system. But we need to do more to create common purpose and common moments in which we can all share.

A new bank holiday could be created on 11 November to allow us to remember why service, sacrifice, duty and democracy are so important. There should be more free-to-air national moments on television – in particular national sports such as football, cricket and rugby – and live broadcasts on free-to-air television and radio from performances at the Royal Shakespeare Theatre and the Royal Opera House. Football's FA Cup could include teams from across the whole of the United Kingdom, rather than just England and Wales. The Guards Division – which attracts huge crowds in London for the Trooping of the Colour and similar events – could parade in towns and cities around the country. The BBC – which needs to transform itself in face of the huge changes in the media – should be reformed to rediscover its original public service ethos established by Lord Reith.

None of these things are likely to happen by chance. Policy-makers need to identify where community can succeed where the market and the state cannot. And they need to steadily and carefully remove the barriers to community action, build up human and social capital, and act as a catalyst for a new community spirit. Community is not a cheap alternative to what the state can do, but it is an important safeguard against abuses of state and market power. And it can reduce the demands upon the state by making society stronger and more prosperous.

We need a new round of enabling legislation to set off a wave of social enterprise and localism. This will include more powers for councils and mayors, more power for communities to take control of their local amenities, and more help for public sector workers to create mutuals and cooperatives. We should encourage municipal leaders to establish new institutions that protect workers, build houses and raise capital for local businesses. Instead of simply creating new quangos or tasking parts of the public sector to meet new challenges – such as the need to advise businesses on how to look after their workers in a changing labour market – we should set up new social enterprises with autonomy and the freedom to think for themselves. Organizations similar to those that help young people to work in public services – like Teach First or Police Now – can be created to help older people at the end of their careers to make a contribution. In education, Now Teach does precisely this, but other institutions are needed to use the experience and social capital of older citizens. Organizations that help people to create social institutions and serve local communities – such as the New Schools Network, which helps people to set up free schools, or Reset, which helps communities to sponsor and welcome refugees – should be established to help create other institutions and initiatives with social value.

One nation once more

We began chapter 1 with an account of how ultra-liberalism is fuelling the twin crises – cultural and economic – that are engulfing British life. It concludes with suggestions as to how we might, by returning to long-held conservative principles and refashioning them to meet the challenges of today and tomorrow, produce a communitarian correction and overcome those crises.

Undoubtedly, some will argue that changes of this kind are 'not conservative'. But there is nothing unconservative about embracing a positive purpose for government, nor for doing all we can to restore community to the strength and vitality it once enjoyed. If these proposals mark a break with any intellectual or ideological tradition, they seek to overthrow the excesses of ideological ultra-liberalism.

Freed from this ideological trap, conservatives can confront the challenges we face with confidence. We can revitalize our economy to increase prosperity and make sure that everybody – from every corner of the country and every social class – can share in it. And we can bring Britain back together by restoring our sense of citizenship, solidarity and proud national identity. There is more to life than the market, more to conservatism than the individual, and more to the future than the destruction of cultures and nations. If we accept this reality, and reveal ideological liberalism's teleological tendency for the myth it has always been, we can start to make the world a better, if not perfect, place. We can discover the solutions to our problems, and we can – like generations of conservatives before us – remake one nation and prosper.

NOTES

Introduction: Out of the Arena

1 *Daily Mail*, 15 July 2016. https://www.dailymail.co.uk/news/article-3691248/MARCH-MERITOCRATS-loads-new-Cabinet-state-educated-Ministers-brutal-day-level-sacking-modern-history.html

2 *Reuters*, 11 October 2018. https://www.reuters.com/article/us-china-usa-nuclear/u-s-tightens-controls-on-china-imports-of-nuclear-components-idUSKCN1ML2V9

3 *Daily Mail*, 5 October 2016 and *Guardian*, 5 October 2016. https://www.dailymail.co.uk/debate/article-3828041/DAILY-MAIL-COMMENT-Theresa-s-bold-vision-enemy-within.html and https://www.theguardian.com/commentisfree/2016/oct/05/the-guardian-view-on-theresa-mays-conference-speech-actions-not-words-will-decide

4 Twitter, 5 October 2016. https://twitter.com/Peggynoonannyc/status/783828734277189632

5 T. May, *The good that government can do*, 5 October 2016. http://press.conservatives.com/post/151378268295/prime-minister-the-good-that-government-can-do

6 *Ibid.*

7 T. May, *We can make Britain a country that works for everyone*, 11

July 2016. https://press.conservatives.com/post/147947450370/we-can-make-britain-a-country-that-works-for

8 T. May, *Leadership campaign launch speech*, 30 June 2016. https://www.conservativehome.com/parliament/2016/06/theresa-mays-launch-statement-full-text.html

9 T. May, *Britain After Brexit: A Vision of a Global Britain*, 2 October 2016. https://press.conservatives.com/post/151239411635/prime-minister-britain-after-brexit-a-vision-of

10 T. May, *The Government's negotiating objectives for exiting the EU*, 17 January 2017. https://www.gov.uk/government/speeches/the-governments-negotiating-objectives-for-exiting-the-eu-pm-speech

11 T. May, *Speech to the Congress of Tomorrow*, 26 January 2017. https://www.gov.uk/government/speeches/prime-ministers-speech-to-the-republican-party-conference-2017

12 Private conversation.

13 *BBC News Online*, 4 January 2017. https://www.bbc.co.uk/news/uk-politics-38503504

14 *BBC News Online*, 24 February 2017. https://www.bbc.co.uk/news/uk-politics-39064149

15 *The Independent*, 15 April 2017. https://www.independent.co.uk/news/uk/politics/theresa-may-s-conservatives-are-21-points-ahead-of-labour-in-a-new-poll-a7685271.html

16 *The Daily Telegraph*, 6 March 2017. https://www.telegraph.co.uk/news/2017/03/06/case-early-general-election-theresa-may-should-free-put-brexit/

17 Conservative Party, *Forward Together: Our Plan for a Stronger Britain and a Prosperous Future*, 18 May 2017. https://s3.eu-west-2.amazonaws.com/conservative-party-manifestos/Forward+Together+-+Our+Plan+for+a+Stronger+Britain+and+a+More+Prosperous....pdf

18 *The Times*, 19 May 2017. https://www.thetimes.co.uk/article/mainstream-may-reaches-out-to-labour-heartlands-j69mrjz6s

19 *The Daily Telegraph*, 19 May 2017. https://www.telegraph.co.uk/news/2017/05/18/theresa-may-redefines-conservatism-tories-move-thatcher/

20 See, for example, the *Guardian*, 19 May 2017 and *The Daily Telegraph*, 19 May 2017. https://www.theguardian.com/commentisfree/2017/may/18/the-guardian-view-on-theresa-may-manifesto-a-new-toryism and https://www.telegraph.co.uk/news/2017/05/18/david-cameron-patronised-old-people-bribes-theresa-may-honest/

21 *The Spectator*, 18 May 2017. https://blogs.spectator.co.uk/2017/05/tory-dementia-tax-backfire-theresa-may/

22 *The Daily Telegraph*, 22 May 2017. https://www.telegraph.co.uk/news/2017/05/22/general-election-2017-latest-news-polls-analysis/

23 *The Economist*, 6 August 2016. https://www.economist.com/britain/2016/08/06/the-sage-of-birmingham

24 *Financial Times*, 22 May 2017. https://www.ft.com/content/4a2a842e-3ed9-11e7-9d56-25f963e998b2

25 *Sunday Times*, 28 May 2017. https://www.thetimes.co.uk/article/general-election-theresa-may-is-trying-hard-to-lose-but-jeremy-corbyn-has-come-to-her-rescue-n6nrk53h7

26 *The Independent*, 30 July 2019. https://www.independent.co.uk/voices/boris-johnson-no-deal-brexit-us-trade-trump-nancy-pelosi-congress-a9026716.html

27 T. Roosevelt, *Citizenship in a Republic*, 23 April 1910.

Chapter 1: The Tyranny of the Minority

1 J. Gray, *Gray's Anatomy: Selected Writings*, Penguin, 2016, p. 78.

2 *Ibid.*, p. 25.

3 T. Hobbes, *Leviathan*, Cambridge University Press, 1996, p. 89.

4 J. Locke, *The Second Treatise of Government*, Barnes and Noble, 2004, p. 56.

5 Cited by I. Berlin, 'Two Concepts of Liberty', *Four Essays on Liberty*, Oxford University Press, 1969. http://cactus.dixie.edu/green/B_Readings/I_Berlin%20Two%20Concpets%20of%20Liberty.pdf

6 A. Smith, *The Theory of Moral Sentiments*, Logos Books, 2018, p. 10.

7 J. Schumpeter, *Capitalism, Socialism and Democracy*, Routledge, 1994, p. 162.

8 J. Schumpeter, cited by T. McCraw, *Prophet of Innovation: Joseph Schumpeter and Creative Destruction*, Harvard University Press, 2009, p. 424.

9 J. Bentham, cited in P. Schofield, C. Pease-Watkin and C. Blamires (eds), *The Collected Works of Jeremy Bentham: Rights, Representation and Reform*, Clarendon Press, 2002, p. 330.

10 J. Bentham, cited by R. Nisbet, *The Quest for Community*, ISI Books, 2014, p. 4.

11 F. A. Hayek, *Law, Legislation and Liberty, Volume 2: The Mirage of Social Justice*, University of Chicago Press, 1976.

12 A. Rand, *The Fountainhead*, Penguin, 2007.

13 J. Carens, 'Aliens and Citizens: The Case for Open Borders', *The Review of Politics*, Vol. 49, No. 2, Spring 1987, p. 252.

14 *Jackson and others v. Her Majesty's Attorney General*, UKHL 56, 2005, https://publications.parliament.uk/pa/ld200506/ldjudgmt/jd051013/jack.pdf

15 *Ibid.*

16 *Ibid.*

17 *Ibid.*

18 *Ibid.*

19 T. Bingham, *The Rule of Law*, Penguin, 2011, p. 167.

20 J. Sumption, *In Praise of Politics*, 2019 Annual Reith Lecture. https://www.bbc.co.uk/sounds/play/m0005f05

21 F. Engels, *Anti-Dühring*, in *Marx/Engels Collected Works Vol. 25*, Lawrence & Wishart, 1987, p. 268.

22 D. Goodhart, *The Road to Somewhere: The New Tribes Shaping British Politics*, Penguin, 2017, p. 15.

23 BBC Trust, *From See-Saw to Wagon Wheel: Safeguarding Impartiality in the 21ˢᵗ Century*, p. 65.

24 *Ibid.*, p. 66.

25 BBC Trust, *A BBC Trust Review of the Breadth of Opinion Reflected in the BBC's Output*, July 2013, p. 28.

26 *Mail on Sunday*, 21 October 2006. https://www.dailymail.co.uk/news/article-411846/We-biased-admit-stars-BBC-News.html

27 Private conversation.

28 Private conversation.

29 R. Tombs and G. Gudgin, 'Our fellow academics must stop push-

ing dishonest anti-Brexit propaganda', *Brexit Central*, 17 February 2018. https://brexitcentral.com/fellow-academics-must-stop-push ing-dishonest-anti-brexit-propaganda/

30 See, for example, J. Brennan, *Against Democracy*, Princeton University Press, 2016.

31 R. Eatwell and M. Goodwin, *National Populism: The Revolt Against Liberal Democracy*, Pelican Books, 2018, pp. 107–11.

32 K. Joseph, 'The Quest for Common Ground', in *Stranded on the Middle Ground? Reflections on Circumstances and Policies*, Centre for Policy Studies, 1976, p. 19.

33 B. Shafer and W. Claggett, *The Two Majorities: The Issue Context of Modern American Politics*, Johns Hopkins University Press, 1995.

34 M. Ashcroft, *The space for a new party isn't just in the centre of politics*, 1 April 2019. https://lordashcroftpolls.com/2019/04/the-space-for-a-new-party-isnt-just-in-the-centre-of-politics/

35 Onward, *Generation Why? What is driving the growing age gap in British politics and how the centre right should respond*, 8 April 2019, p. 3. https://www.ukonward.com/wp-content/uploads/2019/04/Onward-Generation-Why-online-PDF.pdf

36 YouGov study, June 2018. https://d25d2506sfb94s.cloudfront. net/cumulus_uploads/document/07kprp1z3i/Results_180627_rep resentedbyparty_w.pdf

37 J. Gray, *Two Faces of Liberalism*, Polity Press, 2000, p. 105.

38 *Ibid.*

39 Berlin, 'Two Concepts of Liberty'.

40 *Ibid.*

41 R. H. Tawney, cited by T. E. Utley and J. Stuart Maclure (eds), *Documents of Modern Political Thought*, Cambridge University Press, 2013, p. 59.

42 I. Berlin, 'Two Concepts of Liberty'.

43 B. Constant, *The Liberty of the Ancients Compared with that of the Moderns*, lecture to the Athénée Royal of Paris, 1819.

44 T. Penelhum, 'The Analysis of Faith in St Thomas Aquinas', *Religious Studies*, Vol. 13, No. 2, June 1977, pp. 133–54.

45 H. Rosenblatt, *The Lost History of Liberalism: From Ancient Rome to the Twenty-First Century*, Princeton University Press, 2018.

46 J. S. Mill, *On Liberty and Other Essays*, Oxford University Press, 1991, p. 69.

47 D. Hume, *Essays and Treatises on Several Subjects*, p. 254.

48 E. Burke, *Reflections on the Revolution in France*, Penguin, 1986, pp. 150–1.

49 R. Thaler, *Misbehaving: The Making of Behavioral Economics*, W. W. Norton and Company, 2015.

50 D. Kahneman, *Thinking, Fast and Slow*, Penguin, 2011, p. 411.

51 J. Haidt, *The Righteous Mind: Why Good People Are Divided by Politics and Religion*, Penguin, 2013, p. 367.

52 *Ibid.*, p.368

53 *Ibid.*, p. xvi.

54 D. Willetts, quoted in RSA/Prospect Political Debate, *Diversity versus Solidarity*, 28 January 2003.

55 P. Collier, *The Future of Capitalism: Facing the New Anxieties*, Allen Lane, p. 197.

56 E. Kaufmann, *Whiteshift: Populism, Immigration and the Future of White Majorities*, Allen Lane, 2018, pp. 419–20.

57 R. Putnam, '*E Pluribus Unum*: Diversity and Community in the Twenty-First Century', *Scandinavian Political Studies*, Vol. 30, No. 2, 2007, p. 138.

Chapter 2: Destructive Creation

1 B. Clinton, *Speech on China Trade Bill*, 9 March 2000. http://movies2.nytimes.com/library/world/asia/030900clinton-china-text.html

2 *Ibid.*

3 *Ibid.*

4 *Bloomberg Businessweek*, 4 October 2018. https://www.bloomberg.com/news/features/2018-10-04/the-big-hack-how-china-used-a-tiny-chip-to-infiltrate-america-s-top-companies

5 World Bank, https://www.worldbank.org/en/country/china/overview, accessed January 2019.

6 World Bank, https://data.worldbank.org/country/china, accessed January 2019.

7 *Ibid.*

8 HSBC, *The World in 2030*, 28 September 2018. https://www.hsbc.com/news-and-insight/2018/the-world-in-2030

9 *Washington Post*, 26 March 2018. https://www.washingtonpost.com/news/fact-checker/wp/2018/03/26/president-trumps-claim-that-china-caused-60000-u-s-factories-to-close

10 *Ibid.*

11 B. Milanovic, 'Global Income Inequality by the Numbers: In History and Now, An Overview', World Bank Policy Research Working Paper No. 6259, 1 November 2012. https://papers.ssrn.com/sol3/papers.cfm?abstract_id=2173655

12 *Ibid.*

13 *Ibid.*

14 See, for example, A. Corlett, *Examining an Elephant: Globalisation and the lower middle class of the rich world*, Resolution Foundation, September 2016. https://www.resolutionfoundation.org/app/uploads/2016/09/Examining-an-elephant.pdf. Or H. Kharas and B. Seidel, *What's happening to the world income distribution? The elephant chart revisited*, Brookings Institution, April 2018. https://www.brookings.edu/wp-content/uploads/2018/04/workingpaper114-elephantchartrevisited.pdf

15 Kharas and Seidel, *What's happening to the world income distribution?*

16 Corlett, *Examining an Elephant.*

17 Economic Policy Institute, *The Productivity-Pay Gap*, August 2018. https://www.epi.org/productivity-pay-gap/

18 M. Whittaker, *A recovery for all? The evolution of the relationship between economic growth and pay before, during and since the financial crisis*, Resolution Foundation, September 2015. https://www.resolutionfoundation.org/app/uploads/2015/09/Productivity-briefing.pdf

19 Office for National Statistics, *UK labour market: September 2018*, 11 September 2018, Figure 9, Great Britain average weekly earnings at constant 2015 prices, seasonally adjusted. https://www.ons.gov.uk/employmentandlabourmarket/peopleinwork/employmentandemployeetypes/bulletins/uklabourmarket/september2018#average-weekly-earnings

20 Kharas and Seidel, *What's happening to the world income distribution?*

21 Corlett, *Examining an Elephant.*

22 J. Bailey, J. Coward and M. Whittaker, *Painful Separation: An international study of the weakening relationship between economic growth and the pay of ordinary workers*, Resolution Foundation, October 2011. https://www.resolutionfoundation.org/app/uploads/2014/08/Painful-Separation.pdf

23 R. Baldwin, *The Great Convergence: Information Technology and the New Globalization*, Harvard University Press, 2016.

24 *Ibid.*, p. 86.

25 *Ibid.*, p. 136.

26 *Ibid.*, p. 161.

27 House of Commons Library Briefing Paper, *Manufacturing: Statistics and Policy*, 2 January 2018, p. 4.

28 *Ibid.*, p. 6.

29 *Ibid.*, p. 7.

30 *Ibid.*

31 Baldwin, *The Great Convergence*, p. 6.

32 L. Gardiner and A. Corlett, *Looking Through the Hourglass: Hollowing Out of the UK Jobs Market Pre- and Post-Crisis*, Resolution Foundation, March 2015. https://www.resolutionfoundation.org/app/uploads/2015/03/Polarisation-full-slide-pack.pdf

33 M. Taylor, *Good Work: The Taylor Review of Modern Working Practices*, July 2017, p. 25. https://assets.publishing.service.gov.uk/government/uploads/system/uploads/attachment_data/file/627671/good-work-taylor-review-modern-working-practices-rg.pdf

34 D. Autor and A. Salomons, *Is Automation Labor Share-Displacing? Productivity Growth, Employment, and the Labor Share*, Brookings Institution, March 2018. https://www.brookings.edu/wp-content/uploads/2018/03/AutorSalomons_Text.pdf

35 *Robots Aren't Taking the Jobs – Just the Paychecks*, Brookings Institution, 8 March 2018. https://www.brookings.edu/blog/brookings-now/2018/03/08/robots-arent-taking-the-jobs-just-the-paychecks-and-other-new-findings-in-economics/

36 Office for National Statistics, *UK labour market: September 2018*, 11 September 2018, Figure 9, Great Britain average weekly earnings at constant 2015 prices, seasonally adjusted. https://www.ons.

gov.uk/employmentandlabourmarket/peopleinwork/employment
andemployeetypes/bulletins/uklabourmarket/september2018#av
erage-weekly-earnings

37 Office for National Statistics, *Employee Earnings in the UK: 2019*,
29 October 2019. https://www.ons.gov.uk/employmentandlabour
market/peopleinwork/earningsandworkinghours/bulletins/annual
surveyofhoursandearnings/2019

38 S. Clarke and G. Bangham, *Counting the Hours: Two Decades of
Changes in Earnings and Hours Worked*, Resolution Foundation,
January 2018, pp. 2–3. https://www.resolutionfoundation.org/
app/uploads/2018/01/Counting-the-hours.pdf

39 *Ibid.*, p. 11.

40 I. Hogarth, *AI Nationalism*, 13 June 2018. https://www.ianhogar
th.com/blog/2018/6/13/ai-nationalism

41 McKinsey Global Institute, *A Future That Works: Automation,
Employment and Productivity*, January 2017, p. 5. https://www.
mckinsey.com/~/media/McKinsey/Featured%20Insights/Digital
%20Disruption/Harnessing%20automation%20for%20a%20fut
ure%20that%20works/MGI-A-future-that-works_Full-report.
ashx

42 *Politico*, 11 September 2018. https://www.politico.eu/article/
trump-calls-macrons-comments-on-building-a-european-army-
to-defend-against-u-s-insulting/

43 *The Daily Telegraph*, 25 June 2015. https://www.telegraph.co.uk/
technology/internet-security/11699833/The-new-Cold-War-
how-Russia-and-China-are-hacking-British-companies-and-
spying-on-their-employees.html

44 Intelligence and Security Committee, *Foreign Involvement in
the Critical National Infrastructure*, June 2013. https://assets.
publishing.service.gov.uk/government/uploads/system/uploads/
attachment_data/file/205680/ISC-Report-Foreign-Investment-
in-the-Critical-National-Infrastructure.pdf

45 *China Daily*, 29 August 2018. http://www.chinadaily.com.cn/a/
201808/29/WS5b867952a310add14f3887ec.html

46 Council on Foreign Relations, *China's Massive Belt and Road
Initiative*, 21 February 2019. https://www.cfr.org/backgrounder/
chinas-massive-belt-and-road-initiative

47 *Financial Times*, 11 April 2019. https://www.ft.com/content/c098 e654-5bfc-11e9-9dde-7aedca0a081a

48 *Bloomberg*, 15 February 2018. https://www.bloomberg.com/news/ articles/2018-02-15/china-2017-holdings-of-u-s-treasuries-rise-most-in-seven-years

49 Frontex, *FRAN Quarterly, October-December 2015*, 10 March 2016. https://frontex.europa.eu/assets/Publications/Risk_Analysis/FR AN_Q4_2015.pdf

50 *Politico*, 6 January 2016. https://www.politico.eu/article/germany-1-1-million-refugee-arrivals-in-2015/

51 International Organization for Migration. http://migration.iom. int/europe?type=arrivals

52 International Centre for the Study of Radicalisation, *From Daesh to Diaspora*, 23 July 2018. https://icsr.info/wp-content/uploads/ 2018/07/Women-in-ISIS-report_20180719_web.pdf

53 *The Times*, 19 June 2018. https://www.thetimes.co.uk/article/ italian-populist-matteo-salvini-pledges-census-of-gypsies-xb7dnr hds

54 European Council, *Council Conclusions*, 28 June 2018. https:// www.consilium.europa.eu/en/press/press-releases/2018/06/29/ 20180628-euco-conclusions-final/

55 ONS, *Overview of the UK Population*, 1 November 2018. https://www. ons.gov.uk/peoplepopulationandcommunity/populationandmi-gration/populationestimates/articles/overviewoftheukpopulation/ november2018

56 Resolution Foundation, *A New Generational Contract: The Final Report of the Intergenerational Commission*, 8 May 2018, pp. 90–1. https://www.resolutionfoundation.org/app/uploads/2018/05/ A-New-Generational-Contract-Full-PDF.pdf

57 *Ibid.*, p. 92.

58 *Ibid.*, p. 96.

59 *Ibid.*, p. 11.

60 *Ibid.*, p. 13.

61 Ipsos MORI, *Global Trends 2017*. https://www.ipsosglobaltrends. com/financial-security-betterworse-than-parents/

62 ONS, *International Comparisons of UK Productivity*, 6 April 2018. https://www.ons.gov.uk/economy/economicoutputandproductivi

ty/productivitymeasures/bulletins/internationalcomparisonsofpro
ductivityfinalestimates/2016

63 *Ibid.*

64 ONS, *The 2008 Recession Ten Years On*, 30 April 2018. https://
www.ons.gov.uk/economy/grossdomesticproductgdp/articles/
the2008recession10yearson/2018-04-30

65 OECD, *Employment Outlook 2018*, 4 July 2018. https://data.oecd.
org/earnwage/average-wages.htm

66 ONS, *Regional and Sub-Regional Productivity in the UK*, 7 February
2018. https://www.ons.gov.uk/employmentandlabourmarket/peo
pleinwork/labourproductivity/articles/regionalandsubregionalpro
ductivityintheuk/february2018

67 ONS, *Employee Earnings in the UK: 2018*, 25 October 2018. https://
www.ons.gov.uk/employmentandlabourmarket/peopleinwork/
earningsandworkinghours/bulletins/annualsurveyofhoursandearn
ings/2018

68 A. Ward, M. Belén Zinni and P. Marianna, *International Productivity
Gaps: Are Labour Input Measures Comparable?* OECD Publishing,
4 December 2018, pp. 56–7. https://www.oecd-ilibrary.org/docs
erver/5b43c728-en.pdf?expires=1547116884&id=id&accname=
guest&checksum=80B89E665490AC0D855539FBEA39AF64

69 McKinsey Global Institute, *Bridging Global Infrastructure Gaps*,
June 2016, p. 7. https://www.mckinsey.com/~/media/McKinsey/
Industries/Capital%20Projects%20and%20Infrastructure/Our%
20Insights/Bridging%20global%20infrastructure%20gaps/Brid
ging-Global-Infrastructure-Gaps-Full-report-June-2016.ashx

70 *New Statesman*, 15 August 2012. https://www.newstatesman.
com/blogs/politics/2012/08/exclusive-osbornes-supporters-turn-
him

71 *Hansard*, 5 June 2018, col. 168. https://hansard.parliament.uk/com
mons/2018-06-05/debates/ED5F2A14-318D-4A18-8414-E472
C9608DD2/AirportsNationalPolicyStatement

72 Department for Business, Energy and Industrial Strategy, *Prices of
Fuels Purchased by Non-Domestic Consumers in the United Kingdom*,
Table 3.4.2, 20 December 2018. https://www.gov.uk/government/
statistical-data-sets/gas-and-electricity-prices-in-the-non-domest
ic-sector

73 Department for Business, Energy and Industrial Strategy, *Industrial Electricity Prices in the IEA*, Table 5.3.1, 20 December 2018. https://www.gov.uk/government/statistical-data-sets/international-industrial-energy-prices

74 HM Government, *Northern Powerhouse Strategy*, November 2016, p. 12. https://assets.publishing.service.gov.uk/government/uploads/system/uploads/attachment_data/file/571562/NPH_strategy_web.pdf

75 HM Government, *Industrial Strategy: Building a Britain Fit for the Future*, p. 154. https://assets.publishing.service.gov.uk/government/uploads/system/uploads/attachment_data/file/664563/industrial-strategy-white-paper-web-ready-version.pdf

76 *Ibid.*, p. 61.

77 OECD, *Economic Surveys: United Kingdom*, October 2017, p. 36. http://www.oecd.org/eco/surveys/United-Kingdom-2017-OECD-economic-survey-overview.pdf

78 HM Government, *Industrial Strategy: Building a Britain Fit for the Future*, p. 62.

79 OECD, *Economic Surveys: United Kingdom*, October 2017, p. 36.

80 Department for Business, Innovation and Skills, *Geographic breakdown of public research and innovation expenditure*, June 2015, p. 9. https://assets.publishing.service.gov.uk/government/uploads/system/uploads/attachment_data/file/437447/bis-15-350-Public-expenditure-on-research-and-innovation-2013-14.pdf

81 HM Treasury, *Country and Regional Analysis*, November 2018. https://assets.publishing.service.gov.uk/government/uploads/system/uploads/attachment_data/file/759560/Country_and_Regional_Analysis_November_2018_rvsd.pdf

82 OECD, *Economic Surveys: United Kingdom*, October 2017, p. 41.

83 Onward, *Firing on all Cylinders: Building a Strong Economy from the Bottom Up*, 31 May 2019, p. 22. https://www.ukonward.com/wp-content/uploads/2019/05/ONWJ7142-Firing-on-all-cylinders-report-190530-WEB-1.pdf

84 OECD, *Economic Surveys: United Kingdom*, October 2017, p. 46.

85 *Ibid.*, pp. 50–1.

86 *Ibid.*, pp. 51–4.

87 ONS, *International Immigration and the Labour Market, UK: 2016*, 12 April 2017, Table 13. https://www.ons.gov.uk/peoplepopulation andcommunity/populationandmigration/internationalmigration/ articles/migrationandthelabourmarketuk/2016

88 *Ibid.*, Table 1.

89 Home Affairs Select Committee, *Oral Evidence: Post-Brexit Migration*, 9 October 2018. http://data.parliament.uk/writtenevid ence/committeeevidence.svc/evidencedocument/home-affairs-co mmittee/postbrexit-migration/oral/91576.html

90 A. Haldane, *The UK's Productivity Problem: Hub no Spokes*, speech to Academy of Social Sciences, 28 June 2018. https://www.bank ofengland.co.uk/-/media/boe/files/speech/2018/the-uks-product ivity-problem-hub-no-spokes-speech-by-andy-haldane.pdf

91 *Ibid.*

92 C. Mayer, *Firm Commitment: Why the Corporation is Failing Us and How to Restore Trust in it*, Oxford University Press, 2013, p. 85.

93 A. Smith, cited in S. Medema and W. Samuels, *The History of Economic Thought: A Reader*, Routledge, 2003, p. 174.

94 *Financial Times*, 23 October 2017. https://www.ft.com/content/ 9ba9e294-b7d4-11e7-8c12-5661783e5589

95 *Financial Times*, 29 March 2016. https://www.ft.com/content/bbe 57aa6-f1dc-11e5-aff5-19b4e253664a

96 K. Larkin, *Public Sector Relocations*, Centre for Cities, March 2010. https://www.centreforcities.org/wp-content/uploads/2014/09/ 10-03-23-Public-sector-relocations.pdf

97 T. Blair, *Speech to Labour Party Conference*, 27 September 2005. https://www.theguardian.com/uk/2005/sep/27/labourconference. speeches

98 ONS, *Household Disposable Income and Inequality in the UK: Financial year ending 2017*, 10 January 2018, Figure 12. https://www.ons. gov.uk/peoplepopulationandcommunity/personalandhouseholdfi nances/incomeandwealth/bulletins/householddisposableincome andinequality/financialyearending2017

99 OECD Data, *Income Inequality*. https://data.oecd.org/inequality/ income-inequality.htm

100 *Hansard*, 22 November 1990, col. 448. https://publications.par liament.uk/pa/cm199091/cmhansrd/1990-11-22/Debate-3.html

101 Institute for Fiscal Studies, *UK Health Spending*, 3 May 2017. https://www.ifs.org.uk/publications/9186

102 Institute for Fiscal Studies, *2018 annual report on education spending in England*, 17 September 2018. https://www.ifs.org.uk/publicat ions/13306

103 Institute for Fiscal Studies, *Changes in councils' adult social care and overall service spending in England, 2009/10 to 2017/18*, 13 June 2018. https://www.ifs.org.uk/uploads/BN240.pdf

104 OECD, *Inequalities in Household Wealth Across OECD Countries*, 20 June 2018, p. 14. https://www.oecd.org/officialdocuments/public displaydocumentpdf/?cote=SDD/DOC(2018)1&docLanguage= En

105 ONS, *Pension Participation at Record High but Contributions Cluster at Minimum Levels*, 8 May 2018. https://www.ons.gov.uk/employm entandlabourmarket/peopleinwork/workplacepensions/articles/ pensionparticipationatrecordhighbutcontributionsclusteratminim umlevels/2018-05-04

106 House of Commons Library, *Reform of Pension Tax Relief*, 12 October 2018, pp. 7–8. https://researchbriefings.parliament.uk/ ResearchBriefing/Summary/CBP-7505#fullreport

107 OECD, *Inequalities in Household Wealth Across OECD Countries*, p. 21.

108 Ministry of Housing, Communities and Local Government, *English Housing Survey: Home Ownership 2016–17*, 12 July 2018, p. 4. https://assets.publishing.service.gov.uk/government/uploads/ system/uploads/attachment_data/file/724323/Home_ownership. pdf

109 *Ibid.*

110 *Ibid.*, p. 1.

111 Department for Communities and Local Government, *Fixing our broken housing market*, February 2017, p. 9. https://assets.publish ing.service.gov.uk/government/uploads/system/uploads/attachm ent_data/file/590464/Fixing_our_broken_housing_market_-_pri nt_ready_version.pdf

112 *Ibid.*, p. 5.

113 OECD, *Inequalities in Household Wealth Across OECD Countries*, p. 40.

114 ONS, *International Migration and the Changing Nature of Housing in England – What Does the Available Evidence Show?* 25 May 2017. https://www.ons.gov.uk/peoplepopulationandcommunity/popu lationandmigration/internationalmigration/articles/international migrationandthechangingnatureofhousinginenglandwhatdoesthe availableevidenceshow/2017-05-25#international-migration-has-contributed-to-population-growth-in-england-in-recent-years

115 House of Commons Library, *Tackling the under-supply of housing in England*, 12 December 2018, p. 19.

116 National Housing Federation, *England Short of Four Million Homes*, 18 May 2018. https://www.housing.org.uk/press/press-releases/england-short-of-four-million-homes/

117 https://www.helptobuy.gov.uk

118 L. Judge, *Helping or Hindering? The Latest on Help to Buy*, Resolution Foundation, 3 November 2017. https://www.resolutionfoundation.org/media/blog/helping-or-hindering-the-latest-on-help-to-buy/

119 *Ibid.*

120 F. Sá, *The Effect of Foreign Investors on Local Housing Markets: Evidence from the UK*, 30 June 2017. https://www.kcl.ac.uk/sspp/research/economics/people/filipapaper-june2017.pdf

121 Tower Hamlets London Borough Council, *The Impact of Short-Term Holiday Platform Letting*, 13 November 2017. https://democracy.towerhamlets.gov.uk/documents/s116374/Main%20 Report.pdf

122 Mayor of London, *Housing in London: 2018, The evidence base for the Mayor's Housing Strategy*, July 2018, p. 20. https://airdrive-secure.s3-eu-west-1.amazonaws.com/london/dataset/housing-london/2018-08-10T11%3A55%3A25/2018.07.27%20Housing%20in%20London%202018.pdf?X-Amz-Algorithm=AWS4-HMAC-SH A256&X-Amz-Credential=AKIAJJDIMAIVZJDICKHA%2F2 0190201%2Feu-west-1%2Fs3%2Faws4_request&X-Amz-Date=20190201T122436Z&X-Amz-Expires=300&X-Amz-Signature=ceba3f48b1809798127e084edbe6c05ef2f406a372d1b7b6fe3868b 2f1fb985d&X-Amz-SignedHeaders=host

123 P. Bunn, A Pugh and C Yeates, *The Distributional Impact of Monetary Policy Easing in the UK between 2008 and 2014*, Staff Working Paper No. 720, March 2018. https://www.bankofengland.co.uk/-/media/boe/

files/working-paper/2018/the-distributional-impact-of-monet
ary-policy-easing-in-the-uk-between-2008-and-2014.pdf?la=en&
hash=AB17C765D8244FFFBF43E8EF9505FBF10DB65600

124 *Ibid.*, pp. 7–8.

125 *Ibid.*, p. 25.

126 H. Mumtaz and A. Theophilopoulou, 'The Impact of Monetary Policy on Inequality in the UK: An Empirical Analysis', *European Economic Review*, Vol. 98, Issue C, 2017. https://econpapers.repec. org/article/eeeecrev/v_3a98_3ay_3a2017_3ai_3ac_3ap_3a410-423.htm

127 OECD, *Inequalities in Household Wealth Across OECD Countries*, p. 7.

128 A. Haldane, *Whose Recovery?* 30 June 2016. https://www.bankofengl and.co.uk/speech/2016/whose-recovery

129 Department for Business, Energy and Industrial Strategy, *Trade Union Membership 2017: Statistical Bulletin*, May 2018, p. 4. https:// assets.publishing.service.gov.uk/government/uploads/system/up loads/attachment_data/file/712543/TU_membership_bulletin. pdf

130 HM Government, *United Kingdom Labour Market Enforcement Strategy, 2018/19*, May 2018, p. 10. https://assets.publishing.ser vice.gov.uk/government/uploads/system/uploads/attachment_ data/file/705503/labour-market-enforcement-strategy-2018-20 19-full-report.pdf

131 See, for example, A. Kügler, U. Schönberg and R. Schreiner, *Productivity Growth, Wage Growth and Unions*, European Central Bank, 8 June 2018. https://www.ecb.europa.eu/pub/conferences/ shared/pdf/20180618_ecb_forum_on_central_banking/Schoenbe rg_Uta_Paper.pdf

132 Taylor, *Good Work*, pp. 24–5.

133 *Ibid.*, p. 26.

134 HM Government, *United Kingdom Labour Market Enforcement Strategy, 2018/19*, p. 15.

135 Liz Truss, 19 March 2018. https://twitter.com/trussliz/status/97 5822789759389698?lang=en

136 Department for Business, Energy and Industrial Strategy, *Corporate Governance Reform*, November 2016, p. 16. https://ass

ets.publishing.service.gov.uk/government/uploads/system/up
loads/attachment_data/file/584013/corporate-governance-ref
orm-green-paper.pdf

137 Institute for Fiscal Studies, *Higher Education Funding in England:
Past, Present and Options for the Future*, July 2017, p. 17. https://
www.ifs.org.uk/uploads/publications/bns/BN211.pdf

138 A. Wolf, G. Domínguez-Reig and P. Sellen, *Remaking Tertiary
Education*, Education Policy Institute, November 2016, p. 19.
https://epi.org.uk/wp-content/uploads/2018/01/remaking-terti
ary-education-web.compressed.pdf

139 Department for Transport, *Rail Factsheet*, December 2018. https://
assets.publishing.service.gov.uk/government/uploads/system/
uploads/attachment_data/file/761352/rail-factsheet-2018.pdf

140 A. Quine, *A Third Way for Britain's Railways*, Adam Smith
Institute, 3 May 2018, p. 9. https://static1.squarespace.com/static/
56eddde762cd9413e151ac92/t/5b27e3b2352f53260847b9a8/
1529340854106/Railway+paper.pdf

141 ONS, *Labour Disputes in the UK: 2017*, 30 May 2018. https://
www.ons.gov.uk/employmentandlabourmarket/peopleinwork/
workplacedisputesandworkingconditions/articles/labourdisputes/
2017

142 Rail Delivery Group, *Easier Fares for All*, February 2019, p. 9.
https://www.raildeliverygroup.com/files/Publications/2019-02_
easier_fares_for_all.pdf

143 Quine, *A Third Way for Britain's Railways*, p. 9.

144 *Sky News*, 2 January 2018. https://news.sky.com/story/rail-fare-
increase-uk-train-prices-vs-rest-of-europe-11192890

145 Quine, *A Third Way for Britain's Railways*, p. 58.

146 Ofgem, *Retail Market Indicators*, January 2019. https://www.ofgem.
gov.uk/data-portal/retail-market-indicators

147 Citizens Advice, *Frozen Out: Extra Costs Faced by Vulnerable
Consumers in the Energy Market*, March 2017, p. 5. https://www.
citizensadvice.org.uk/Global/CitizensAdvice/Energy/Frozen%20
out.pdf

148 *Ibid.*

149 *Ibid.*, p. 4.

150 *Financial Times*, 12 September 2019.

151 Department for Business, Energy and Industrial Strategy, *Modernising Consumer Markets*, April 2018, p. 15. https://assets. publishing.service.gov.uk/government/uploads/system/uploads/ attachment_data/file/699937/modernising-consumer-markets-green-paper.pdf

152 National Audit Office, *The Economic Regulation of the Water Sector*, October 2015, p. 7. https://www.nao.org.uk/wp-content/ uploads/2014/07/The-economic-regulation-of-the-water-sector. pdf

153 *City AM*, 26 July 2015. http://www.cityam.com/220942/former-of wat-boss-ian-byatt-calls-london-super-sewer-real-disaster-and-says-its-unnecessary

154 M. Gove, *A Water Industry that Works for Everyone*, 1 March 2018. https://www.gov.uk/government/speeches/a-water-industry-that-works-for-everyone

155 Citizens Advice, *Energy Consumers' Mission Billions*, July 2017, p. 27. https://www.citizensadvice.org.uk/Global/CitizensAdvice/ Energy/EnergyConsumersMissingBillions.pdf

156 Gove, *A Water Industry that Works for Everyone*.

157 S. D. Anthony, S. P. Viguerie, E. I. Schwartz and J. Van Landeghem, *2018 Corporate Longevity Forecast: Creative Destruction is Accelerating*, February 2018. https://www.innosight.com/wp-content/uploads/2017/11/Innosight-Corporate-Longevity-2018. pdf

158 J. Bartlett, *The People Vs Tech*, Ebury Press, 2018, p. 120.

159 B. Obama, *We Now Stand at a Crossroads*, Nelson Mandela Memorial Lecture, Johannesburg, 17 July 2018. http://time.com/ 5341180/barack-obama-south-africa-speech-transcript/

160 *Guardian*, 25 April 2016. https://www.theguardian.com/business/ 2016/apr/25/bhs-philip-green-family-millions-administration-arcadia

161 House of Commons Work and Pensions and Business, Innovation and Skills Committees, *BHS*, July 2016, p. 4. https://publications. parliament.uk/pa/cm201617/cmselect/cmworpen/54/54.pdf? utm_source=54&utm_medium=module&utm_campaign=module reports

162 *Guardian*, 25 April 2016. https://www.theguardian.com/business/

2016/apr/25/bhs-philip-green-family-millions-administration-arcadia

163 House of Commons Business Innovation and Skills Committee, *Mike Ashley Must Be Accountable for Sports Direct Working Practices*, 22 July 2016. https://www.parliament.uk/business/committees/committees-a-z/commons-select/business-innovation-and-skills/news-parliament-2015/working-practices-at-sports-direct-report-published-16-17/

164 House of Commons Business Innovation and Skills Committee, *Employment Practices at Sports Direct*, 19 July 2016, p. 4. https://publications.parliament.uk/pa/cm201617/cmselect/cmbis/219/219.pdf?utm_source=219&utm_medium=module&utm_campaign=modulereports

165 *Guardian*, 21 March 2016. https://www.theguardian.com/business/2016/mar/21/sports-direct-founder-mike-ashley-snubs-call-mps-parliamentary-select-committee

166 *Guardian*, 15 December 2017. https://www.theguardian.com/business/2017/dec/15/persimmon-chair-resigns-chief-executive-obscene-bonus

167 *Guardian*, 9 January 2018. https://www.theguardian.com/business/2018/jan/09/persimmon-profits-chief-bonus-scheme

168 Office for National Statistics, *Average Weekly Earnings by Sector*, 19 February 2019. https://www.ons.gov.uk/employmentandlabourmarket/peopleinwork/earningsandworkinghours/datasets/averageweeklyearningsbysectorearn02/current

169 Gove, *A Water Industry that Works for Everyone*.

170 HM Government, *United Kingdom Labour Market Enforcement Strategy, 2018/19*, p. iv.

171 *The Daily Telegraph*, 26 November 2014. https://www.telegraph.co.uk/news/uknews/terrorism-in-the-uk/11253518/Facebook-could-have-prevented-Lee-Rigby-murder.html

172 *Daily Mirror*, 31 January 2019. https://www.mirror.co.uk/news/uk-news/amazon-storm-over-tax-bill-13936012

Chapter 3: E Pluribus Nihil

1 M. Young, *The Rise of the Meritocracy*, Penguin Books, p. 94.

2 *Ibid.*, p. 106.

3 *Ibid.*, pp. 107–8.

4 Twitter, 20 November 2014. https://twitter.com/emilythornb erry/status/535450556199075840

5 *The Times*, 6 September 2014. https://www.thetimes.co.uk/article/ tories-should-turn-their-backs-on-clacton-j0k5h6zld08

6 *Observer*, 19 June 2016. https://www.theguardian.com/comm entisfree/2016/jun/18/eu-referendum-vote-leave-campaign-poi sonous

7 V. Cable, *Speech to Liberal Democrat Spring Conference*, 11 March 2018. https://www.libdemvoice.org/in-full-vince-cables-speech- to-conference-56902.html

8 See, for example, comments by Barry Sheerman MP. *BBC News Online*, 29 October 2017. https://www.bbc.co.uk/news/uk-engl and-leeds-41795133

9 *Guardian*, 5 October 2016. https://www.theguardian.com/ politics/2016/oct/05/trump-brexit-education-gap-tearing-polit ics-apart

10 Sutton Trust, *Britain's Dying Dream of Social Mobility*, 26 September 2018. https://www.suttontrust.com/newsarchive/britains-dying- dream-of-social-mobility/

11 Social Mobility Commission, *State of the Nation 2017: Social Mobility in Great Britain*, November 2017, p. iii. https://assets.publishing. service.gov.uk/government/uploads/system/uploads/attachment_ data/file/662744/State_of_the_Nation_2017_-_Social_Mobility_ in_Great_Britain.pdf

12 *Ibid.*

13 Young, *The Rise of the Meritocracy*, p. 176.

14 Department for Education, *Early Years Foundation Stage Profile Results: 2017 to 2018*, underlying data, 18 October 2018. https:// www.gov.uk/government/statistics/early-years-foundation-stage- profile-results-2017-to-2018

15 Department for Education, *Analysing Family Circumstances and Education: Increasing Our Understanding of Ordinary Working Families*, April 2017, p. 38. https://dera.ioe.ac.uk/28896/1/Techni cal%20consultation%20document.pdf

16 Department for Education, *House Prices and Schools: Do Houses Close to the Best-Performing Schools Cost More? Ad Hoc Research Note*, April

2017, p. 3. https://assets.publishing.service.gov.uk/government/uploads/system/uploads/attachment_data/file/600623/House_prices_and_schools.pdf

17 Sutton Trust, *Access to Advantage*, 7 December 2018. https://www.suttontrust.com/research-paper/access-to-advantage-university-admissions

18 Sutton Trust, *Social Mobility Fact Sheet*. https://www.suttontrust.com/wp-content/uploads/2018/01/Socialmobility_SuttonTrust_Factsheet_.pdf

19 Sutton Trust, *Britain's Dying Dream of Social Mobility*.

20 OECD Data, *Income Inequality*. https://data.oecd.org/inequality/income-inequality.htm

21 Social Mobility Commission, *State of the Nation 2017*, p. 7.

22 *Ibid.*, p. v.

23 OECD, *A Broken Social Elevator? How to Promote Social Mobility*, 15 June 2018, p. 27. https://read.oecd-ilibrary.org/social-issues-migration-health/broken-elevator-how-to-promote-social-mobility_9789264301085-en#page28

24 Social Mobility Commission, *State of the Nation 2017*, p. v.

25 *The Independent*, 17 February 2018. https://www.independent.co.uk/voices/first-time-buyers-economic-crisis-bank-mum-dad-wealth-property-a8215571.html

26 Channel Four, *Death of a Revolutionary*, 13 April 2013. https://www.youtube.com/watch?v=7VlcjyNwA10

27 J. Greening, *Unlocking the Potential of a New Generation*, 30 March 2017. https://www.gov.uk/government/speeches/justine-greening-unlocking-the-potential-of-a-new-generation

28 *The Spectator*, 6 January 2018. https://www.spectator.co.uk/2018/01/why-isnt-angela-rayner-a-tory/

29 Goodhart, *The Road to Somewhere*, p. xv.

30 A. Haldane, *Whose Recovery?*

31 Centre for Cities, *The Great British Brain Drain: Where Graduates Move and Why*, November 2016, p. 1. https://www.centreforcities.org/wp-content/uploads/2016/11/16-11-18-The-Great-British-Brain-Drain.pdf

32 Centre for Cities, *Competing with the Continent: How UK Cities Compare with their European Counterparts*, September 2016, p. 12.

https://www.centreforcities.org/wp-content/uploads/2016/09/16-09-21-Competing-with-the-continent.pdf

33 *Ibid.*, p. 13.

34 Joseph Rowntree Foundation, *Uneven Growth: Tackling City Decline*, p. 1. https://www.jrf.org.uk/sites/default/files/jrf/files-research/tackling_declining_cities_report.pdf

35 *Ibid.*, p. 18.

36 Onward, *Human Capital: Why We Need a New Approach to Tackle Britain's Long Tail of Low Skills*, 3 July 2019, p. 24. https://www.ukonward.com/wp-content/uploads/2019/07/ONWJ7193-Human-Capital-report-190626-WEB.pdf

37 Centre for Cities, *Talk of the Town: The Economic Links between Cities and Towns*, September 2018. https://www.centreforcities.org/wp-content/uploads/2018/09/18-10-04-Talk-of-the-Town.pdf

38 *Ibid.*

39 Centre for Social Justice, *Turning the Tide: Social Justice in Five Seaside Towns*, August 2013, pp. 26–7. https://www.centreforsocialjustice.org.uk/core/wp-content/uploads/2016/08/Turning-the-Tide.pdf

40 N. Steel et al., 'Changes in Health in the Countries of the UK and 150 English Local Authority Areas 1990–2016: A Systematic Analysis for the Global Burden of Disease Study 2016', *The Lancet*, 24 October 2018. https://www.thelancet.com/journals/lancet/article/PIIS0140-6736(18)32207-4/fulltext

41 ONS, *Employee Earnings in the UK: 2018*, 25 October 2018. https://www.ons.gov.uk/employmentandlabourmarket/peopleinwork/earningsandworkinghours/bulletins/annualsurveyofhoursandearnings/2018

42 Goodhart, *The Road to Somewhere*, p. 3.

43 *Financial Times*, 4 September 2016. https://www.ft.com/content/7f49b034-7126-11e6-a0c9-1365ce54b926

44 C. Ainsley, *The New Working Class: How to Win Hearts, Minds and Votes*, Policy Press, 2018, p. 20.

45 G. Evans and J. Mellon, 'Social Class: Identity, Awareness and Political Attitudes: Why Are We Still Working Class?', *British Social Attitudes 33*, 2016. https://www.bsa.natcen.ac.uk/media/39094/bsa33_social-class_v5.pdf

46 *Ibid.*

47 Ainsley, *The New Working Class*, p. 25.

48 *Ibid.*, pp. 25–26.

49 *Ibid.*, p. 26.

50 *Ibid.*

51 Department for Education, *Analysing family circumstances and education*, p. 5.

52 *Ibid.*, p. 23.

53 Cabinet Office, *Race Disparity Audit: Summary Findings from the Ethnicity Facts and Figures Website*, October 2017 (revised March 2018), p. 41. https://assets.publishing.service.gov.uk/government/uploads/system/uploads/attachment_data/file/686071/Revised_RDA_report_March_2018.pdf

54 *Ibid.*, p. 10.

55 D. Snoussi and L. Mompelat, *We Are Ghosts: Race, Class and Institutional Prejudice*, Runnymede and CLASS, 9 July 2019, p. 16. https://www.runnymedetrust.org/uploads/publications/We%20Are%20Ghosts.pdf

56 Cabinet Office, *Race Disparity Audit*, pp. 13–15.

57 L. Casey, *The Casey Review: A Review into Opportunity and Integration*, December 2016, p. 32. https://assets.publishing.service.gov.uk/government/uploads/system/uploads/attachment_data/file/575973/The_Casey_Review_Report.pdf

58 *Guardian*, 7 January 2018. https://www.theguardian.com/commentisfree/2018/jan/07/british-education-failure-white-working-class

59 Department for Education, *National Curriculum Assessments at Key Stage 1 And Phonics Screening Checks in England, 2018*, 13 December 2018. https://www.gov.uk/government/publications/phonics-screening-check-and-key-stage-1-assessments-england-2018/national-curriculum-assessments-at-key-stage-1-and-phonics-screening-checks-in-england-2018

60 Department for Education, *Key Stage 4 including Multi-Academy Trust Performance, 2018*, 24 January 2019, pp. 29–30. https://assets.publishing.service.gov.uk/government/uploads/system/uploads/attachment_data/file/774014/2018_KS4_main_text.pdf

61 UCAS, *End of Cycle Report, 2018: Patterns of Equality in England*, Data Table 4: 'Entry rates for England domiciled 18 year old state school students by ethnic group', 12 March 2019. https://www.ucas.com/data-and-analysis/undergraduate-statistics-and-reports/ucas-undergraduate-end-cycle-reports/2018-end-cycle-report

62 *Financial Times*, 14 December 2018. https://www.ft.com/content/d53298f8-fe2d-11e8-ac00-57a2a826423e

63 A. Spielman, *Speech to the Wellington Festival of Education*, 22 June 2018. https://www.gov.uk/government/speeches/amanda-spielmans-speech-at-the-wellington-festival-of-education

64 ONS, *Regional Ethnic Diversity*, 1 August 2018, Updated 8 March 2019. https://www.ethnicity-facts-figures.service.gov.uk/british-population/national-and-regional-populations/regional-ethnic-diversity/latest

65 Social Mobility Commission, *State of the Nation 2017*, pp. 16–17.

66 ONS, *Estimated Number of Parents in Families with Dependent Children by Ethnic Group of the Parent, UK*, 2016, 12 October 2017. https://www.ons.gov.uk/peoplepopulationandcommunity/birthsdeathsandmarriages/families/adhocs/007594estimatednumberofparentsinfamilieswithdependentchildrenbyethnicgroupoftheparentuk2016

67 Goodhart, *The Road to Somewhere*, p. 202.

68 Mill, *On Liberty and Other Essays*, pp. 13–14.

69 *Ibid.*, p. 14.

70 *Ibid.*

71 Gray, *Two Faces of Liberalism*, p. 89.

72 Gray, *Gray's Anatomy*, pp. 516–17.

73 F. A. Hayek, *The Constitution of Liberty*, Routledge, 2006, p. 343.

74 *Ibid.*, p. 354.

75 *Ibid.*, p. 349.

76 M. Foucault, *The Order of Things: An Archaeology of the Human Sciences*, Routledge, 2002, p. 183.

77 Combahee River Collective, *Combahee River Collective Statement*, 1977. https://warwick.ac.uk/fac/arts/english/currentstudents/undergraduate/modules/fulllist/special/en304/syllabus2017-18/combahee_statement.pdf

78 K. Crenshaw, 'Demarginalizing the Intersection of Race and Sex: A Black Feminist Critique of Antidiscrimination Doctrine, Feminist Theory and Antiracist Politics', *University of Chicago Legal Forum*, Vol. 1989, No. 1, p. 140.

79 J. Butler, 'Performative Acts and Gender Constitution: An Essay in Phenomenology and Feminist Theory', *Theatre Journal*, Vol. 40, No. 4, December 1988, pp. 519–20.

80 A. Lentin, 'Beyond Denial: "Not Racism" as Racist Violence', *Continuum: Journal of Media and Cultural Studies*, Vol. 32, 2018.

81 Goodhart, *The Road to Somewhere*, p. 40.

82 Twitter, 26 July 2019. https://twitter.com/labourlewis/status/115 4650631547871233

83 Twitter, 26 July 2019. https://twitter.com/themendozawoman/ status/1154664706201858048?s=11

84 *Guardian*, 4 March 2019. https://www.theguardian.com/edu cation/2019/mar/04/birmingham-school-stops-lgbt-lessons-aft er-parent-protests

85 Home Office, *Counter-Extremism Strategy*, October 2015. https:// assets.publishing.service.gov.uk/government/uploads/system/up loads/attachment_data/file/470088/51859_Cm9148_Accessible. pdf

86 *Guardian*, 1 February 2019. https://www.theguardian.com/ society/2019/feb/01/fgm-mother-of-three-year-old-first-person- convicted-in-uk

87 A. Jay, *Independent Inquiry into Child Sexual Exploitation in Rotherham, 1997–2013*, August 2014, p. 30. https://www.rotherh am.gov.uk/downloads/file/1407/independent_inquiry_cse_in_ro therham

88 CEOP, *Threat Assessment of Child Sexual Exploitation and Abuse*, June 2013, p. 19. https://www.norfolklscb.org/wp-content/up loads/2015/03/CEOP_Threat-Assessment_CSE_JUN2013.pdf

89 Jay, *Independent Inquiry into Child Sexual Exploitation in Rotherham*, p. 147.

90 L. Casey, *Report of Inspection of Rotherham Metropolitan Council*, February 2015, p. 35. https://assets.publishing.service.gov.uk/gov ernment/uploads/system/uploads/attachment_data/file/401119/ 46966_Rotherham_Report_PRINT.pdf

91 *The Voice*, 21 March 2019. https://www.voice-online.co.uk/article/tension-labour-over-all-women-party-shortlists

92 See, for example, *Guardian*, 9 October 2015. https://www.theguardian.com/commentisfree/2015/oct/09/no-platform-universities-julie-bindel-exclusion-anti-feminist-crusade

93 *Guardian*, 20 February 2019. https://www.theguardian.com/sport/2019/feb/20/lgbt-group-drops-martina-navratilova-over-trans-gender-comments

94 *Sky News*, 2 July 2017. https://news.sky.com/story/grenfell-tower-inquiry-chair-sir-martin-moore-bick-urged-to-walk-with-victims-10933962

95 *The Independent*, 27 June 2017. https://www.independent.co.uk/news/uk/home-news/grenfell-tower-fire-cover-up-death-toll-stop-riot-david-lammy-mp-labour-london-prevent-a7809911.html

96 G. Lukianoff and J. Haidt, *The Coddling of the American Mind: How Good Intentions and Bad Ideas are Setting Up a Generation for Failure*, Penguin, 2018.

97 YouGov, *How Britain Voted*, 27 June 2016. https://yougov.co.uk/topics/politics/articles-reports/2016/06/27/how-britain-voted

98 *Observer*, 24 February 2019. https://www.theguardian.com/uk-news/2019/feb/24/labour-councils-remove-embedded-immigration-officers

99 *New York Times*, 18 November 2016. https://www.nytimes.com/2016/11/20/opinion/sunday/the-end-of-identity-liberalism.html

100 J. Gest, *The New Minority: White Working Class Politics in an Age of Immigration and Inequality*, Oxford University Press, 2016.

101 Eatwell and Goodwin, *National Populism*, p. 215.

102 E. Kaufmann, *Whiteshift: Populism, Immigration and the Future of White Majorities*, Allen Lane, 2018, p. 7.

103 *Ibid.*, pp. 520–1.

104 Eatwell and Goodwin, *National Populism*, p. 174.

105 Kaufmann, *Whiteshift*, p. 457.

106 DCLG, *Integrated Communities Strategy Green Paper*, March 2018, p. 43. https://assets.publishing.service.gov.uk/government/uploads/system/uploads/attachment_data/file/696993/Integrated_Communities_Strategy.pdf

107 Kaufmann, *Whiteshift*, pp. 391–411.

108 Social Integration Commission, *Kingdom United? Thirteen steps to tackle social segregation*, March 2015, p. 6. http://socialintegration commission.org.uk/images/sic_kingdomunited.pdf

109 Kaufmann, *Whiteshift*, pp. 416–17.

110 DCLG, *Integrated Communities Strategy Green Paper*, p. 11.

111 Casey, *The Casey Review*, p. 11.

112 Kaufmann, *Whiteshift*, p. 412.

113 *Ibid.*, p. 139.

114 *Ibid.*, pp. 409–10.

115 YouGov, *Where the Public Stands on Immigration*, 27 April 2018. https://d25d2506sfb94s.cloudfront.net/cumulus_uploads/docume nt/dqjh8rbx2e/InternalResults_180425_Immigration.pdf

116 Ipsos MORI, *Shifting Ground: 8 Key Findings from a Longitudinal Study on Attitudes towards Immigration and Brexit*, 17 October 2017, p. 4. https://www.ipsos.com/sites/default/files/ct/news/documen ts/2017-10/Shifting%20Ground_Unbound.pdf

117 ONS, *Provisional Long-Term International Migration Estimates*, 28 February 2019. https://www.ons.gov.uk/peoplepopulationand community/populationandmigration/internationalmigration/data sets/migrationstatisticsquarterlyreportprovisionallongterminter nationalmigrationltimestimates

118 Labour Party, *Because Britain Deserves Better*, April 1997. http:// www.politicsresources.net/area/uk/man/lab97.htm

119 Conservative Party, *An Invitation to Join the Government of Britain*, April 2010, p. 21. https://conservativehome.blogs.com/files/con servative-manifesto-2010.pdf

120 ONS, *Provisional Long-Term International Migration Estimates*, 28 February 2019. https://www.ons.gov.uk/peoplepopulationand community/populationandmigration/internationalmigration/data sets/migrationstatisticsquarterlyreportprovisionallongterminter nationalmigrationltimestimates

121 Private conversation.

122 ONS, *Provisional Long-Term International Migration Estimates*.

123 D. Goodhart, *The British Dream: Successes and Failures of Post-War Immigration*, Atlantic Books, 2013, p. 215.

124 OECD, *Is Migration Good for the Economy?* May 2014, p. 2. http://

www.oecd.org/els/mig/OECD%20Migration%20Policy%20De
      bates%20Numero%202.pdf

125 R. Rowthorn, *The Costs and Benefits of Large-Scale Immigration*,
      December 2015, p. 71. http://www.civitas.org.uk/pdf/Largescale
      Immigration

126 Migration Observatory, *The Labour Market Effects of Immigration*,
      14 December 2018. https://migrationobservatory.ox.ac.uk/resour
      ces/briefings/the-labour-market-effects-of-immigration/

127 ONS, *International migration and the changing nature of housing in
      England*.

128 Department for Education, *National Pupil Projections – Future
      Trends in Pupil Numbers*, 12 July 2018, p. 3. https://assets.publi
      shing.service.gov.uk/government/uploads/system/uploads/attach
      ment_data/file/723851/2018Release_Projections_Text.pdf

129 Kaufmann, *Whiteshift*, p. 204.

130 *Ibid.*, p. 53.

131 T. Phillips, *After 7/7: Sleepwalking to Segregation*, 26 September
      2005. https://www.jiscmail.ac.uk/cgi-bin/webadmin?A3=ind0509
      &L=CRONEM&E=quoted-printable&P=60513&B=——_%
      3D_NextPart_001_01C5C28A.09501783&T=text%2Fhtml;%20
      charset=iso-8859–1&pending=

132 Casey, *The Casey Review*, p. 10.

133 DCLG, *Integrated Communities Strategy Green Paper*, p. 12.

134 Casey, *The Casey Review*, p. 11.

135 DCLG, *Integrated Communities Strategy Green Paper*, p. 12.

136 *Ibid.*, p. 35.

137 *Ibid.*, p. 36.

138 Casey, *The Casey Review*, pp. 13–14.

139 T. Cantle, *Community Cohesion: A Report of the Independent Review
      Team*, December 2001, p. 9. http://tedcantle.co.uk/pdf/communi
      tycohesion%20cantlereport.pdf

140 Casey, *The Casey Review*, p. 5.

141 Cabinet Office, *Race Disparity Audit*, p. 8.

142 R. Nisbet, *The Quest for Community*, ISI Books, 2014,
      pp. 247–8.

143 *Ibid.*, p. 28.

144 D. Phillips, J. Curtice, M. Phillips and J. Perry (eds), *British Social*

Attitudes 35, 2018, p. 13. http://www.bsa.natcen.ac.uk/media/39284/bsa35_full-report.pdf

145 C. Hakim, 'Competing Family Models, Competing Social Policies', *Family Matters*, Number 64, Autumn 2003. http://www.catherine hakim.org/wp-content/uploads/2011/07/AIFSarticle.pdf

146 Phillips et al. (eds), *British Social Attitudes 35*, p. 12.

147 *Ibid.*

148 Edelman, *2019 Edelman Trust Barometer, UK Supplement*, 22 February 2019. https://www.slideshare.net/Edelman_UK/edel-man-trust-barometer-2019-uk-results-132908642

149 A. Park, C. Bryson, E. Clery, J. Curtice and M. Phillips (eds), *British Social Attitudes 30*, 2013, p. xvi, http://www.bsa.natcen.ac.uk/media/38723/bsa30_full_report_final.pdf

150 Reuters Institute, *Digital News Report 2018*, 2 April 2018, p. 63. ht tp://media.digitalnewsreport.org/wp-content/uploads/2018/06/di gital-news-report-2018.pdf?x89475

151 Bartlett, *The People Vs Tech*, p. 152.

152 Facebook website, accessed 5 April 2019. https://newsroom. fb.com/company-info/

153 *Guardian*, 19 March 2018. https://www.theguardian.com/tech nology/2018/mar/19/snapchat-uk-ad-revenue-overtake-twitter-next-year

154 *Washington Post*, 10 April 2018. https://www.washingtonpost. com/news/the-switch/wp/2018/04/10/transcript-of-mark-zucker bergs-senate-hearing/?utm_term=.cc7e444a8568

Chapter 4: Reflections on Two Revolutions

1 Eatwell and Goodwin, *National Populism*, p. 32.

2 N. Davis, K. Goidel, C. S. Lipsmeyer, G. D. Whitten and C. Young, 'Economic Vulnerability, Cultural Decline, and Nativism: Contingent and Indirect Effects', *Social Science Quarterly*, Vol. 100, No. 2, April 2019.

3 Gest, *The New Minority*.

4 Berlin, 'Two Concepts of Liberty'.

5 Nisbet, *The Quest for Community*, p. 28.

6 J. Müller, *What is Populism?*, Penguin, 2017, p. 20.

7 *Ibid.*, p. 46.

8 The McDonnell quotations were widely reported but can be found at: https://www.theguardian.com/politics/2015/sep/18/john-mcdonnell-apologises-for-ira-comment-labour; https://www.dailymail.co.uk/news/article-2832286/Labour-MPs-cheered-jokes-lynching-Tory-minister-killing-royal-sick-alternative-poppy-day-comedy-night.html; https://reaction.life/john-mcdonnell-supporting-rioting-students-kicking-shit-london/

9 *Guardian*, 26 September 2018. https://www.theguardian.com/politics/2018/sep/26/labour-mps-call-for-general-strike-to-topple-tories-rejected-laura-smith

10 *Local Government Chronicle*, 26 September 2018. https://www.lgcplus.com/politics/finance/labour-leaders-refuse-to-back-corbyns-illegal-budget-comments/7026129.article

11 *Guardian*, 29 June 2011. https://www.theguardian.com/commentisfree/2011/jun/29/blue-labour-attacks?INTCMP=SRCH

12 *Guardian*, 8 April 2011. https://www.theguardian.com/commentisfree/2011/apr/08/blue-labour-maurice-glasman

13 M. Oakeshott, 'On Being Conservative', in *Rationalism in Politics and Other Essays*, Methuen, 1962, p. 169.

14 E. Burke, *Reflections on the Revolution in France*, Penguin, 1986, p. 106.

15 Hayek, *The Constitution of Liberty*, p. 344.

16 A. Trollope, *Phineas Finn*, p. 522.

17 R. Scruton, *Conservatism: Ideas in Profile*, Profile Books, 2017, p. 33.

18 I. Gilmour, *Inside Right: Conservatism, Policies and the People*, Quartet Books, 1978, p. 159.

19 E. Burke, 'Letter to a Member of the National Assembly', in L. Mitchell, *The Writings and Speeches of Edmund Burke, Volume 8: The French Revolution 1790–1794*, Oxford University Press, 1989.

20 P. Stanlis (ed.), *Edmund Burke: Selected Writings and Speeches*, 2009, p. 509.

21 A. Smith, cited in S. Medema and W. Samuels, *The History of Economic Thought: A Reader*, Routledge, 2003, p. 160.

22 Gilmour, *Inside Right*, p. 188.

23 D. Willetts, *Modern Conservatism*, Penguin, 1992, p. 81.

24 A. Smith, cited in *ibid.*, p. 80.

25 Haidt, *The Righteous Mind*, p. xvi.

26 See, for example, R. Putnam, '*E Pluribus Unum*: Diversity and Community in the Twenty-First Century', *Scandinavian Political Studies*, Vol. 30, No. 2, 2007, p. 138.

27 See, for example, OECD, *Family Violence*, January 2013. https://www.oecd.org/els/soc/SF3_4_Family_violence_Jan2013.pdf

28 Burke, *Reflections on the Revolution in France*, p. 151.

29 Gilmour, *Inside Right*, p. 109.

30 *Ibid.*, p. 126.

31 Willetts, *Modern Conservatism*, pp. 88–9.

32 *Ibid.*, p. 11.

33 D. Skelton, *Little Platoons: How a Revived One Nation Can Empower England's Forgotten Towns and Redraw the Political Map*, Biteback Publishing, 2019, p. 180.

34 I. and A. Maude (eds), *One Nation: A Tory Approach to Social Problems*, Conservative Political Centre, 1950.

35 Burke, *Reflections on the Revolution in France*, p. 135.

36 E. Burke, 'The First Letter on a Regicide Peace', in I. Hampsher-Monk (ed.), *Burke: Revolutionary Writings*, Cambridge University Press, 2014, pp. 316–17.

Chapter 5: Remaking One Nation

1 Populus, poll conducted between 22 and 24 March 2019. https://www.populus.co.uk/poll/dignity-in-dying-2/

2 See, for example, PWC, *The World in 2050: How Will the Global Economic Order Change by 2050?* February 2017. https://www.pwc.com/gx/en/world-2050/assets/pwc-the-world-in-2050-full-report-feb-2017.pdf

3 *Libération*, 30 August 2019. https://www.liberation.fr/france/2019/08/30/pionnier-des-bus-gratuits-dunkerque-suscite-l-interet-de-nombreuses-villes_1748292

4 Tech Nation, *UK Tech on the Global Stage*, June 2019. https://technation.io/report2019/#introduction

5 *Ibid.*

6 Estimate provided by Credit Suisse. https://www.credit-suisse.com/microsites/events/china-investment-conference/en/blog/china-making-good-progress-semiconductor-development.html

7 Federal Ministry for Economic Affairs and Energy, 4 December 2018. https://www.de.digital/DIGITAL/Redaktion/EN/Standard artikel/artificial-intelligence-strategy.html

8 L. Martinelli, *The Fiscal and Distributional Implications of Alternative Universal Basic Income Schemes in the UK*, IPR Working Paper, March 2017. http://www.bath.ac.uk/publications/the-fiscal-and-distributional-implications-of-alternative-universal-basic-in come-schemes-in-the-uk/attachments/Basic_Income_Working_Paper.pdf

9 A. Dube, 'Using Wage Boards to Raise Pay', *Economics for Inclusive Prosperity*, February 2019. https://econfip.org/policy-brief/using-wage-boards-to-raise-pay/

10 Rail Delivery Group, *Easier Fares for All*, p. 25.

11 Digital Competition Expert Panel, *Unlocking Digital Competition*, March 2019, p. 12. https://assets.publishing.service.gov.uk/gove rnment/uploads/system/uploads/attachment_data/file/785547/un locking_digital_competition_furman_review_web.pdf?mc_cid=b0 e006f1d2&mc_eid=657cb43256%20https://www.bennettinstitu te.cam.ac.uk/blog/making-digital-competition-possible/?mc_cid= b0e006f1d2&mc_eid=657cb43256

12 House of Lords Library Briefing, *House Building in the UK*, 5 January 2018, p. 13.

13 House of Commons Library, *Tackling the Under-Supply of Housing in England*, 12 December 2018, p. 19.

14 House of Commons Library, *Reform of Pension Tax Relief*, 12 October 2018, pp. 7–8.

15 HM Government, *National Insurance: How much you pay*. https://www.gov.uk/national-insurance/how-much-you-pay

16 Resolution Foundation, *A New Generational Contract*, pp. 90–1.

17 See, for example IMF, *Inequality of Opportunity, Inequality of Income and Economic Growth*, February 2019. https://www.imf.org/en/Publications/WP/Issues/2019/02/15/Inequality-of-Opportunity-Inequality-of-Income-and-Economic-Growth-46566

INDEX